120°W

Los Angeles

NORTH AMERICA

30°N

Guadalupe

20°N

Revilla Gigedo
Islands

Mexico City

Acapulco

Caribbean Sea

Clipperton

Panama

10°N

Pearl
Islands

Cocos

Equator

Galapagos
Islands

Quito

SOUTH
AMERICA

10°S

Lima

La Paz

20°S

Pitcairn
Islands

Tropic of Capricorn

Pitcairn

San Felix

San Ambrosio

Easter

Sala-y-Gomez

30°S

Juan Fernandez
Islands

Santiago

40°S

Cartography by Manoa Mapworks, Inc., 1990.
Map not to be used for navigation

120°W

90°W

Other cruising guides and nautical books published by
Wescott Cove Publishing Co., Box 130, Stamford, CT 06904

Cruising Guide to Belize and Mexico's Caribbean Coast including
Guatemala's Rio Dulce by Freya Rauscher

Irma Quaterdeck Reports by Harley L. Sachs with cartoons by Peter Wells

Cruising Guide to the Turquoise Coasts of Turkey by Marcia Davock

Cruising Guide to Tahiti and the French Society Islands by Marcia Davock

Cruising Guide to Maine—Volume I, Kittery to Rockland by Don Johnson

Cruising Guide to Maine—Volume II, Rockport to Eastport by Don Johnson

Cruising Guide to the Abacos and Northern Bahamas by Julius M. Wilensky

Yachtsman's Guide to the Windward Islands by Julius M. Wilensky

I Don't Do Portholes, a compendium of useful boatkeeping tips
by Gladys H. Walker and Iris Lorimer with cartoons by Peter Wells

Lights and Legends—a historical guide to the lighthouses of Long Island
Sound, Fishers Island Sound, and Block Island Sound by Harlan Hamilton

Beachcombing and Beachcrafting by Anne Wescott Dodd

Visiting canoe at Abemama

2

PACIFIC WANDERER

by

Earl R. Hinz

Edited by Julius M. Wilensky

**All photos by the author unless otherwise indicated
Scenic sketches by Lorraine de Preta**

Copyright © *by* **Earl R. Hinz**
published by **Wescott Cove Publishing Company**
P.O. Box 130, Stamford, CT 06904

1st Edition — 1991

Library of Congress Card No. 91-65015
ISBN No. 0-918752-13-2
SAN No. 210-5810

TABLE OF CONTENTS

Quinn's Bar, Papeete, Tahiti, a gathering place for cruising sailors until
the 1970s when Papeete's waterfront was redeveloped

AUTHOR'S INTRODUCTION

For 15 years I have been writing magazine stories of my experiences and observations while living, cruising and flying over the Pacific Ocean. My readers seem to relish this first-hand information, but as most magazine stories go, they have a limited lifetime, about as long as it takes for the next issue to arrive in the mailbox. This was evident in my two columns, "Pacific Update" (Sea) and "Pacific Tidings" (Cruising World), which have carried letters from my readers for the 10 years of their existence. Many of the same questions would resurface time and again. With that problem in mind, and with the help of a sympathetic publisher, I decided to gather the most pertinent and timely articles into an anthology, thus putting between durable covers useful Pacific cruising stories which could hold their head high even with dog-eared pages.

Dog-eared pages are not in themselves bad. When I am invited aboard cruising boats passing through my home port of Honolulu, I am often asked if I will autograph a copy of "Landfalls of Paradise" which the thoughtful skipper has put aboard. I am most honored when it is a dog-eared copy, for that meant it has been used as it should be. The same is true of magazine stories, but magazine designers see to it that the best stories are scattered throughout the publication making it impossible to collect them without also memorializing large numbers of advertisements. This anthology will save you the effort of clipping, punching and correlating recent stories on Pacific cruising. Keep it with your copy of "Landfalls of Paradise," it is a companion volume.

A Look Back

A few years back, Joe Brown (Editor, Sea) related to me his plans for an anniversary issue of Sea magazine which was born in 1908, I got to wondering what bluewater cruising was like at the time the magazine was founded. As you well imagine, accounts of early bluewater cruising are sparse. Captain Joshua Slocum had already completed a circumnavigation in his yawl *Spray* in which he touched at many familiar islands such as the Marquesas, Societies, Samoas, Fiji and Australia. Later he wrote the first popular cruising yarn, "Sailing Alone Around the World" (1900). but Sea had not yet been born then.

Then came Captain John Voss in that wonderful Indian canoe *Tillicum*. He departed Victoria, B.C. in 1901, and touched Cooks, Samoas, Fiji, Australia and New Zealand before continuing on into the Indian Ocean on his circumnavigation. Voss became another bluewater storyteller with his book, "The Venturesome Voyages of Captain Voss," which didn't come out until 1913; by then Sea was 5 years old.

Enter Jack London, that prolific writer of outdoor tales who in 1907 departed San Francisco for the South Seas in the fabled *Snark*. The custom-built *Snark* measured 55 feet LOA, 43 feet LWL, 15-foot beam and a 7 foot 8 inch draft. It was a gaff-rigged ketch with a 70-hp gasoline auxiliary— very modern for its day and it cost $30,000, a hefty sum at the time.

The first leg of the *Snark*'s cruise took it to Hawaii in 27 days, a distance of 2,080 miles, which today's cruising boats make in an average time under 20 days. From Hawaii, London went south to the Marquesas and that's where he was when Sea magazine was born in 1908. London continued along the now-popular Coconut Milk Run from the Marquesas through the Society Islands, Samoas, Fiji and Solomons where illness ended his cruise.

From London's book, "Cruise of the Snark," published in 1917, I learned that cruising boats could then enter Pearl Harbor, Oahu, now a secure Navy base; the nau-nau (pronounced no-no) flies had already occupied the Marquesas; and cannibalism was still common in the islands of Melanesia.

There have been many other changes in the Pacific cruising scene since London's time. Most of the islands then were colonies or territories of world powers; today they are either independent countries or on their way to becoming independent. Copra and guano were leaders in the economy and copra schooners abounded. Immigration rules were lax and seamen and beachcombers melded with the indigenes producing the mixed bloodlines in evidence today.

As best as I can determine, Quinn's Bar appeared on the Papeete waterfront in the 1920s becoming the most famous watering hole in the Pacific. It existed until the 1970s when misguided civic officials decided to improve Tahiti's image by destroying the colorful waterfront that had made her famous. Today, Tahiti's waterfront is sterile, a real tragedy.

But we still have Aggie Grey's Hotel in Apia, which had the clean reputation that Quinn's did not and is not only a tourist drawing card today, but an oasis of dignified colonial hospitality to jet-setter and cruiser alike.

Yes, the Pacific has indeed changed since Sea magazine was born in 1908. But cruising boats and adventurous souls can still reach outlying islands that have not yet been tainted by the tourist masses. Take heart, salty reader, there are 10,000 islands in the Pacific waiting to be found by bluewater cruisers.

—Sea

Earl Hinz

Other books by the same author:

The Offshore Log, 1968
C. Plath North American Division, 222 Severn Ave., Annapolis, MD 21403

Landfalls of Paradise—The Guide to the Pacific Islands, 1986. Western Marine Enterprises, Inc., 3611 Motor Ave., Suite 102, Los Angeles, CA 90034

The Complete Book of Anchoring and Mooring, 1986 and
Understanding Sea Anchors and Drogues, 1987
Cornell Maritime Press, Inc. P.O. Box 456, Centreville, MD 21617

Nautical Almanac Sight Reduction Tables SIGHT SOLVER
Celestaire, Inc., 416 South Pershing, Wichita, KS 67218

EDITOR'S PREFACE

Earl Hinz is the guru of South Pacific sailing. How did he get that way? Decades of living aboard and cruising the far-flung lovely isles of Polynesia, Melanesia, and Micronesia. Not only sailing—making the passages and landfalls; but exploring every harbor, walking every village and settlement, seeing all the sights to behold and then writing about it. I know first hand that if you're going to write authentic cruising articles and books, you have to go into your explorations much more thoroughly than any tourist. Earl Hinz has done this. You also have to do extensive research on the history, economy, government, and people of each island. Earl Hinz has done this. You also have to be dedicated enough, well organized enough, and talented enough as a writer to get all this authentic information into good form that magazine editors and book publishers will want. Earl Hinz has done this also.

Earl came to us with his idea for this anthology. We didn't want old information, nor to leave the reader groping for atlases to learn where on earth are these places. For this anthology covers both little known and popular corners of the vast Pacific Ocean. What Earl did for you (and us!) is to make the beautiful sketch charts that you see in this book and to update all of the articles. After each section, credit is given to the magazine that first published the article. To make this book more complete, he has added some previously unpublished material.

Mr. Hinz gave us rough sketches which were turned into finished art by Don Johnson, the Maine Coast cruising guru, who is not only a great commercial artist, but has sailed as many miles as Earl, but in the Atlantic Ocean, European waters, Caribbean, and the East Coast of the USA. Although this is not intended as a cruising guide, and these charts are not to be used for navigation, we think you'll enjoy this book more because points of interest afloat and ashore are located on these charts. The end papers in the front and rear of this book were drawn by Manoa Map Works in Honolulu, Hawaii. Together, these end paper charts show the entire area described in this book, with some overlap for orientation.

Wescott Cove is proud of its books, every one an authentic reference for the area it covers. We're also proud that we've been able to bring you the work of Earl Hinz and other dedicated and talented authors. None of them do it for money alone because they are all well-educated and could all earn more money putting their time into more lucrative pursuits. They do it as a service to people who want to sail to these places, and to people who only want to learn about them. I've cruised all over the French Society Islands, and this has whetted my appetite for cruising other groups of isles in the South Pacific, so I qualify as someone who will find the book useful, and also as an armchair sailor.

I'm delighted with Earl Hinz's book and we hope you will be too.

Julius M. Wilensky, Stamford, CT., January, 1991

LIST OF CHARTS IN THIS BOOK

Editor's Note: If you only want to learn about these isles, Earl Hinz's sketch charts in this book are good enough. But if you intend to cruise these lovely isles, please get yourself a complete set of charts, numbers given below. **THE CHARTS IN THIS BOOK ARE NOT INTENDED TO BE USED FOR NAVIGATION.**

Charts beginning with BA are British Admiralty charts. Our sketch charts were redrawn from these with the kind permission of the Hydrographer of the British Navy. DMA charts are those of the U.S. Defense Mapping Agency, readily available from many chart agents. So is the NOAA chart for the Hawaiian Islands. The chart recommended for the Lord Howe Island is an Australian Hydrographic Service chart.

Although the charts in this book are as accurate as we could make them, neither the author nor the publisher can accept responsibility for any errors. If you find any discrepancies, we'd love to hear from you. Please write to the author, Earl Hinz, care of the publisher, address on the title page. It will help us update the charts for the next edition.

Magazines which originally published the stories in this anthology:

Cruising World, Newport, Rhode Island

Sea, Newport Beach, California

Pacific, Honolulu, Hawaii

Ocean Navigator, Portland, Maine

Guam and Micronesia Glimpses, Tamuning, Guam

Western Boatman, Carson, California

CHAPTER 1

WESTWARD HO!

*"Millions upon millions of years ago, when the contin-
ents were already formed and the prinicpal features of
the earth had been decided, there existed then as now,
one aspect of the world that dwarfed all others . . . a
mighty ocean, resting uneasily to the east of the largest
continent, a restless ever-changing, gigantic body of water that would later be described as Pacific."*

James A. Michener, "Hawaii"

The Cruising Scene Evolves

Ever since Josh Slocum made his famous circumnavigation in 1898,
yachties have been following in the wake of the *Spray* to enjoy the good
life in the tropics. The early singlehanders like Slocum, Pidgeon and
Gerbault were followed much later by delightful cruising couples like the
Hiscocks, Smeetons and Roths providing enticing tales of tropic moons,
swaying palms, friendly natives and balmy trade winds that have spurred
many of us to shuck the cares of the world and head south.

But is cruising today anything like it was for those pioneers? Certainly
not, the world is changing and the tropical paradise changes with it. The
question is, how fast is the cruising scene changing and are the changes
for better or for worse?

Betty (*Horizon's* First Mate on all our Pacific voyages) and I got our
first taste of South Pacific sailing in 1970 and that just created the urge for
more. By the mid-1970s, we were able to make the full Coconut Milk Run
through Polynesia* with a two-year cruise that took us to New Zealand.
In the early 1980s, we returned again to full-time cruising and as the decade closed, we observed that many changes were taking place—boats,
equipment and bureaucracy had collectively altered the cruising scene.

---

*Footnote: If you are a little confused by these "nesia" names, let me ex-
plain. Anthropologists long ago saw fit to categorize the peoples of Oceania into three groups having ethnically similar backgrounds and characteristics. the regions in which these three groups lived were called
Polynesia, meaning "many islands," Melanesia meaning "black islands,"
and Micronesia meaning "small islands." Of course, these terms are not
mutually exclusive since all three regions are made up of many islands,
most of which are small and they are inhabited by indigenous people
having skin tones ranging from copper to ebony. Also, travel, first by outrigger canoe and now airplane, have mixed the peoples of Oceania just
like other parts of the world.

First of all, there were more cruising boats on the high seas. Secondly, advancing technology had found its way into all aspects of cruising and, thirdly, several new Pacific countries had come into being. There seemed to be only two things that did not change—the urge to go and the sea itself.

Most cruising boats now seen in Pacific ports are built of fiberglass. Whether they are 20-footers sailed by intrepid singlehanders or luxury 60-footers sailed by professional hands, fiberglass hulls are now the "in" thing. It would be safe to say that without fiberglass, synthetic fibers and stainless steel, fewer of us would be on the cruising scene today. Modern materials have become so maintenance-free and durable that now we can enjoy boats for what they were intended to be, namely, means of getting across the water. Love of boating is no longer synonymous with love of working on a boat and that change has attracted the masses to the water and cruising.

Sailing rigs have changed over the years, not only with the introduction of aluminum spars and stainless steel rigging, but the growing use of roller furling jibs and, occasionally, a roller furling mainsail. People who have not experienced the fury of Pacific gales or hurricanes swear by these aids. Some of the rest of us cling to the flexibility of individual headsails, reefable genoas and mainsails. Separate sails are more work,

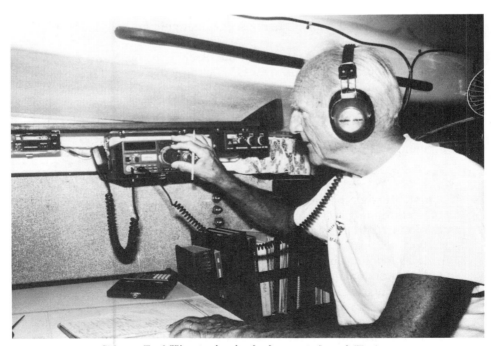

Skipper Earl Hinz tuning in the ham set aboard *Horizon*

but they also offer maximum opportunity for storm survival and that requirement hasn't changed since the days of Noah.

Of all the creature comforts that seem to be gaining popularity with the cruising fleet, refrigeration is the leader. We can do without television, air conditioning, soft beds and the corner store, but we cannot do without a cold drink. In 1975, *Horizon* was a rarity with its built-in refrigeration and, personally, I did not think that we needed it. Today, probably one-half of the cruising boats, certainly all of the larger ones, have either or both refrigeration or freezer capability. It does make life a whole lot easier for the cook who is also entitled to some comforts in this cruising game and it also provides a good income for refrigeration servicemen in port.

Although you can buy a virtually trouble-free refrigerator for home use for a mere $500, a smaller box with fewer features for a boat will cost you three to four times as much and requires frequent servicing. But the luxury of a cold gin and tonic in the tropics can be priceless and who am I to drink warm beer, if I don't have to?

Bluewater cruising has not escaped the growing onslaught of high technology electronics. While few of us find the need for time diversions such as video games when anchored in a moonlit lagoon, other products of the chip factories have found their way to sea helping with navigation, communications, safety and even cooking. (Yes, the microwave oven is quite common.) None of these items are what an old salt would call needed and he may even abhor the thought of them. Nevertheless, they have appeared on the scene and are making long-distance cruising more appealing to more sailors, rightly or wrongly.

SatNav is probably the outstanding new electronic device to find its place on the cruising boat. Of course, the present system is not new, having been released by the federal government for commercial use way back in 1967. But it wasn't until the 1980s that miniaturization and price breakthroughs made it practical for cruising boats. At this time, I would estimate that as many as one-half of the boats cruising the Pacific have a SatNav on board. For those who do not yet have SatNav, navigation has been greatly improved by the introduction of quartz time-keepers and the hand calculator. These instruments have become so cheap that no boat should be without them.

I still meet diehards who take only noon sun sights and challenge the need for more accurate or frequent position-fixing. I think that this is hazardous nonsense when such good nav gear, so easily operated, is available at modest prices. These improvements in nav gear not only make passages more efficient and landfalls safer, but, properly used, you can consider more exciting ports of call like the entire Tuamotu Archipelago where currents can wreak havoc with old-fashioned dead reckoning.

In the early 1970s, ham radio was just taking hold in bluewater cruising and a few maritime mobile nets had been opened. Many cruisers found out along the way how much fun ham radio could be and simply bought

a ham transceiver (oft-times at a duty-free port) and went on the air. Things were pretty loose initially and a lonely sailor at sea, bootlegging a call sign, was overlooked for the moment. It didn't take long, though, for the expanding numbers of unlicensed boats to become a problem. The nets made up of licensed amateurs ceased servicing unlicensed maritime mobiles because the law makes it an offense for licensed opeators to knowingly converse with unlicensed operators except in the case of a bona fide emergency.

Licensing of radio transmissions is nothing new, but when ham rigs first appeared aboard cruising boats, operators thought that they may be exempt from such landside bureaucracy. But that was not to be. The licensed maritime mobile operator has now become the norm and the self-discipline that made the amateur radio service so successful, has been preserved on the high seas.

Another electronic device changing the cruising scene is the autopilot. Few boats are seen nowadays that depend solely on a person at the wheel to keep the boat on course. Virtually all boats have some kind of a steering aid. Early bluewater sailors developed a form of self-steering in which they rigged sheets to the tiller to hold the boat's heading relative to the wind. Downwind sails became a part of this rig and permitted long runs without the need to hang onto the tiller. But being able to self-steer only when running or reaching, limited the ports of call too much and many interesting upwind ports had to be bypassed. So, out of the bag of tricks of the singlehanded sailors came wind vane self-steering and it became the bluewater boat's trademark in the 1970s.

Practically everybody installed wind vanes except a few visionaries who saw in high-tech electronics, autopilots that would not clutter up the transom of a boat and could be tuned, trimmed and otherwise adjusted from the comfort of wheelhouse or cockpit. While the first autopilots were bulky, cantankerous electro-mechanical-hydraulic assemblages of considerable cost and upkeep, new technology has greatly reduced their size, increased their reliability and brought their price within reach of at least the larger boats. Now, probably, one in four boats has an autopilot on board to keep it on course.

While all of these electronic devices have found their niche in the cruising world, they have not done it alone. Simultaneously, new electric power sources have evolved to a practical stage where they can be considered as a regular part of the boat's electrical system.

Stored electricity has always been a precious commodity on a sailboat and a limiting factor in adding electrical gadgets. It was not only the finite capacity of the batteries to hold at least 24 hours worth of electricity, but the capability to replace that electricity the next day.

Boating started in the '70s with generators and alternators running off the auxiliary engine which was one argument for not being a purist—we wanted electric power besides propulsion. But we soon found out that to depend on an engine for electric power in time of need could be just as

foolhardy as to depend on it when wind and tide were against you. Large boats had the capability to add an off-line auxiliary generator to provide 110-volt AC and 12-volt DC electric power, but boats under 40 feet could not afford the precious below-decks space. So there had to be another answer and that was found in solar, wind and water power. OPEC has something to do with it because it gave the incentive for users to look for new power sources and sailors, long on ingenuity, adapted new technology to the problem of smaller boats.

Whatever the reason, recent years have seen the successful application of solar, wind and water power to recharging the boat's batteries. With such additional power now available, we can add electronic navigation, improved communications, better lighting, stereo players and a whole new line of computer-aided sailing instruments. My mechanical Sumlog, vintage 1972, with some 30,000 plus Pacific miles on it, seems rather archaic compared to the electronic instruments I see on new boats sailing the Pacific. But the old Sumlog still works and I know how to fix it.

Bluewater sailors are the world's greatest traditionalists and the most conservative sailors to leave a dock. And well they should be, for when they are a thousand miles from nowhere, they can ill-afford to have a vital piece of sailing gear fail and not be repairable with their own hands. But electronic devices in general are not repairable by the average sailor in the confines of a small boat, so reliability had to increase and it did with the introduction of the myriad of solid-state devices at the heart of today's electronics. Low power consumption, small packaging, good reliability and modest price tags have combined to make electronics an integral part of the cruising scene of the 1980s.

Author's *Horizon* anchored off Palmyra

While it is clear that the technology of cruising is undergoing change, what about the cruising environment? Is it changing and in what direction?

No area on earth is escaping the social and political changes of the 20th century. More officialdom, more automobiles, more pollution and more tourists are becoming a way of life for everyone. Even on the tiny atoll of Funafuti in the young Republic of Tuvalu, there are now street lights to guide lovers home where before there was only the glint of the tropic moon.

In the last 10 years, nine more of the 33 island groups which make up Oceania have become independent countries. They have thrown off the yoke of colonial masters and have set out on their own with democratic governments and budget deficits. Fortunately, their former colonial masters have not entirely abandoned them, for it is outside aid that keeps the little countries afloat.

While governments are ostensibly created for the social good of the governed, it does not take them long to find out that they, too, must grow for survival. More and more paperwork becomes the answer. Even the unsophisticated society of the Republic of Kiribati has learned the value of photocopy machines and printing presses. And as soon as a government gets the capability to process paper, it finds uses for it.

As far as cruising is concerned, tropical bureaucracy has kept pace with the rest of the world. No longer can you aimlessly roam the islands of Oceania. In practically all island countries you must first clear in at a port of entry. There you get your passport stamped, a tourist permit issued and approval is given to cruise the outer islands of the group. In most places this is still a formality, but it is getting stickier by the year because of excesses wrought by past visitors to the islands. Immigration rules have grown to protect jobs of the indigenes and the resources of the island from the aggressive outsider. In 1975, we were among the last yachts allowed to enter New Zealand without a visa obtained before arrival. Now you absolutely must get your visa outside of New Zealand before you enter unless you are satisfied with a 30-day stay. Papua New Guinea also demands a pre-entry visa but they go further; no short-stay permit and they make it very difficult to extend visas.

The islands of the former United States Trust Territory in Micronesia have always been tough to visit because Uncle Sam with his well-developed bureaucracy, ran them like stateside subdivisions and even made it hard for U.S. citizens to visit them. Well, the training worked and you now have to get prior written permission from each of the individual governments (Marshalls, Federated States of Micronesia, Palau and the Northern Marianas) to visit them. But once there, it is easy (and good) cruising.

While most of the Pacific island countries welcome visitors for a short stay, they all keep an eye out for beachcomber types who come to live off the land, and the down-at-the-heels yachtie who is cruising on a mini-

mum budget, seeking work wherever he can get it. These are the reasons why immigration rules have been tightened up and requirements for bonds and onward airline tickets have come into being in recent years.

Customs, too, has become more wary of cruising boats. Not so much that they will compete with the local copra boat trade, but that they have been known to traffic in drugs; sell high customs-duty electronic products without paying the duty; and also bring in firearms and ammunition which makes new governments shudder.

Four-legged crew members have not fared well either in recent years. In the mid-1970s cruising period, we saw may pets on boats—dogs, cats and birds. Usually the animals were kept on board without the need for bonds. But the numbers increased to the point that island governments began to worry about the possible introduction of western animal diseases such as rabies and Newcastle's disease. This forced them to introduce strict controls on pets; none can be brought ashore under any circumstances in most countries. In New Zealand, you now have to post a NZ$1,000 bond swearing that you will keep the pet aboard at all times and will remove it from the country after three months, or they will destroy it. The country of Vanuatu will turn away from its waters any boat that is carrying a pet aboard.

But while pet entry problems have been getting more difficult, human problems have been gettting easier. At one time, pratique was the overwhelmingly important inbound clearance consideration. On arrival in a new port, the port health officer was the first on on board and he had to clear you before any other inspection was made. Now it is rare to undergo even minimal probing of the health of the crew members unless the boat has arrived from a known epidemic area. Although some ports no longer have port health officers, you must still fly the yellow Q-flag when entering.

Taxes go hand in hand with government and the trend in the Pacific Islands is to charge cruising boats for "services rendered and facilities used." Sometimes there is an overcharge as in the Solomon Islands, where the cruising boat has to pay the same SI$100 "light fee" as commercial vessels. The new country of the Marshall Islands now charges a port fee of US$10 on departure. Mooring or port fees are routinely charged in Papeete, Pago Pago, Rarotonga, Honolulu, Whangarei, Port Vila, Tarawa, Wreck Bay and, in fact, in most ports of entry of the more westernized islands of Oceania.

Speaking of Wreck bay, the Galapagos are a classic example of cruising boats overdoing a good thing when the government does not impose strict rules. In the early 1970s, it was possible to visit the Enchanted Islands without prior permission, just check in and then go gunkholing. But too many yachts and too much damage to the environment—flora, fauna and geologic features—led the government of Ecuador to clamp down on the freedom of the cruising boat, so it is now almost impossible to see the islands in your own boat.

Aside from the growing bureaucracy, which has its roots in our own western civilization, are cruising boats still welcome in the islands? Yes, and I think they always will be welcome. The peoples of Oceania have a sailing heritage and they live close to the water. Visitors who come from across the sea by small boat are one with them. At the popular ports of call, though, you sense a more blasé attitude by the local people because they are seeing so many boats these days.

Papeete in 1973 was officially visited by 160 overseas boats, by 1977 the numbers had increased to over 300 and in 1985 to over 400 boats. In 1986, 250 boats signed in at the Oa Oa Hotel on Bora Bora alone. Rarotonga cleared 38 boats in 1971 and 112 in 1980, and that doesn't count the dozens that stop at Suvarow and never check in. American Samoa records 38 yachts stopping at Pago Pago in 1971 and 275 in 1978. In the first five months of 1988, 278 cruisers had already checked into Pago Pago. Tonga was visited by 599 cruising boats in 1987, 342 visiting Vava'u alone.

These are all popular ports on the Coconut Milk Run and, as far as I am concerned, they should be seen by all cruising boats, but the numbers of visitors have changed the attitude of the locals toward cruisers.

I remember our 1975 visit to the small village of Haka Maii on the island of Ua Pou in the Marquesas. We had no sooner set our anchors than we were surrounded by laughing kids in canoes, on logs, and some just plain swimming. It was the sort of welcome that Captain Bligh got at Tahiti in 1788, although these kids were more formally dressed. That sort of thing no longer can be expected in the major ports along the Coconut Milk Run, but it is still prevalent in the smaller villages and the lesser-visited of the 10,000 islands of the Pacific. For these places, you have to get off the beaten path and become your own Captain Cook, Explorer.

Some islands, however, seem not to have lost their native luster in spite of the numerous visiting boats. Ahe in the Tuamotus is one of those. In the early 1970s, 30 to 40 yachts a year would stop at this delightful atoll and receive a warm native welcome. By 1977, the official count of visiting yachts had risen to over 170, yet even today I hear only good things about the reception given to boats by these warm and friendly Paumotuans. I guess some islands just wear better than others.

The cost of cruising, ignoring exchange rates for the moment and exclusive of your boat, has probably not changed much more than inflation has raised prices at home, which is a great deal. Our cruise into Micronesia in the mid-1980s cost about twice as much per month as our South Pacific cruise of the mid-1970s. Boat, crew and modus operandi were similar although the cruising grounds were different. Fuel costs were obviously higher, but when you sail most of the way, they are unimportant. Food costs vary depending on your location, but you make menus to suit local food availability. The closer you get to New Zealand, the lower your meat costs will be, but the higher your bread costs. Labor costs for boat repairs and maintenance become considerably less when you get away from Uncle Sam's shores.

All in all, I would say that most of the cost of cruising is no greater now than in the 1970s and, since more islands of the Pacific are tied economically to large western nations, I see no reason for the prices of their goods and services to get out of line. The one exception is Papeete, whose economy seems to be controlled from way back in France.

It is difficult to make any sweeping statements on the cost of cruising, since so much depends on your cruising style. If you lived an austere life on land, you can get by cheaply in cruising; conversely, if you live a high life on land, expect to also pay the price in cruising.

Probably the largest unknown in the cruising budget is the rate of exchange of the U.S. dollar compared with other monies of the Pacific. Most Pacific islands, except U.S. territories and former Trust Territory countries, use money that is related to the French franc, the New Zealand dollar and the Australian dollar.

Most of the changes we have seen in two decades of sailing the blue Pacific have been inspired by our own western civilization. Government, materialism and a cash economy have all contributed to changes in the cruising scene. But there is one thing that has not changed, and that is the sea. It is still its restless, dynamic and tempestuous self—quick to please and even quicker to slap the unwary. At sunset, there is nothing more beautiful; at the height of a storm, nothing more awesome. Its depths still harbor creatures ranging in size from microscopic plankton to leviathans. Its saline environment still provides a life-giving habitat to the mysterious chambered nautilus, the fearsome shark, the cowardly octopus, the graceful seal, the playful porpoise, the colorful reef fish and tasty mahimahi.

Terrestrial winds caress its surface while shafts of sunlight induce photosynthetic plant life in its depths. On a clear night, the moon casts a slivery glow upon it while thousands of stars look down from above as they have for eons.

The only thing that changes in the sea is the outsider—man. He pursues the sea with a relentless passion to make capital of its natural resources.

While I say it is never too late to see the Pacific, it is changing and what you read about today is not what it is going to be tomorrow. Fortunately, there are 10,000 islands in Oceania and when you get away from ports of entry, you are still able to see a native lad scampering up a tree for a drinking nut; outrigger canoes with woven mat sails; women making fine tapa cloth; men fishing by the light of candlenut torches; and native dancing under the palms.

Be of good cheer, most of the changes are the better for today's cruisers. Without modern boats and technology, most of us would not undertake long bluewater cruises. As for bureaucracy, you live with it every day no matter where you are. Ports of entry are now modernized so that you can get fresh-water showers, eat in restaurants, telephone home via satellite,

receive your mail in reasonable time, and enjoy many of the niceties to which you have become accustomed.

If you ask me what one thing I miss in the new Pacific that I found in the old, I would answer Quinn's Bar in Papeete. But Tahiti's Hinano beer tastes just as good in a modern setting. Manuia!

— Sea

ISLAND ENCHANTMENT INDEX

Several readers of my column (Pacific Update) have asked for my opinion of various Pacific Islands as desirable cruising destinations. There are so many islands in the Pacific that it is not surprising a first-time cruiser becomes confused on which ones to include in the vacation of a lifetime; certainly they cannot all be seen.

The Coconut Milk Run—French Polynesia, Cook Islands, the Samoas, Tonga, Fiji, New Zealand, etc.—was originally developed as the best of the downwind routes when ships were square-rigged and small boats were driven by downwind headsails. Now, however, most cruising boats can make good progress to windward, so the rules of the game have changed. It is no longer necessary to make a circumnavigation of the world or even the Pacific in order to see the islands of the South Seas. Naval architects and sailmakers have freed us from the necessity of running with the wind, so maybe, the Coconut Milk Run should be looked at again in a less constrained manner.

With a can of Fosters in one hand and a pencil in the other, I took a stab at developing an Island Enchantment Index for the island groups of the Pacific. It had some surprises in it.

The evaluation factors and their weightings were as follows, in descending order of their cruising importance:

Factor	Weighting
Pristine nature of the island group	1 coconut
Personality of the indigenous population	"
Shelter and accommodations for the visiting boat	"
Sailing conditions	½ coconut
International communications availability	"
Boat service and supplies	"
Provisioning resources and cost	"

In considering the pristine nature of the islands, places like the Marquesas, Tuamotus, Tonga, Vanuatu and the Galapagos rated the full coconut. Hawaii, American Samoa, Marshall Islands, New Caledonia, Northern Marianas and Guam only got half a coconut because of either too much tourist development, or the environment has been allowed to deteriorate. All of the islands got some credit in this category because these are islands of the fabled South Seas and they can still weave a spell of romance and adventure over the traveler.

The personality of the indigenous population varied from a one coconut level for most of the islands of Polynesia to only a partial coconut in the case of Hawaii, Fiji, New Zealand and New Caledonia where the indigenous dwellers have been outnumbered by immigrants. I also sliced some coconut off the score for Melanesian and Micronesian islands because these races tend to be more stolid and less fun-loving than the Polynesians. In the case of the Galapagos, though, I gave the indigenous population (tortoises, seals, lizards and other Darwinian subjects) a full coconut for their natural personality.

Shelter and accommodations for cruising boats rated one full coconut of importance primarily for the first-time cruiser who lacks the experience for handling difficult anchorages. Only three island groups got a full coconut for adequate shelter (hurricanes excepted), and they were the Societies, New Zealand and Papua New Guinea. These places all offered good shelter behind reefs or inside enclosed harbors. Reef anchorages like Easter, Pitcairn, Tokelau, Niue and Nauru got zero because they are not recommended anchorages for the majority of boats. Open bight anchorages like those in the Marquesas, Cooks and Western Samoa only got a partial coconut. Hawaii also received only a partial coconut in this category because of a lack of natural anchorages and limitations on visiting boats in state harbors.

Sailing conditions are something that the cruiser has to put up with, but some areas of the Pacific are better than others. The best were worth half a coconut and even the worst still got some credit because the worst weather of the tropical Pacific isn't really too bad—hurricanes excepted again. Islands getting the least good weather credit were mostly in the Intertropical Convergence Zone like Micronesia, the Galapagos and the Line Islands.

International communications were important to the tune of half a coconut since few of today's cruisers truly want the solitary life of a Slocum, Voss or Gerbault. Mail, telephone and airline connections are important to the modern day cruiser and places like Hawaii, New Zealand, Fiji and Guam offer a full measure of world-wide communications. The Tuamotus, Pitcairn, Tokelau, Wallis, Galapagos and the Line Islands offer essentially zero contact with the outside world and they got zero credit. But if you like your isolation, have your boat properly outfitted and your crew psyched-up to leave civilization behind, then by all means go to these interesting islands.

But no matter how well you have provisioned and mentally conditioned your crew for going it alone, you will eventually have to put into a well-equipped port for boat repairs and supplies as well as for reprovisioning. These two categories each warranted half a coconut and, in most cases, the islands received the same value in both categories. Hawaii, New Zealand and Fiji got a half coconut for each factor. The Society Islands, Cook Islands, American Samoa, Papua New Guinea, Solomons, New Caledonia and Guam all turned out to be average ports for replenishing and repairing and received only a quarter of the coconut. Western Samoa got a half coconut as a replenishing port but nothing for boat services. Many islands like the Marquesas, Tuamotus, Australs, Easter, Pitcairn, Tokelau, Niue, Wallis and Nauru had little or nothing to offer in either of these categories. You must have your vessel and stores in top shape before even thinking of visiting those islands.

Native dwellings on Antebuka Island on the south rim of Tarawa Atoll, Kiribati

The maximum possible score in this game of Island Enchantment was five coconuts. The tentative standings (subject to much haggling and personal bias by others who have had different experiences cruising these islands) came out as follows:

Coconut Index	Island Group
4½ coconuts	Society Islands
	New Zealand
4 coconuts	Cook Islands
	Tonga
	Fiji
	Solomon Islands
	Vanuatu
	Kiribati
	Papua New Guinea
3½ coconuts	Hawaii
	Marquesas
	Austral Islands
	American Samoa
	Western Samoa
	New Caledonia
	Guam
	Palau
	Tuvalu
3 coconuts	Tuamotus
	Wallis and Futuna
	Federated States of Micronesia
	Marshall Islands
	Galapagos Islands
	Line Islands
2½ coconuts	Easter Island
	Pitcairn
	Tokelau
	Niue
	Northern Marianas
2 coconuts	Nauru

Overall, I was not surprised that the Societies and New Zealand rated high as did many others of the islands along the Coconut Milk Run. They have withstood the test of time. Some of the lesser-visited islands that rated high like Vanuatu, Australs, Kiribati and New Caledonia are just

waiting their turn at the cruising traffic. I was a little surprised that the Tuamotus rated only three coconuts but they lost on material things like communications, boat services and provisioning while still getting full credit for their natural beauty and people. They also lost a little for difficult sailing conditions—they are not called the Dangerous Archipelago for nothing.

Well, it was fun, and the Coconut Milk Run isn't all that bad after all, just getting a little crowded in some spots. I hope newcomers to Pacific cruising can see the relative desirability of islands to visit with this Island Enchantment Index. Your first problem is to separate yourself from the workaday world and the second is to blend your sailing around the hurricane seasons. Now about that Fosters beer . . .

— Sea

Transportation on Aitutake

PRIME PACIFIC LANDFALLS

Anyone familiar with Pacific Ocean cruising has heard the expressions "Yellow Brick Road" and the "Coconut Milk Run," which are used to describe the popular cruising routes from North America to New Zealand and back. Along this waterway that stretches for thousands of miles are such well-known and romantic ports of call as Papeete, Tahiti; Pago Pago, American Samoa; Suva, Fiji; Neiafu, Tonga; Auckland, New Zealand; and Honolulu, Hawaii, to name just a few.

There are many other ports in the Pacific, however, that are less frequented by cruisers but are equally attractive as those along the Coconut Milk Run. to see these lesser-known ports, one must be a little adventurous and eager to do some independent exploring. Let's take a look at five "alternative" Pacific ports to illustrate the rewards that can be found by getting off the beaten path.

Rarotonga, Cook Islands

Nowhere in the Pacific will you find a more mellow blend of native culture and Western civilization than in the Cook Islands. Here, amidst the coconut palms that for many years sustained the local economy, you will now find small but thriving industries such as fruit processing, garment manufacturing and electronics assembling. Of course, you will also find tourists, but the numbers are small compared to spots like Papeete.

In the Cook Islands you will also find a unique spirit that I can only attribute to its close ties with New Zealand. When you first hear the Kiwi accent of the Cook Islanders, you might think that you are in New Zealand. But the islanders have adopted more than the Kiwi accent; they also have much of the independent nature that is found in New Zealanders.

Mt. Te Manga, 2140 ft. high, dominates Rarotonga Island

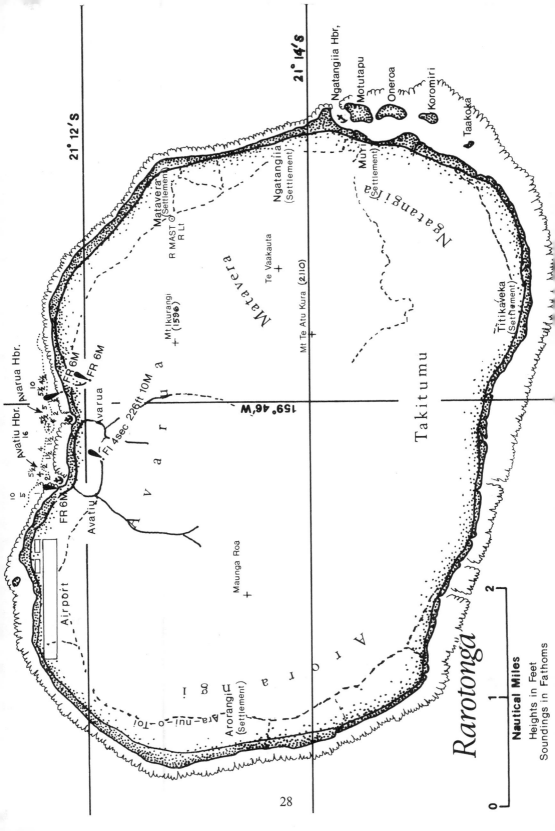

Rarotonga

Nautical Miles

Heights in Feet
Soundings in Fathoms

0   1   2

28

Without mineral or timber resources, the Cook Islanders have built an economy that takes advantage of what resources they do have—abundant sunshine, the fertile soils of the high islands, the pearl cultures in the atolls and the Polynesian's inherent zest for life.

The Cook Islanders are every bit as attractive and fun-loving as the Tahitians who seem to get all the attention from cruising boats. The reason for this, of course, is that French Polynesia is a destination in itself, while the Cook Islands are considered way points for boats transiting between the Society Islands and the Samoas. By following the Coconut Milk Run, one passes through the Cook Islands without really coming close to any of them, although uninhabited Suvarov is but a slight downwind hitch and does get its share of cruisers.

Rarotonga is a good reason to make a detour. Rarotonga is the largest, highest, greenest and most populous (10,000 persons) of the Cook Islands. It is one of three ports of entry into the country. Avatiu is the only real harbor on Rarotonga and is located near the main town of Avarua. Avarua Harbor is small but capable of accomodating a few cruising boats since it was fixed up following Cyclone Sally in late 1986.

The main harbor of Avatiu is closed to cruising boats now except for clearing-in and provisioning. It, too, is being redeveloped after the cyclone, but predominantly for commerce. The western part of the harbor is planned for a marina, but funds have been diverted for the more important commercial harbor, instead. Cruisers being a resourceful lot, though, have found that Aitutake Island to the north is an off-the-beaten path landfall with real outer island hospitality to offer. So, once the needs of Rarotonga have been satisfied, cruisers sail north to Aitutake and go native. (See Chapter 3 for more on the Cook Islands.)

Tarawa Atoll, Gilbert Islands

A lesser-known destination that is universally popular among all who visit it, is Tarawa Atoll in the Gilbert Islands (one of the three island groups making up the Republic of Kiribati). For those of us with gray in our hair, Tarawa is remembered as the site of the first American amphibious landing in World War II. On Betio Islet, barely one-half square mile in area, a furious battle by land, sea and air went on for 72 hours before American forces wrested it from Japanese occupiers. Today, the violence of war has been forgotten and the rusting hulks of tanks, amtracs and landing craft along the shoreline are mute evidence of the past. Inland, rusting Japanese coastal batteries point their guns aimlessly at peaceful skies, and battered concrete bunkers mingle with the rustling palms and the bright laundry of local households.

The Gilbert Islands are the westernmost archipelago in the sprawling nation of Kiribati (pronounced keer-i-bas), which encompasses 1½ million square miles of water. The archipelago spans the equator just west of the International Date Line. They are exciting islands (all atolls) and the indigenous population is, in my estimation, the friendliest of all Micronesian peoples. While there is a Gilbertese language, practically all Kiribati people speak English with an accent that reminds me that these islands once were a British colony.

Tarawa is not a sailing destination in itself, but, rather, a welcome stopover for boats making east–west passages near the intersection of the equator and the International Date Line. Boats headed from Hawaii to the Solomon Islands or Papua New Guinea usually call at Tarawa. It is a reasonable resupply point and has boatyard facilities and shops capable of doing essential, if not exotic, boat work. There is little boat hardware available, but local shops can fabricate or repair most basic equipment.

On and around Tarawa Atoll, one finds a living cross section of Pacific life ranging from hand fishing to jet flying. Starting with the busy islet of Betio, which is the industrial and shipping center of Kiribati, you go next to Bairiki islet via a new mile-long causeway, to the government and financial center. Farther along, on Bikenibeu islet is a hotel, hospital and school. At the eastern corner of this triangular-shaped atoll is Bonriki islet, with aquaculture farms and a more or less modern jet airport. And beyond Bonriki to the northwest are many, many isolated islets where canoes, footpaths and thatched roofs are the order of the day. On Tarawa, there is something for everybody.

(See Chapter 7 for more on the Gilbert Islands.)

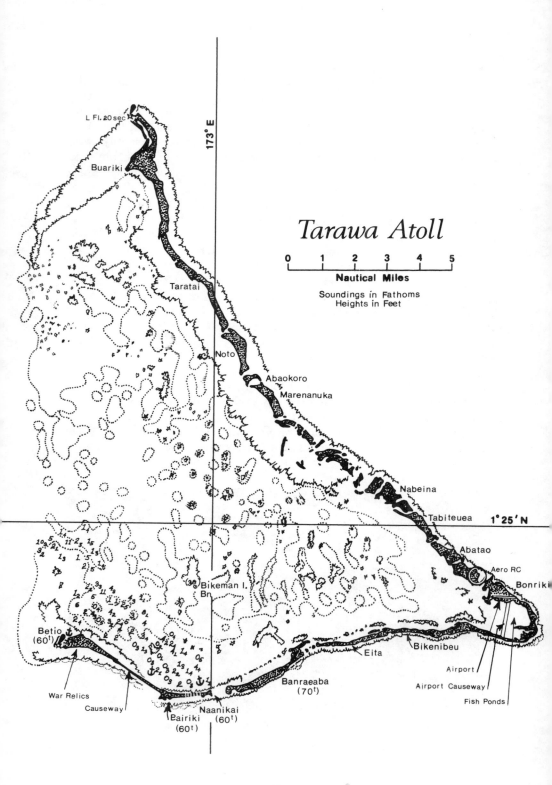

Tarawa Atoll

0 1 2 3 4 5
Nautical Miles
Soundings in Fathoms
Heights in Feet

L Fl. 20 sec

Buariki

173° E

Taratai

Noto

Abaokoro

Marenanuka

Nabeina

Tabiteuea

1° 25′ N

Abatao

Aero RC

Bonriki

Bikeman I.
Bn

Betio
(60ᵗ)

War Relics

Causeway

Bairiki
(60ᵗ)

Naanikai
(60ᵗ)

Banraeaba
(70ᵗ)

Eita

Bikenibeu

Airport

Airport Causeway

Fish Ponds

Honiara, Guadalcanal

The mystique of the Solomon Islands is readily apparent in the people, dark-skinned Melanesians with a happy disposition that says "welcome" with the best King's English you have ever heard. The Solomons are called the Happy Isles for good reason. With red hibiscus in their hair and broad smiles on their faces, one cannot help but like these folks who 45 years ago were unknown except to copra traders and beachcombers.

Out of the rubble of World War II rose a new capital city for the Solomon Islands—Honiara. It was in a most unlikely place for a center of commerce and national administration because it had no harbor. Before World War II, it was just an insignificant shoreline village on Guadalcanal, one of the larger islands in the British Solomon Islands Protectorate. World War II, though, not only brought the Solomon Islands out of their stone age culture, but provided a unique basis for its new capital.

During the British colonial period of 1884–1942, the Colonial Administration ensconced itself on the island of Tulaghi, a place well-sheltered from the strong southeast tradewinds and one having a good harbor. Come World War II, the invading Japanese took up this same administrative area and that proved the end of Tulaghi as the Solomon Islands capital. For when the Allies arrived to drive out the Japanese, Tulahgi was leveled by aerial bombardment causing the Japanese to move their forces across New Georgia Sound to Guadalcanal. There they built an airfield and it became not only the key to the battle for the Solomon Islands, but the root of the new capital.

To supply the Allied war effort on Guadalcanal, once the key airfield on Guadalcanal had beeen secured, a massive supply dump was created

Friendly people at home on Honiara

Honiara

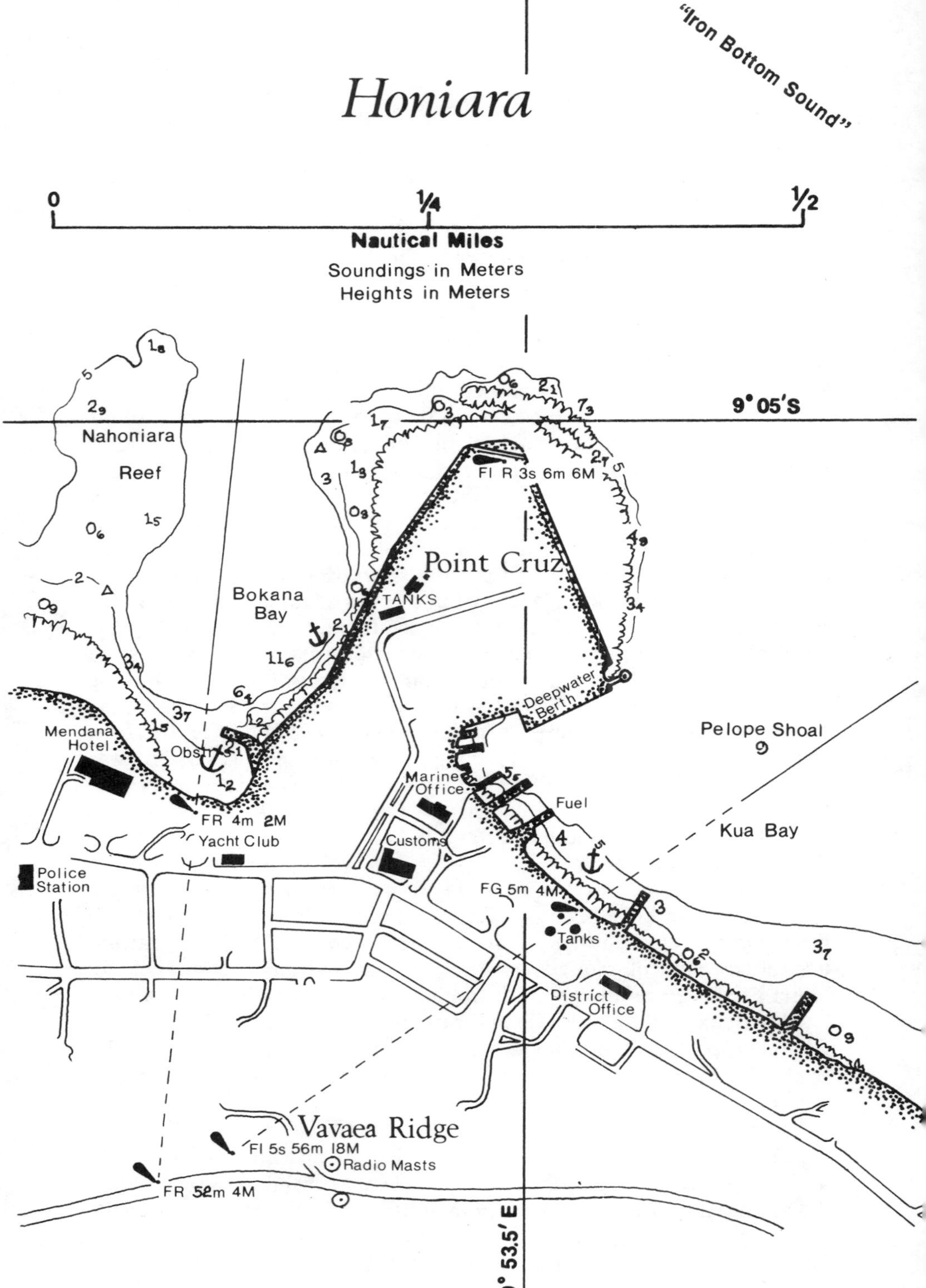

0   ¼   ½

Nautical Miles

Soundings in Meters
Heights in Meters

9° 05'S

Nahoniara

Reef

Point Cruz

FI R 3s 6m 6M

Bokana
Bay

TANKS

Pelope Shoal

Deepwater
Berth

Kua Bay

Mendana
Hotel

Obstn

Marine
Office

Fuel

FR 4m 2M

Yacht Club

Customs

FG 5m 4M

Police
Station

Tanks

District
Office

Vavaea Ridge

FI 5s 56m 18M

Radio Masts

FR 52m 4M

159° 53.5' E

33

at nearby Point Cruz, the only place along the island's windward shoreline where topography was at all favorable for any kind of harbor operations. The indigenous name for Point Cruz was Naho-ni-ara, meaning facing the southeast (trade) winds. For six months of the year, April to October, it is a reasonable harbor, but for the remaining six months, it is less than desirable. Nevertheless, when the Japanese retreated from the Solomon Islands with the Allies close behind, the large supply dump with its network of Quonset huts and hordes of leftover war equipment was an attractive place for the British Colonial Administration to restore itself. And so they did, maintaining a colonial administration there until 1978, when the Solomon Islanders gained full independence.

It was only natural that the new nation of the Solomon Islands would also select Honiara as its capital in spite of the lack of a natural harbor. They reasoned that harbors can be built by man and that is what has been done. Point Cruz has been reshaped many times giving a capability to handle all the cargo, passenger and fishing needs of the Solomon Islands.

The yacht anchorage is on the west side of Point Cruz directly in front of the Point Cruz Yacht Club. It is but a short dinghy ride into the club and once out the back door, you are in downtown Honiara. The convenience can't be beat nor can prices of foodstuffs and other provisions.

World War II's supply dump has blossomed into a town of close to 30,000 persons, the largest in all the Solomon Islands. But poor economy and a reluctant tourist industry has let slip through the country's hands an irreplaceable attraction—the unique relics of World War II. Here, where the southern advance of the Japanese war machine was halted, was a natural location for a Pacific War Museum. But slow reaction by government allowed souvenir hunters to cart away most of the priceless relics and, what hasn't been pirated, is rapidly being destroyed by nature in a tangle of tropical growth.

Honiara has tried in other ways to keep pace with the rest of the world in preserving and displaying its culture in a downtown museum. It also has a fine botanical garden providing a nice slice of nature's magnificent tropical environment. Flowers grow in profusion and multitudes of colorful butterflies flit gracefully about its tropical forest. East of town is the well-known Betikama Carving Center run by the Seventh Day Adventist Church as part of its mission. Original carvings are produced here and it is also the distribution center for carvings brought in from the outer islands.

The Solomon Islands are located out of the Southwest Pacific hurricane belt so it is an ideal region to continue cruising while cyclones come and go to the south during the months of November through April. When the southeast trades give way to strong north winds blowing right into the unprotected anchorage at Point Cruz, it is time to sail across "Iron Bottom Sound" to Tulaghi Island and haul out for bottom painting and other maintenance work at one of the boatyards. When through, pay a visit to nearby Ghavutu Harbor, a wonderfully secure anchorage in all weather.

From Honiara you can sail to the other Solomon Islands where anchorages abound and the natives are the epitome of friendliness. Yes, there are reefs to avoid and periods of calm when you will need the iron genny, but the profusion of islands will add spice to your cruise. (See Chapter 5 for more on the Solomon Islands.)

Madang, Papua New Guinea

One of the prettiest ports in all the Southwest Pacific is Madang, Papua New Guinea, on the eastern shore of the very large island of New Guinea. Madang Harbor is located at the southern end of a coastal waterway that is protected from winter's southeasterlies by 10 miles of coral reef and assorted islets. One can enter these waters from the north through Ottilien Pass and cruise through a wonderland of islands, or take Dallman Pass at the south end to enter Madang Harbor directly.

Madang town sits on a low flat peninsula that separates its harbor from Astrolabe Bay to the east. Its low elevation has also created a number of

Marketplace, Madang

lakes which the city fathers have turned into botanic gardens and a waterlily park. One would think the area ripe for mosquitoes, but rigorous controls have eliminated the pests.

Madang is the ideal place for cruising boat crews to begin their safaris by road or air to the famous Sing Sings in the highland towns of Mount Hagen and Goroka. The reason is that one can leave a boat in a safe harbor under the watchful eye of reliable local people.

The yacht anchorage is actually located in an inner harbor. It is large in area with many coves and inlets and is well out of ship traffic lanes and within walking distance of stores, banks and government offices.

This is also a good port to take care of your boat needs. Several good slipways and repair shops can handle most problems. English is spoken by most of the people in addition to a native dialect (of which there are some 700 in all Papua New Guinea), and there are many Australian expatriates in business and government who are helping to modernize the local commerce. For this reason, Americans find themselves at home in this tropical country.

Papua New Guinea has not been cursed by the inflow of vast quantities of foreign aid to distort the local lifestyle. In rural villages near Madang, time seems to have stood still for centuries. The houses are made of thatch and woven bamboo, water buffalo provide motive power to plows and wagons. It is easy to develop a languid feeling in this land for it is hot (only five degrees south of the equator), but the living is easy and worth the stop, if for no other reason than to replenish fresh provisions at the famous Madang People's Market.

(See Chapter 5 for more on Papua New Guinea.)

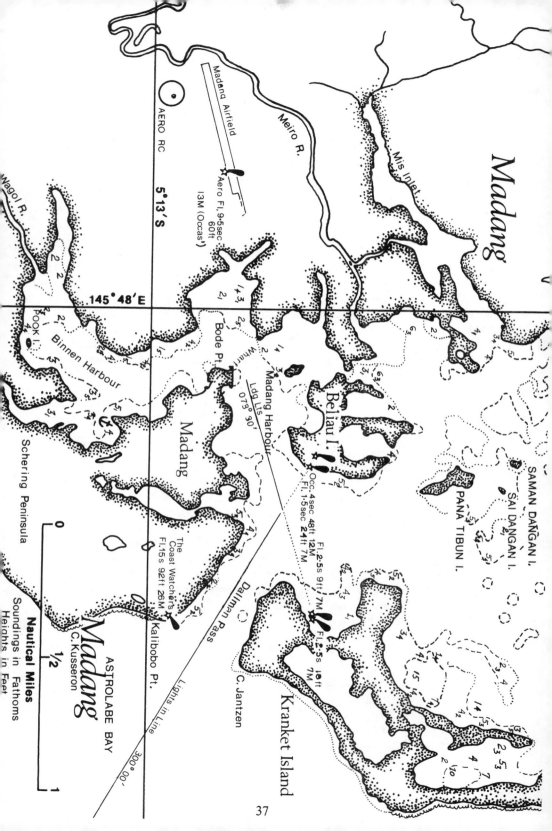

37

Guam, Mariana Islands

Guam is to the Western Pacific what Hawaii is to the Eastern Pacific—the gateway to an extensive cruising area. If there were such a thing as a Coconut Milk Run in the Northern Pacific, Guam would surely be part of it because of its strategic cruising position relative to Micronesia and the Orient. Practically any sailing one does in the Western Pacific will involve Guam—if not from a routing standpoint, then from a reprovisioning one.

Guam is an American Territory and has most of the benefits associated with the 50 states—domestic postage as part of the U.S. Postal Service; commercial airline service at domestic fares; an English-speaking population; U.S. currency; supermarket stocks of U.S. goods (as well as many Japanese goods); and one of the world's largest McDonald's fast food restaurants.

Although Guam has been politically separated from the rest of the Mariana Islands chain since the Spanish American War of 1898, it is only a short sail to the neighboring islands of Rota, Tinian and Saipan in the new United States Commonwealth of the Northern Mariana Islands.

Historical records of Guam's past begin with Magellan's landing at Umatac Bay in 1521. From then until 1898, the Spanish church cruelly administered the island and was responsible for the near total devastation of the Chamorro peoples, the island's original inhabitants. What the Spanish failed to destroy, the Japanese completed in World War II. True Chammoros are hard to find today, but there is a resurgence of Chamorro culture among those who remain. Of the civilian population on Guam, almost half claim a descendancy from the original Chamorros.

Guam is also a military island with both Navy and Air Force installations. Apra Harbor is the main Navy base and the sheltered waters are shared with commercial shipping, a fishing fleet and the Marianas Yacht Club.

The island is fairly young geologically and, as a result, there are no natural harbors. Apra has been made into a good harbor by an extended breakwater built on the coral reef, suppplemented by extensive dredging inside the breakwater to make it safely navigable. A second small craft harbor has been constructed at Agana near the business district.

Both the Apra and Agana harbors are ports of entry to Guam. The kind folks at the Marianas Yacht Club make Apra Harbor attractive for cruising boats that are going to stay awhile. Agana Harbor is better suited to provisioning because of it proximity to stores and it also boasts the only haul-out facilities for small craft.

Wherever your travels take you in the Western Pacific, put Guam on your itinerary as a scenic and historic reprovisioning stop. It will acclimate you to the upcoming cultures of either rural Micronesia or the exotic lands of the Orient.

— Cruising World

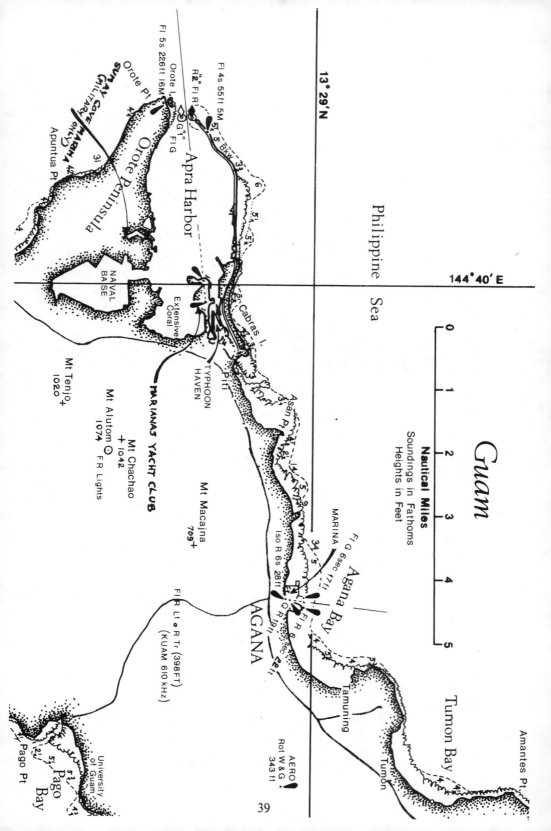

Guam

Nautical Miles

Soundings in Fathoms
Heights in Feet

Philippine Sea

13° 29′ N

144° 40′ E

Fl 5s 226ft 16M
Orote Pt

SUMAY COVE MARINA
(MILITARY ONLY)

Apuntua Pt

Orote I.
Fl 4s 55ft 5M

Orote I. Fl R
"R2" Fl R

Fl 3s
"G1" Fl G

Apra Harbor

Orote Peninsula

NAVAL
BASE

Cabras I.

Extensive
Coral

TYPHOON
HAVEN

Piti

Asan Pt

MARIANAS YACHT CLUB

Mt Tenjo
1020 +

Mt Chachao
+ 1042

Mt Alutom ⊙
1074 F R Lights

Mt Macajna
705 +

Iso R 6s 28ft

MARINA

Fl G 6sec 47ft

Agana Bay

Fl G 6sec
Fl R 6
sec

Q R 19ft

28ft

AGANA

Fl R Lt ● R Tr (398FT)
(KUAM 610 kHz)

University
of Guam

Tamuning

Tumon

Tumon Bay

AERO
Rot W & G
343 ft

Amantes Pt

Pago Pt
Pago
Bay

39

One of Guam's magnificent churches

FRIENDLY PACIFIC ISLES

The islands of Oceania are destinations for cruising boats from Europe, United States, Canada, New Zealand, Australia and, occasionally, South America, Mexico and Japan. At any one time in mid-year, there are in excess of 1000 sailing craft winging their way through the Pacific, stopping at well-known ports, rarely visited ports and those special ports that have become known for an extra measure of hospitality.

The cruising sailor is seeking lands that have figured in the romantic history of years gone by—islands made popular by such early story tellers as Maugham, Stevenson, London, Melville, Nordhoff & Hall and Heyerdahl. Their characters, whether true or fictional, may be long gone, but they are not forgotten by today's cruising sailors who approach a new landfall in anticipation of meeting some of their descendants and participating for a brief interlude in traditional island life.

It is quite common to find a local person or family who will help the visitor into the mainstream of island life. A brief cultural exchange ensues, which is welcomed by both parties, and usually results in an exchange of gifts long remembered by the cruiser. At major ports and government capitals, however, such hospitality no longer exists. The cruiser gets his official clearance and is on his way.

Betty and I have traveled widely about the Pacific on our ketch *Horizon* and have met wonderful people all over, but a few meetings stand out above the rest and I would like to tell you about them.

One year in Bora Bora, we anchored off the pier of the government meteorologist. He not only welcomed us, but allowed us the use of his shower and water supply. Daily we saw and talked to him and his family as we pursued our island visits. The highlight, though, came the night before our departure when we were invited to dinner with his family and given our first taste of octopus prepared Tahitian style. And if that weren't enough, his daughters left bouquets of fragrant frangipani flowers on our dinghy the day we departed.

Another atoll long to be remembered for its hospitality was Fanning. We arrive there after a difficult four-day passage from Palmyra and we were just glad to set the hook in calm waters. A local canoe came alongside and the lone occupant introduced himself and offered us loaves of a most delicious homemade bread, fresh from the oven. Tears came to our eyes at the generosity of this islander to the weary traveler. Fanning's people were so hospitable that we stayed for 17 days and left with regrets.

But not all initial meetings are that pleasant. Years before, we had stopped at Vava'u, Tonga, on our way to New Zealand and got the hard sell even before setting the anchor. Trading boats would come alongside a new arrival selling fruits and vegetables at prices double what we learned to pay just a hundred yards away at the Neiafu Saturday market. And that wasn't the worst. If you allowed a trader on board, you had a permanent guest for your stay. We later learned that this was an innocent local custom, but it was far removed from what we have experienced elsewhere.

The arrival of a trading ship at an island port provides yet another variation on a cruising boat's reception. Since the trading ship is the island's lifeline, business comes first. Fatu Hiva's unofficial boat host at the time of our arrival was Jean, a local bachelor. Jean showed us the way around his pleasant valley and helped us purchase tapa cloth and fresh fruit. But when the trading ship arrived, Jean became all business selling his copra and we were left on our own.

At Abemama, *Horizon* again experienced island friendliness. We had just anchored off the now unused copra pier, when we were visited by a local family. This was an unusual meeting for they came out in their sailing canoe and we invited them aboard for a visit and refreshments. We saw this family many times when going ashore, but they maintained a friendly distance so that we were free to visit other parts of the atoll. On departure eve, we asked them out to *Horizon* for the last time and to our surprise, the lady presented Betty with a Gilbertese fan she had just crafted. This became one of our most treasured momentos from years of cruising.

Ahe atoll, in the Tuamotus, has long been a favorite port of call for cruisers. It has not one, but a whole village of greeters. This is probably the friendliest port in all Polynesia. Our days ashore were spent visiting and dining with local people and attending church social functions. A copra economy and an occasional tropical cyclone limits their resources,

but not their hearts. The inevitable departure from Ahe takes on a different meaning for you are leaving behind a newly-found family.

What is most amazing about the peoples of Oceania is their continued friendliness and generosity. Year after year, dozens of yachts visit them. New generations of local families take over, yet the welcome mat is always out for the salt-laden traveler from overseas. One has to believe in the commonality of man.

— Pacific Magazine

Socorro children (Chapter 2)

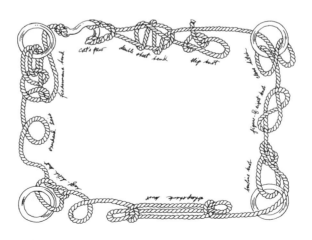

CHAPTER 2

EASTERN PACIFIC OUTLIERS

"The thought of how wonderful it would be to quit the rat race, someday, somehow, and go off to live on a tropic island occurs to many of us. To flee, once and for all, the hurrying crowds, and the smog—to live on an island where it's always warm, the air is fresh, the sky is clear, and the pace is slow—is something we long to try. An impossible dream, we know, but still worth pondering now and again."

Ross Norgrove, "Blueprint for Paradise—How to Live on a Tropic Island"

When we think of the South Seas, visions of Tahiti, Samoa and Fiji dance through our minds, but actually the South Seas start right at the door step of the Americas. It was in 1513 that Vasco Nunez de Balboa first sighted the waters which someday would be known as the Pacific Ocean. He had traveled overland at the Isthmus of Panama (although at the time he didn't know it was an isthmus) and arrived at a western shore. Because the Isthmus of Panama runs east and west at this location, he was in fact looking south and called the endless body of water he saw, Mar del Sur or, South Seas.

It was many years and many explorers later before the extent of his pronouncement became common knowledge. In the meantime, Spanish and English ships roamed the Pacific coastlines of the Americas discovering many islands in and near the tropics. These offshore islands lie along many sailing routes from the Americas to the better known islands of the Pacific. Geographically, they are called outliers and they make welcome intermediate landfalls on passages to Polynesia.

Islas de Revillagigido

Almost dead on the cruising tack from Mazatlan to Nuku Hiva lies an archipelago of volcanic islands belonging to Mexico. It is called Islas de Revillagigido and they are visited by few persons not having business there. They are valuable not for the mineral deposits nor for the fertile soil well watered by warm rains because that is marginal, but because of the vast ocean area they create by today's 200-mile Exclusive Economic Zone. The area abounds in fish and when migratory species are not to be found, the rocky points and nearshore areas offer abundant smaller species including shellfish.

Four islands make up the archipelago—San Benedicto, Socorro, Partida (more a rock) and Clarion, spead over about 240 miles of the ocean. There is little homegeneity to the group and only Socorro and Clarion have any inhabitants.

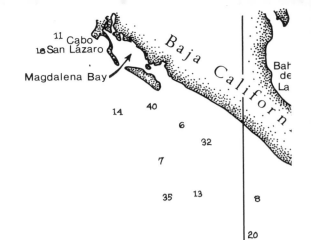

Baja Californ...

11 Cabo
18 San Lázaro

Magdalena Bay

Bah
de
La

14   40

6

32

7

35   13

8

20

110° 57' W

28

Isla d
• Ben

Islas Revillagigedo

Isla Roca
• Partida

ISLA S

Isla Clarion

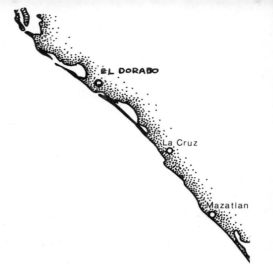

Pta. Coyote

Paz

Isla Cerralvo

La Paz

Sur

Punta
Arena

Todos
Santos

Cabo
San
Lucas

9   Cabo Falso

EL DORADO

La Cruz

Mazatlan

ISLAS MARIAS

Islas de Revillagigedo

```
0              60             120
├──────────────┼──────────────┤
```
Nautical Miles

Soundings in Meters

le San
edicto

OCORRO   18° 43' N
_____

These islands are geologically rather young; San Benedicto experienced a volcanic outburst as recent as 1952 and it has a unique lava delta building in the sea along its southeast side. There is virtually no fringing coral growth around the islands although coral is found on cove bottoms.

There is little known history to these islands. Prior to the Mexicans establishing an outpost on Socorro in 1957, the only sign of past habitation was the residue of an Australian sheep farm from the mid-1800s. The islands are said to be rich in both sulphur and guano, but the difficulty of mining and the spartan living conditions on the islands have discouraged development.

Socorro, the largest island (18° 43' N, 110° 57' W) is 10 miles in length and 5 miles wide with a single volcanic peak rising 3700 feet. The lack of rainfall, more than anything else, has depressed activity on this island. Less than 24 inches of rain falls in a single season, wells and springs provide the water supply for the outlying ranches and the few dwellings that exist.

Cruisers visiting Socorro are advised to make landfall at the southern tip in the cove between Bahia Braithwaite and Cabo Ragla. The anchorage is good and protected from the north and west winds common to the January to June period. The cove has a rocky beach, poor for landing a dinghy, but you can use the concrete landing belonging to the Navy. Clearance procedures are relatively simple and the Navy garrison will introduce you to the small population of the village.

Snorkeling and scuba diving are said to be fantastic around all of the islands with exellent visibility as deep as 100-plus feet. Lobster, octopus, manta ray, shark, bottlenose dolphin and trumpetfish abound along the steep walls of the island.

The preferred time of the year for visiting the Islas de Revillagigedo is December to May. During the rest of the year the islands can be affected by Eastern North Pacific hurricanes, some of which generate in the vicinity of the islands. The minimal size of the protected coves and the abundance of rocks surfacing about the islands tells you that this is not a good place to ride out a storm; but, in clear, settled weather, it can be a memorable port of call.

— Cruising World

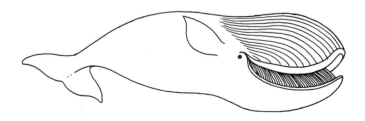

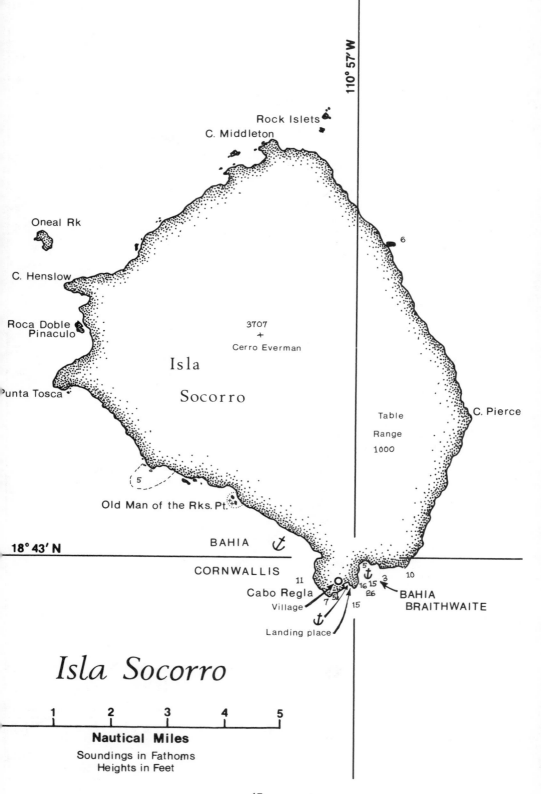

Rock Islets

C. Middleton

Oneal Rk

C. Henslow

Roca Doble
Pinaculo

Punta Tosca

3707
+
Cerro Everman

Isla

Socorro

6

C. Pierce

Table

Range

1000

5

Old Man of the Rks. Pt.

18° 43′ N

BAHIA

CORNWALLIS

11

Cabo Regla

Village

7 5

5

16 15

26

3

10

15

**BAHIA
BRAITHWAITE**

Landing place

110° 57′ W

Isla Socorro

| 1 | 2 | 3 | 4 | 5 |

Nautical Miles

Soundings in Fathoms
Heights in Feet

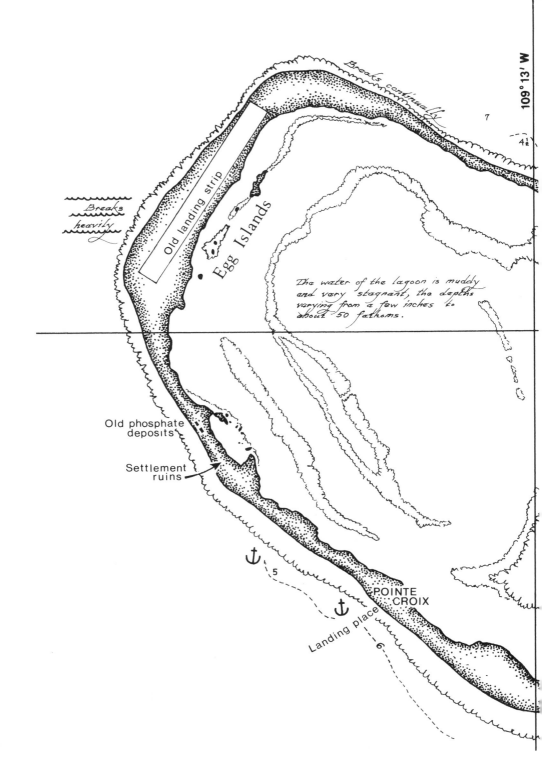

Breaks continually

109° 13' W

7

4½

Breaks heavily

Old landing strip

Egg Islands

The water of the lagoon is muddy and very stagnant, the depths varying from a few inches to about 50 fathoms.

Old phosphate deposits

Settlement ruins

5

POINTE CROIX

Landing place

6

Clipperton Island

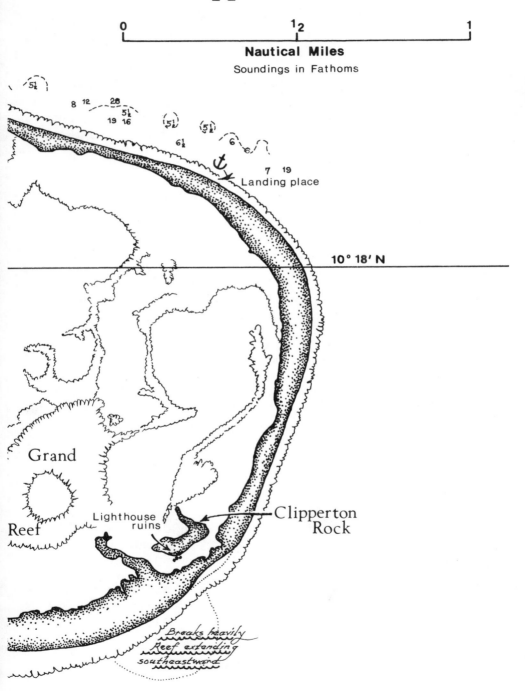

0   1 2   1

Nautical Miles

Soundings in Fathoms

Landing place

10° 18' N

Grand

Reef

Lighthouse
ruins

Clipperton
Rock

Breaks heavily
Reef extending
southeastward

CLIPPERTON ISLAND

See end paper charts for location.

This solitary island lies astride the sailing route from Acapulco to Nuku Hiva (670 NM from Acapulco) and it is a rare speciman of forgotten history. Clipperton (10° 18′ N, 109° 13′ W) today is a deserted island belonging to France, but at one time it had pirates, miners and aviators as its cohorts. Its name, in fact, comes from John Clipperton, an otherwise trusted mate with William Dampier's English exploring expedition of 1704, who mutinied along with 21 other seamen. They seized the barque they were sailing on and, turning pirates, made this lovely isloated island into their hideout.

The bouncing ball history of Clipperton had only started. France annexed it in 1855, the United States laid claim to it under the Guano Act of 1856, and the Mexicans seized it in 1897. France regained ownership in 1935, and it is today a dependency of France, ruled from faraway Europe in spite of its closeness to French Polynesia.

Mexico was the only country to make economic use of Clipperton. It engaged the British Pacific Islands Company to work the phosphate deposits between 1906 and 1917. For that operation, approximately 100 settlers and Mexican Army personnel were supplied by sea from the Mexican mainland. With the outbreak of World War I, this outpost was literally forgotten and in the three years following the last supply ship, the people left on Clipperton slowly died off, except for the keeper of the lighthouse—a giant of a man, three women and eight children. With the inevitable facing the women, one woman took an axe and dispensed with the lighthouse keeper. But the threat of starvation, sickness and loneliness was still with them. In a most unusual coincidence, though, the U.S. Navy vessel *Yorktown* hove to off the island the very next day and rescued the survivors.

During World War II, the Australians surveyed the island for use as a refueling stop for airplanes flying from Acapulco to the Marquesas. They landed PBY flying boats on the lagoon and mapped a 5,000-foot airstrip on the western end of the island. Nothing further was done, however, because the tide of battle changed for the Allies in the Pacific, and there were more direct routes to the battle zones.

Clipperton was also the site of a French scientific base in 1957/58 for the International Geophysical Year and it is regularly used by hams as an unusual location for long distance communications contests.

Contrary to most descriptions, Clipperton is not an atoll. At best it can be defined as an "almost atoll" for at its east end is "Rocher Clipperton," a 70-foot high rock that is part of the original island. Geologists following Darwin's theory of atolls believe that this island was a cratered volcano that slowly slipped back into the sea—all but The Rock. What now forms the barrier reef around the lagoon, was the wall of the crater with an opening to the sea along the northeast side allowing sea water inside.

This, in turn, fostered coral polyp growth both inside and outside. It is also believed that this opening was once large enough to accommodate Clipperton's pirate ship.

Somewhere along the way, the opening was closed and the water of the lagoon turned mildly brackish, effectively killing the coral inside. Lagoon depths now range from inches to 50 fathoms. The water is stagnant and muddy, with patches of weeds covered with brown algae.

> "A passage in the old Sailing directions informs us that there is "one rock seventy feet high, on which there is an old lighthouse. Vessels have sometimes mistaken this rock for the sail of a ship on the horizon."
> — P.G. Taylor, "Forgotten Island", 1948

Yachts visiting Clipperton can use "The Rock" with its lighthouse ruins as a navigation aid on approach. The preferred landing place in north or easterly winds is on the sourthwest side. As with atolls, you must anchor in close for the coral shelf drops precipitously. Exercise care in going ashore because the surf can be rough and the coral sharp.

When the West German yacht *Jambo* stopped there recently, there was another boat already anchored—almost a crowd! They spent one day ashore exploring the ruins of the phospate workings and the old settlement. It would probably have taken a second day to visit The Rock and lighthouse ruins.

If French visionaries have their way, the former entrance to the lagoon will be reopened and a yacht haven with marina amenities built inside the barrier reef. Weather statistics show Clipperton to be relatively free from the Eastern Pacific hurricanes. But remember, when you anchor on a reef, be doubly sure that your ground tackle can do its job or your home will float out to sea.

— Cruising World

ISLA DEL COCO

Refer to end paper charts for location.

For those who cannot resist the lure of buried treasure, what better place to visit than the fabled "treasure island," Isla del Coco? But be aware there have already been more than 500 treasure hunting expeditions to Isla del Coco, including one sponsored by the Costa Rican government itself. None have found even the slightest trace of treasure.

So maybe it isn't the gems and precious metals that are the treasures of Cocos, just possibly it is the island itself. Cocos Island (5° 32' N, 87° 04' W) lies 300 NM south southwest of Costa Rica's major seaport of Puntarenas. It is the largest unihabited island in the world at approximately 20 sq. mi., and most certainly it is one of the prettiest with its hundreds of waterfalls cascading down 200-foot cliffs while fed by 300 inches of rain per year.

Along the mountain ridges and in the valleys are lush tropical rain forests with enormous ferns, giant tropical trees, strangler figs and gaily colored orchids everywhere.

Cocos Island sits atop the Cocos Ridge, a submarine plateau that stretches from Peninsula de Osa on the mainland southwest to the Galapagos Islands. Don't expect to anchor on the ridge, though, since it lies 1500 to 2000 meters below the surface. Like the Galapagos Islands, Cocos Island has its own unique endemic species of birds and plants, but any mammals or reptiles you may see (except two small lizards) are not indigenous critters but were brought by ships in recent years.

Isla del Coco

0   1   2

Nautical Miles

Soundings in Meters
Heights in Meters

The actual source of the legends of Cocos' buried treasure is not clear, but one can surmise that such a lonely island with a couple of good harbors and lots of fresh water must have been well known to 16th and 17th century mariners. One legend seems to have some basis in fact because it dovetails with an actual happening on land. During a Peruvian uprising in the early 1800s, a Captain Thompson of the schooner *Mary Deare*, took the country's treasure of gold, pearls, gems, and religious objects on board, ostensibly for safe keeping. Captain Thompson, however, was not quite as honorable as assumed and he sailed away to Cocos Island where he reportedly buried the loot.

Other pirates including the notorious Benito Bonito also deposited loot in the Cocos bank, and estimates of the total assets of the Cocos Island bank vary from as little as $20 million to $500 million.

There are only three secure harbors on the island—Chatham Bay and Wafer Bay on the north coast, and the less desirable Inglesias Bay on the south coast. Cocos Island is a National Park (if not a national treasure) and three of four Park Service rangers are on duty at Wafer Bay. They keep an eye out for visitors to Chatham Bay and will cross over the isthmus between bays to welcome the newcomers. That crossing is a three-hour hike through a rain forest over a rough trail which is constantly being infiltrated by tropical bush. The only supplies that you can get on the island are fresh water and abundant scenery.

Scuba divers find the reefs around the island loaded with spectacular tropical fish as well as such oddities as hammerhead sharks, which are fed so well by natural means they show little interest in rubber fins and diving masks. There is only one wreck to dive on and that is an early 1900s German sailing ship which is in the shallow water of Wafer Bay. Maybe the sight of a ship's bones won't interest you, but surely, the profusion of lobsters will drive your taste buds into demanding action.

Being so far south, this island is not bothered by eastern Pacific hurricanes. In the northern hemisphere winter the winds tend to east and east southeast, while in the summer, the Intertopical Convergence Zone oscillates over the island with westerlies reported to the north and northeasterlies to the south. Most of the year there is some measure of rain and often the drizzle can completely obscure the island from sight. Good navigation, however, will tell you that it is close and patience will get you those lobsters for your arrival dinner.

— Cruising World

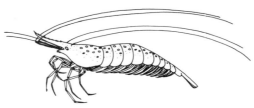

Cocos Island

ARCHIPIELAGO DE LAS PERLAS

Cruising boats departing Panama for the Galapagos Islands will find their first South Seas islands just 45 miles from Balboa. These are the Las Perlas Islands in the Gulf of Panama. There are 183 of them, many simply rocks breaking the surface, but 39 are sizeable islands. Largest and highest of the islands is Isla del Rey, which rise 727 feet above sea level. At the north end of Isla del Rey is the largest village in the archipelago, San Miguel (8° 27' N, 78° 56' W). Although there are many islands, the population of the total group is only about 3000 persons.

One island is significantly different from the rest and that is Isla Contadora. It is a modern resort island just 17 minutes by air from Panama City. Here can be found a luxury hotel with casino, golf course and fine waterfront homes for the jetset. Contadora's most famous guest was the Shah of Iran who took refuge there in 1979.

There are no stores in these islands but fresh fruit and vegetables such as yams, plantains and coconuts can be bought from local residents. As a word of caution, though, stay away from the south shore of Isla del Rey where some of Panama's special brand of pot is grown. Strangers are simply not welcome.

In the colonial period, pearl gathering was the primary economic activity, but it has been replaced by general fishing. Shelling and diving is good except when the north wind blows and the waters then become turbid. This should not be surprising since the Gulf of Panama is relatively shallow.

Panama, like its neighboring countries, is jealous of its sovereignty and cruisers are advised to have a cruising permit when sailing in her waters. There is no Customs office in the Las Perlas Islands so all the paper work must be taken care of on the mainland. Your *zarpe* can be endorsed giving you clearance to stop in the Las Perlas Islands on your way to the Galapagos.

— Cruising World

PANAMA

AERO Al Fl WG

Oc G 20M

PANAMA CANAL

Rio Chepo

COROZAL

9   4₅   2
                  Fl 5M

20
29₅   16

Oc(2) WR 19M

Bahia Chorrera

30
L Fl WR 14M

Isla Taboga

18₅
20

21₅

Fl 4M

27

BAHIA DE PANAMA

Fl 7M

Isla Contadora
Isla El Pelado

16₅
Punta Chamé

Isla Saboga

27

Archipielago de las

Isla Otoque
Isla Bona

2
4₅   20   SAN MIGUEL

17₅

16

8° 27' N

3

13

24₅

Perlas

Isla Pedro González

Isla del Rey

9   3

Isla de San Jose

22₅

18₅   12

Fl 14M   *3₅

3

12

20   27₅

Isla Galera

Archipielago de las Perlas

0   15   30
Nautical Miles

Soundings in Meters

78° 56' W

ARCHIPIELAGO DE COLON
(Galapagos Islands)

Spanning the equator 850 miles southwest of the Panama Canal, on the way to the Marquesas Islands, are the 34 islands that make up the Archipielago de Colon—the Galapagos Islands, a province of Ecuador. Everyone knows the attractions of the Galapagos—giant tortoises; huge but harmless iguanas; a managerie of marine life and an abundance of incredibly tame birds. Because the wildlife has not learned to fear man, it became necessary for the Ecuadorian government to put restrictions on visits to these islands in order to protect the species. Man's past depredations are a black mark in seafaring history.

First it was the English pirates of the 17th century, who found the islands a useful refuge, visiting often to restock food and water supplies. Unfortunately, they found the tortoise an excellent source of fresh meat and one that could be stored for many months (alive on its back!). They were followed by the whalers who continued the same practice almost driving the tortoise to extinction. Lastly, it was early cruising boats who landed on many islands destroying flora and fauna. The worst story to my recollection concerns a boat that visited there and later bragged how they had killed one living creature of each species. After hearing that story, I had full sympathy with the Ecuadorian government for clamping tight controls on this group of islands where Darwin formulated his controversial theory of evolution.

There are three ways to visit the Galapagos Islands today—by air, cruise ship or your own boat. The air and cruise ship visits are easily implemented. The visit in your own cruising boat is a bit sticky.

Assuming that you only want to spend enough time to say you have been there, you can make a casual stop at either San Cristobal's Wreck Bay or Santa Cruz's Academy Bay. With the Port Captain's permission, you will be permitted to stay at anchor for 72 hours in each place and go ashore for local walks on each island.

A 72-hour stay only at Academy Bay, though, can still give you a tantalizing snapshot of the wonders of the Galapagos. It is possible to take a half-day trip by charter boat to Plaza Island for a quick look at the sea birds, land iguanas, sea lions and an ancient landscape. You can visit the famous Darwin Research Station at Puerto Ayoro and a tortoise reserve. You can also dine ashore at the Hotel Galapagos owned by Forrest Nelson, a well-known and hospitable cruiser of a generation back.

There is another option, though, if you can wheedle enough time out of the Academy Bay Port Captain, and that is to take passage on a local charter boat leaving your own boat at anchor while you are gone. The anchorage is safe and the Port Captain will keep an eye on your unattended boat. This will give you time to see parts of Darwin's representation of species evolution in its natural habitat.

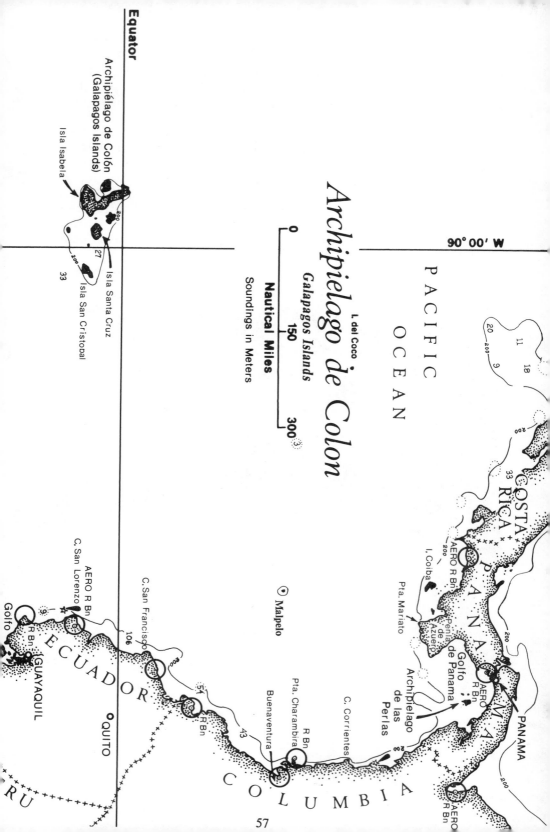

Equator

Archipiélago de Colón
(Galapagos Islands)

Isla Isabela

Isla Santa Cruz

Isla San Cristobal

200

27

200

33

Archipiélago de Colon

Galapagos Islands

L del Coco

PACIFIC

OCEAN

90° 00′ W

0

150

300

3

Nautical Miles

Soundings in Meters

⊙ Malpelo

20
11
18
9
200

200

COSTA
RICA

33

AERO R Bn

I. Coiba

Pta. Mariato

Peninsula
de
Azuero

PANAMA

Golfo de Panama

Archipiélago
de las
Perlas

AERO
R Bn

AERO
R Bn

PANAMA

200

C. San Lorenzo

AERO R Bn

C. San Francisco

Golfo

R Bn

GUAYAQUIL

ECUADOR

QUITO

106

800

54

R Bn

43

Pta. Charambira

Buenaventura

R Bn

C. Corrientes

200

AERO
R Bn

COLUMBIA

PERU

9

57

To be able to see all the islands in your own boat is an entirely different problem. The Ecuadorian government is holding in abeyance its once-issued "permit to foreign vessels to visit the territorial sea, the coasts and islands of the Galapagos Archipelago for scientific, cultural, or tourist purposes." The latter was a misnomer since few permits were issued for tourist purposes only, although the original intent was to promote tourism. Even with limitations on visitor permits, excessive numbers of tourists came by sea and air and the whole permit system was halted to minimize the strain on facilities and the ecology.

To pass the Galapagos Islands without stopping would certainly leave a void in your Pacific cruise memoirs. Take the proffered 72-hour stays in Wreck Bay and Academy Bay and make your South Pacific cruise complete.

— Cruising World

Iguana, Galapagos Islands

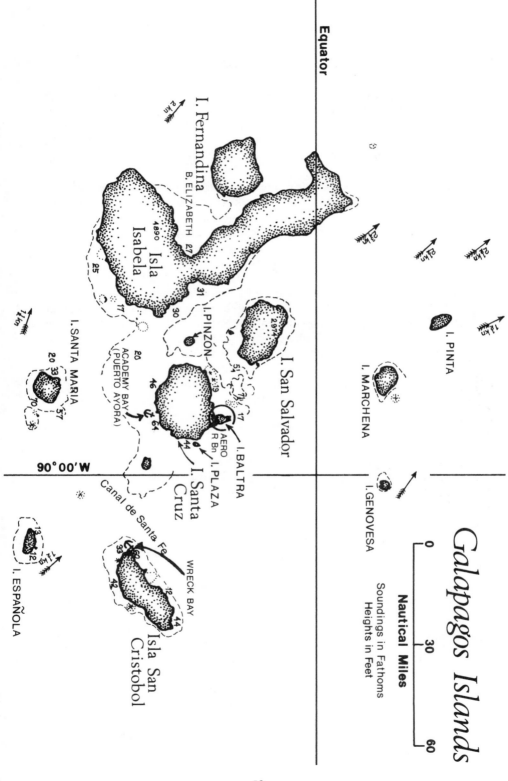

Galápagos Islands

Nautical Miles

Soundings in Fathoms
Heights in Feet

Equator

I. Fernandina

B. ELIZABETH

Isla
Isabela

4890

27

25

31

30

17

I. PINZÓN

ACADEMY BAY
(PUERTO AYORA)

20

46

16

I. SANTA MARIA

20 33

57

70

I. San Salvador

2974

54

19

17

AERO
R Bn   I. PLAZA

I. BALTRA

I. Santa
Cruz

64

44

Canal de Santa Fe

WRECK BAY

33

42

12

44

Isla San
Cristobol

I. ESPAÑOLA

13

12

I. PINTA

I. MARCHENA

I. GENOVESA

90°00'W

0   30   60

59

ISLAS JUAN FERNANDEZ

The outlying islands farthest south of general interest to cruisers are the Islas Juan Fernandez. They are a possession of Chile and lie approximately 370 miles west of Chile's principal port of Valparaiso. The group consists of two islands and several "rocks," but only one of the islands, Robinson Crusoe (33° 37' S, 78° 50' W), is inhabited and it with less than 500 hardy souls.

Where have you heard that name before? It was back in grade school when you read Daniel Defoe's book—Robinson Crusoe. Although Defoe's Robinson Crusoe lived on a fictional island in the Caribbean, Defoe got his inspiration for the book from the exploits of a Scottish seaman named Alexander Selkirk, who was put ashore on this island at his own bequest in 1704, and was later rescued from his self-imposed exile in 1709. There is no record of a man Friday sharing his island.

Selkirk's reward for his memoirs, which made him a household name, was to get the second island of the Juan Fernadez group, 80 miles farther to the west, named after him—Alexander Selkirk Island. The names were given to the islands in 1935 when the popularity of the folk hero was well established and the archipelago was made into a National Park.

In Memory of
Alexander Selkirk
Mariner

- - - - - - - - - -

A native of Larco, in the country of
Fife, Scotland.

- - - - - - - - - -

Who lived on this island in complete solitude for four years
and four months.

- - - - - - - - - -

He was landed from the Cinque
Ports galley, 90 tons, 16 guns, A.D.
1704, and was taken off in the
Duke, privateer, 12 February 1709.

- - - - - - - - - -

He died Lieutenant of H.M.S. Wey-
mouth, A.D. 1728, age 47 years.

- - - - - - - - - -

This tablet is erected
near Selkirk's lookout by
Commodore Powell and the
Officers of H.M.S. Topaz, A.D. 1868.

— Bronze Plaque, Robinson Crusoe Island

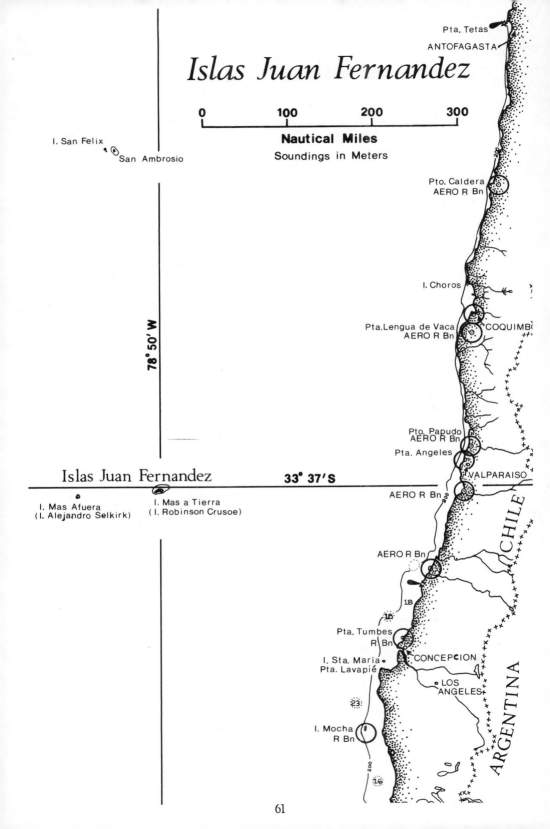

Islas Juan Fernandez

0   100   200   300
Nautical Miles
Soundings in Meters

Pta, Tetas
ANTOFAGASTA

I. San Felix
San Ambrosio

Pto. Caldera
AERO R Bn

I. Choros

Pta.Lengua de Vaca
AERO R Bn   COQUIMBO

78° 50' W

Pto. Papudo
AERO R Bn
Pta. Angeles

Islas Juan Fernandez   33° 37'S
                                VALPARAISO
                            AERO R Bn

I. Mas Afuera   I. Mas a Tierra
(I. Alejandro Selkirk) (I. Robinson Crusoe)

CHILE

AERO R Bn

18

15

Pta. Tumbes
R Bn
I. Sta. Maria   CONCEPCION
Pta. Lavapié
                        LOS
                     ANGELES

23

I. Mocha
R Bn

ARGENTINA

16

The Juan Fernandez Islands are not on any common cruising route unless you have rounded the Horn and are bent for warmer climes of the Pacific. A less demanding way of visiting these islands, though, is to come from the west (New Zealand or French Polynesia), making your easting in the "roaring forties." You can get under the South Pacific high and sneak up on the islands as if you were coming from Cape Horn. Bear in mind that the South Pacific "high" rotates counterclockwise, making wind directions opposite to what they are around the North Pacific "high" and a benefit in this case.

If you are headed for Easter Island from, say, the Galapagos and are willing to put in a few days of sailing to weather, then you are also a candidate to visit these islands and be one of the few that do. The Southern Hemisphere summer (December to April) would be the best time of year, for the northerly current is weaker, and the seas lower and the winds are still a good 10 to 12 knots.

There is only one place to make landfall at Robinson Crusoe Island. That is Cumberland Bay, along whose shores the bulk of the residents live in a village called San Juan Bautista. Cumberland Bay is quite deep owing to the shorelines being steep-to, so plan on using at least 300-ft. anchor rodes. The best anchorage for small boats is in the southwestern part of the bay, and the bottom provides good holding. Set two anchors in a hurricane hawse because the williwaws coming down Anson's Valley will seek to drive your craft out to sea. A prudent mariner will leave a capable crewperson aboard to handle the boat if that should occur. As you might expect, the good anchorages (shallow water and good bottom) are taken up by local fishing boats. There is a mooring buoy available when the island supply boat is not in port and the harbormaster may allow you to use that. Officials will come out to your boat to effect clearance procedures.

Ashore you will find the inhabitants (1982 population was 516) busy with their lobster fishery. Lobsters are caught in deep water (80 feet plus) and retained in traps along the shoreline until they can be shipped to Valparaiso by air or ship. Lobsters are the principal meat that you can buy on the island and the price is reasonable. Other than lobster and some limited homegrown vegetables and fresh bread, there are no provisions to be obtained at San Juan Bautista. Likewise, there are no boat supplies and the only way to get fuel is to buy some from a local fisherman. Water is usually plentiful, espeically during the rainy season of May to November.

When visiting ashore, the only way to get around is on foot. The only road, as such, leads to the mountains to an airstrip at the west end. Ashore you will find the expected temperate climate growth of pines, cypress, acacias and eucalyptus plus an abundance of wild berries on the fertile hillsides. If your timing is right, you may be there when beef is butchered and can get a few small cuts of fresh meat.

Visiting the Juan Fernandez Islands is an experience in sailing off the beaten path and seeing peoples who are rarely visited by cruising boats. The other way to get there is by air, but that wouldn't be half as much fun, would it?

— Cruising World

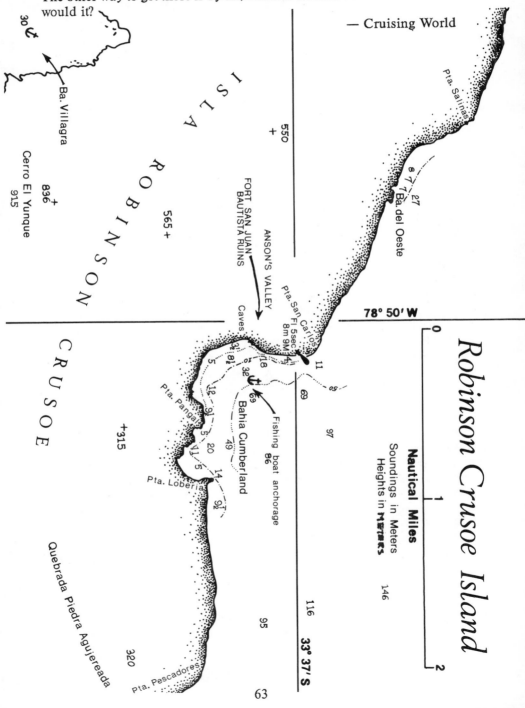

63

CHAPTER 3

SOUTH SEAS ORIGINALS

*"You are here to . . . what? . . . search for Gauguin?"
smiled a Papeete tourism official when I explained my
mission in Tahiti. "Monsieur Gauguin, is it? Then you
must have a poster, you know, a souvenir." He handed
me a Gauguin poster depicting a Tahitian vahine (woman) in a sleeping pose. Then in a voice conveying a
sense of puzzled amusement, he asked, "Wherever will you
begin?"*

— John W. Perry, "Pacific Travelogue"

The reader may wonder about the current broad use of the words Tahiti and Tahitian—often applied with seeming indifference to a specific island or group of people. Tahiti is, always has been and, I hope, always
will be an island wreathed in folklorian glamour. The people who lived
on the island of Tahiti in Captain Cook's time, were Tahitians, as they are
now. But common usage in the tourist industry has resulted in the application of the names Tahiti and Tahitians to all islands and peoples indigenous to French Polynesia. While in truth, we still have Raiateans,
Tuamotuans, Raivavaens, and the like, they are all broadly referred to as
Tahitians. It is a pity to homogenize such interesting people, but that is
what is happening "by popular demand." So, when the tourism official
asked, "Wherever will you begin?" he was not being facetious, he just
wanted to know where in French Polynesia will the search start.

The Enduring Tuamotus

Nowhere in the Pacific are there more enticing atolls than in the
Tuamotu Archipelago of French Polynesia. These atolls (a few are still islands) have become cardinal destinations of world cruising boats as well
as for tourists who want to see the South Seas in their natural state. What
makes the atolls of the Tuamotus so attractive is that they are classic atolls—
ribbons of motus (islets) covered with coconut palms surrounding placid
jade green lagoons. Ravaged by hurricanes, scarred by nuclear blasts and
exploited by adventurers, the Tuamotus live on as one of Nature's most
exotic geologic creations.

The Tuamotu Archipelago is a 1000-mile long string of coral atolls lying between the Society and Marquesan groups of French Polynesia. The
76 islands of the archipelago have only 343 square miles of land area and
range from unbroken circles of coral reefs to glistening chains of coral islets with one or more navigable passes opening into shimmering turquoise lagoons. The only geologic stranger in this archipelago is Makatea, which
is a raised coral atoll.

The Tuamotus were long known in history as the Dangerous Archipelago because of its clutching coral reefs and the perverse currents that pervade the area. Many a sailing ship has left its bones drying on the reefs of a Tuamotu atoll. Even today, Oriental fishing boats and some sailboats manage to find their way onto the jagged reefs, for the atolls sit low on the horizon. Yet, these islands are so attractive that hundreds of overseas yachts visit them every year.

This archipelago was also once known as the Paumotu Archipelago, a name that local residents still prefer. They would also prefer their own language, Paumotuan, however, it is rapidly disappearing as Tahitian, French and, yes, even English take over in the daily world.

Thirty of the atolls are uninhabited, the rest support small populations limited by food, water and space. In bygone days, atoll populations were balanced by infanticide and migration of adults, but today the bright lights of Papeete draw the youth away from their atoll homes and families. An estimated 6700 persons live throughout the inhabited atolls, scraping together an economic subsistence from copra, fish and black pearls.

The atolls were known to Europeans as early as 1615, when the Dutch explorer Jacob LeMaire sailed past the western end. To him, they were dangerous low-lying islands to be avoided, but in the early 1800s, adventurers became aware that a fortune awaited them in the lagoons. Pearls and mother of pearl shells became a source of easy money. Harvesting of the black pearls was made possible by hardy Tuamotuan divers who could descend to unbelievable depths of 50 to 100 feet without diving apparatus and gather the valuable mollusks from the bottom. Of course, it was dangerous and many a native diver paid a high price in permanent disability and even death for his swimming prowess.

The first Tuamotu atoll to get worldwide attention was Raroia. It was the unplanned landing site for Thor Heyerdahl's balsa wood raft *Kon Tiki* in 1947. Hyerdahl believed South Americans were the first persons to

Cruising boats at the village pier, Ahe, Tuamotus

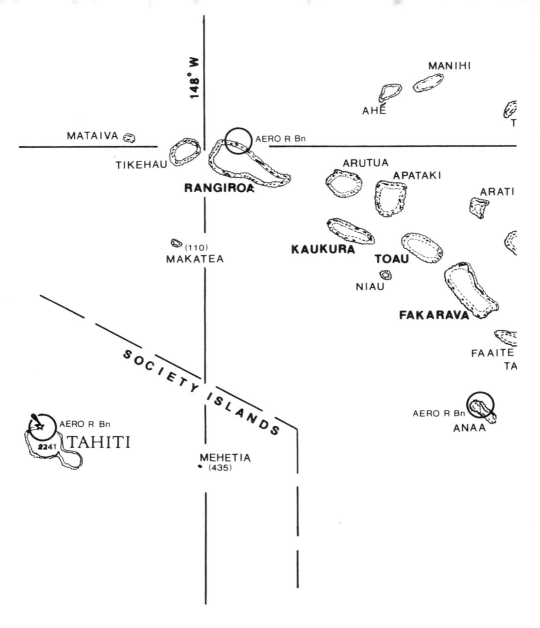

Tuamotu Archipelago
Leeward End

0   60   120

Nautical Miles

Heights in Meters

TÉPOTO
NAPUKA

TAKAROA

Nuclear Activities
Test Base

AKAPOTO

TIKEI

PUKAPUKA →

15° S

KA

TAIARO

TAKUME

FANGATAU

KAUEHI

FAKAHINA →

RARAKA

KATIU

TAENGA

RAROIA

MAKEMO

NIHIRU

TUANAKE

HITI

REKAREKA

TÉPOTO

MARUTEA NORD

HANEA

MOTU TUNGA

TOKOKOTA

TAUERE

HIKUERU

HARAIKI

REITORU

AMANU

AERO R Bn

MAROKAU

HAO

RAVAHERE

NENGO NENGO

PARAOA

MANUHANGI

HEREHERETUE

AERO R Bn

ANUANURARO

ANUANURUNGA

NUKUTEPIPI

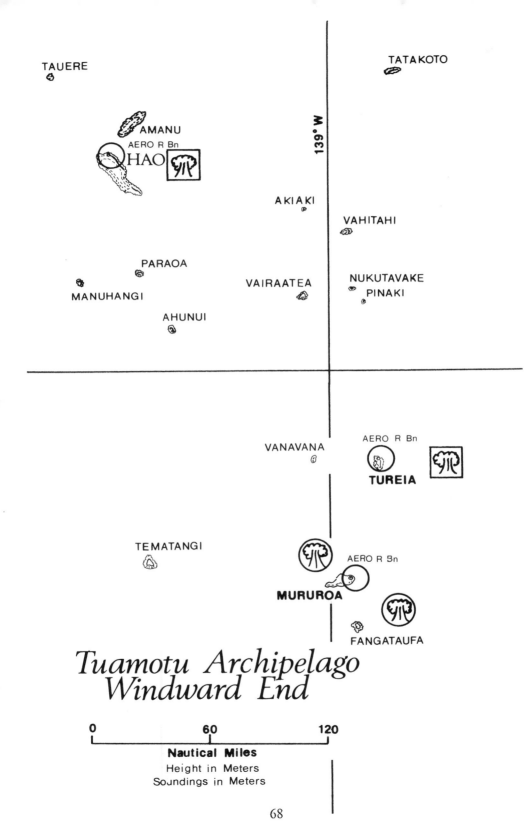

TATAKOTO

TAUERE

AMANU

AERO R Bn

HAO

139° W

AKIAKI

VAHITAHI

PARAOA

VAIRAATEA

NUKUTAVAKE

MANUHANGI

PINAKI

AHUNUI

VANAVANA

AERO R Bn

TUREIA

TEMATANGI

AERO R Bn

MURUROA

FANGATAUFA

Tuamotu Archipelago
Windward End

0   60   120

Nautical Miles

Height in Meters

Soundings in Meters

 PUKARUKA

REAO
AERO R Bn

Nuclear Activities

Test Site

Test Base

20° S

 TENARARO

VAHANGA
TENARUNGA

MARUTEA SUD

MATUREIVAVAO

MARIA

 14 Récif de la Minerve

AERO R Bn

 MORANE

 ILES GAMBIER
(441)
TEMOE

 9 11

populate these islands and to prove it, he drifted for 3½ months over a distance of 4300 miles from Peru before unexpectedly landing on Rarioia. His westerly drift theory, however, is still doubted in anthropologic circles.

More recently, five of the atolls—Mururoa, Fagataufa, Tureia, Hao and Anaa—have received notoriety as the French atomic test area. While the actual explosions were underground in basalt rock on Mururoa, they are monitored and logistically supported from the other atolls. That the fragile-looking atoll has survived numerous nuclear explosions is a tribute to the structural engineering of the minute coral polyp.

It is not only the meager economy of these atolls that has limited their population. Nature takes a hand every few years by sending devastating tropical cyclones across the low-lying atolls in the austral summer. Little is heard about them for the area is large; weather reporting stations few and the people uncomplaining. Most village structures are built of local materials and easily rebuilt after a storm, hence they are considered expendable. A few, though, are heavy concrete structures, usually churches, which provide needed storm-proof shelters for the population.

And now tourists have also found their way to them via airplanes and island trading ships. Some atolls such as Manihi and Rangiroa have hotels for guests; others such as Takapoto, can furnish guests informal lodging with local families. During the austral winter months (May–October), the climate is at its best and balmy tradewinds temper the ever-present sun. These are the islands for travelers tired of bustling Papeete or stereotyped Moorea.

Although there is no "capital," as such, for the Tuamotus, Rangiroa Atoll has, by default, taken over as the most important atoll. It is the largest in the archipelago and now the most populous. Once known as Rairoa,

Outrigger canoe carrying copra, Ahe, Tuamotus

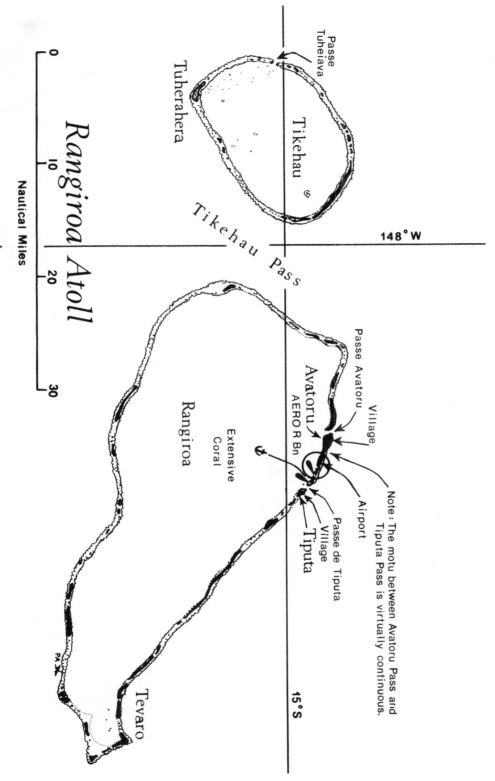

Passe
Tuheiava

Tuherahera

Tikehau

Passe
Tuheiava

148°W

Tikehau Pass

Rangiroa Atoll

Nautical Miles

0

10

20

30

Rangiroa

Extensive
Coral

Avatoru

Passe Avatoru

Village

AERO R Bn

Note: The motu between Avatoru Pass and
Tiputa Pass is virtually continuous.

Airport

Passe de Tiputa

Village

Tiputa

Tevaro

PA

15°S

71

its sparkling lagoon is 400 square miles in area, making it the third largest atoll in the world (Kwajalein is the largest followed by Nanonuito). Rangiroa, however, is the first in the number of motus making up the barrier reef—150. On these 150 motus live 1200 persons striving to maintain a hereditary system of government while under the domination of a strong central government in Tahiti.

Two passes lead into Rangiroa's expansive lagoon—Avatoru and Tiputa, each of which has its own adjoining village. Avatoru is the "business" center while Tiputa is the "administrative" center. To go between villages, you must take to the water and traverse lively Tiputa Pass with its swift currents—exciting but not dangerous.

Both villages are somewhat alike with houses built of coral blocks and corrugated iron roofs, others of brightly painted clapboard construction, and still others of traditional thatch construction. In spite of fresh water problems common to all atolls, many homes are surrounded with well-manicured lawns punctuated with brilliant hibiscus and fragrant frangipani and shaded by stately tropical trees. Traffic is never a problem because most people walk the coral roads to their destinations while airport buses and delivery trucks signal their approach with clouds of dust.

The weather in French Polynesia is normally the finest in the Pacific Basin, but it can become obstreperous at times. Tropical storms and hurricanes occasionally appear in the December through April time period and the Tuamotus are a favored breeding ground for them. Good weather forecasting, however, has reduced the danger to the inhabitants, but the strong winds and storm surge still devastate property. The hardy people of these atolls take such occurrences in stride and continue a way of life that accepts hurricanes as unavoidable nuisances.

Rangiroa's economic resources are the lagoon, motus and endless sunshine. From the lagoon, the local people take fish for their tables as well as for Tahiti restaurants where it is shipped daily by air. They also cultivate pearls in the shallows of the lagoon. This industry replaced the black pearl diving in deep waters of years back. Sharks abound in the lagoon passes where they feed on fish stemming the swift currents. Most of the sharks are black-tipped reef sharks which are quite indifferent to human beings. Ten years ago, a flourishing fish processing plant stood on the banks of Avatoru Pass, but it closed after years of intensive fishing depleted the schools of fish.

Rangiroa captured the attention of tourists as soon as jet airplane travel to Tahiti because popular. Now a traveler can take an additional one-hour flight to Rangiroa at a modest fare of $150 (round trip) and enjoy a part of the Pacific seen by few other people. Or, if he is truly adventurous, he can board an interisland freighter at the low fare of $20 (one way) and enjoy a two-day copra schooner cruise to Rangiroa. The return trip may be a little indefinite, though, since it depends on the arrival of another trading ship headed back to Tahiti.

Tourists have, indeed, taken to this tropical paradise and several hotels now serve their needs. Best of these is the bungalow-style Kia Ora Hotel located near the village of Avatoru which is, itself, only minutes from the airport. Tourism has caused development of many small associated enterprises taking advantage of the paradisical environment. Visitors can snorkel, windsurf, water ski, scuba dive and take excursions to neighboring motus where copra-making is still pursued.

On an atoll such as Rangiroa, the visitor falls into a relaxed way of life for the sun is hot and the rustling palms tell him to slow down. The trappings of distant civilization are stripped away by the subtle sound of the waves' ceaseless lapping on the reef.

The bronze-skinned native peoples that live on 46 of the atolls have been at one with their environment for a thousand years. Modern society has minimal influence on native life for it is the sun, sea and sand that shapes its destiny. While the rest of the world lives in turmoil, mostly of its own creation, the Tuamotu atolls bask in the sun as they have for eons. Their future is assured as long as the coral polyps are left alone to do their job.

— Pacific

Avatoru Pass, Rangiroa Atoll, Tuamotus Archipelago

FRENCH POLYNESIA'S BEST KEPT SECRET

Sitting astride the Tropic of Capricorn, due south of Tahiti, are some of the prettiest islands in the entire Pacific. These are the Austral Islands, the southernmost islands of French Polynesia. Because they are 300 to 400 miles off the usual sailing track through the South Pacific, only a handful of boats visit them each year, and those that do, find unspoiled islands like few others in the Pacific.

The Australs are comprised of five inhabited islands—Rimatara, Rurutu, Tubuai, Raivavae and Rapa—flanked by two uninhabited atolls—Marie (Hull) Island to the west and Marotiri (Bass) Island to the east. Forget the atolls for they are uninhabited, but don't run into them if you are in the area.

You may as well also forget Rapa (also called Rapa Iti to distinguish it from Rapa Nui, the Polynesian name for Easter Island). The French government does not approve of casual visitors to Rapa. It is the highest of the Austral Islands and the least touched by civilization. At 27° 36′ S, it is out of the tropics and in the temperate zone of weather. There is no barrier reef to shelter the harbor, which is a volcanic crater with lots of foul ground, well-protected from the sea but subject to severe downdrafts off the surrounding crater walls. Unless you are an anthropologist, you probably will not be visiting Rapa, but if you do, anchor with great care.

The Austral Islands are an extension of the vast submerged mountain chain which also forms the base of the Cook Islands to the northwest. The main Austral islands are high islands; although none exceeds 2000 feet. They are mountainous and surrounded by the barrier reefs with passes through the reefs and up to the copra wharves so there is little danger, if you have learned your eyeball navigation. While you can occupy a copra wharf as long as there is no copra vessel there, it is better to anchor out for peace, quiet and freedom from the cockroaches and rats that abound on copra wharves.

There are two ways to get to the Austral Islands—either as a side trip from Tahiti, or as a stopover on the return passage from New Zealand. We were introduced to them in the latter fashion. During *Horizon*'s first trip to Tahiti, she was moored alongside the 27-foot New Zealand sloop *Landfalls II*, which had just arrived from Auckland with an intermediate stop at Raivavae. Her crew extolled the virtues of this island to such an extent that we decided to stop on our return from New Zealand the next year.

We departed Whangarei, New Zealand, in late March (the South Pacific hurricane threat diminishes earlier to the east of New Zealand than to the north and west). The southeast trades were brisk and we stayed above the Roaring Forties. For 19 days we held on a starboard tack until a wandering storm from the Cook Islands forced us to flip over to port tack for the last two days before reaching Raivavae. It was not a particularly

cold trip and we were headed by only one gale, but each crew member ended up with one leg shorter than the other!

Passage time records indicate that two-thirds of the boats make the passage from Auckland to Tubuai in 15 to 22 days. Raivavae takes one day longer. While it is among the longer passages in the Pacific, the reward is in the destination.

The passage from Tahiti is really a milk run and I don't know why more boats don't take two weeks to see these unsullied islands. If you

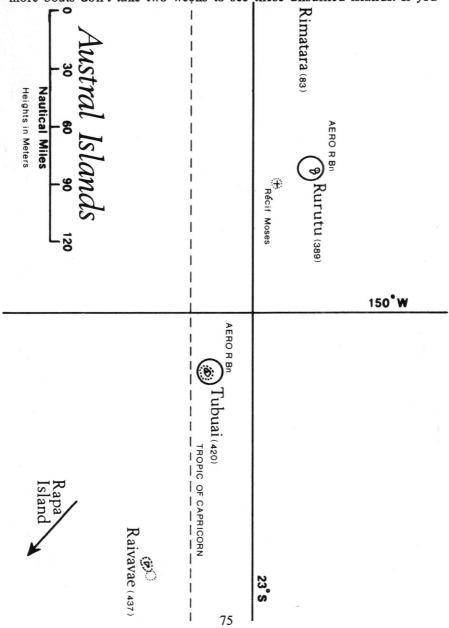

Loading copra boat *Tahaa Pae*, Raivavae, Austral Islands

want to do it the easy way, pick Rurutu as your destination and enjoy a close reach down and a broad reach back. If you feel more weatherly, sail for Raivavae at the eastern end and then lope downwind to see Tubuai and Rurutu. The passage to and from Tahiti should take about three days each way.

Weather in the Austral Islands is much like that of the windward Societies—excellent during the midyear, with the most pleasant weather occurring in September and October. After that, it's the hurricane season and the Australs get the tail ends of many of the cyclonic storms that pass through the Tuamotus and Societies.

Tubuai is the administrative center for the Austral Islands but both Raivavae and Rurutu have their own gendarmeries so you can make temporary entries there. Do not expect to get visas in the Australs; the best you can hope for is a 30-day permit which will have to be converted to a visa at Papeete, Tahiti. If you sailed down from Tahiti, you will already have your visa for French Polynesia, which includes the Australs. Be sure to officially clear before leaving Tahiti for the Australs; the French do not take kindly to random wandering about their islands.

The economy of these islands is agrarian with crops consisting of taro, arrowroot (manioc), copra, vanilla, coffee, bananas and wonderful green oranges. Some European vegetables are grown here for the tables of Tahiti and, as in all French Polynesia, French bread baked twice daily is the prize local product.

Another segment of the economy of interest to the cruiser is handicraft production. Woven hats and mats are superior grade and bring a high price in the markets of Papeete. In fact, when you buy handicrafts in the Australs, you will be bidding against the prices paid by the Papeete dealers. You have an advantage in that these friendly people will offer a bargain to their visitors. Don't spend too much time looking for carvings. That skill was lost many years ago even though rosewood and sandalwood still grow on the islands.

Also don't look for history even though these islands had a rich past. Before Captain Cook arrived in 1777, the islands had a sophisticated civilization numbering about 9,000 persons and rivaling Raiatea. In subsequent years, diseases for which the natives had no immunity swept the islands and by 1830 less than 1,000 persons remained. Barely able to sustain life itself, their rich cultural past vanished into the bush. Few antiquities of pagan days exist today and those that do are in the museums around the world. The nearest evidence of Raivavae's rich past is the large tiki *Heiata* now on display at the Gauguin Museum on Tahiti.

Today, the Australs' 5,000 inhabitants have such modern conveniences as airplane service from Tahiti to Rurutu and Tubuai; electricity by home generating plants; a few trucks to raise dust on the coastal roads and, of course, radios and VCRs. It is, however, still a very much laid-back society that welcomes cruising boats as a diversion from a routine existence. You will find none of the gaiety here that exists in Papeete; on the other hand, you will also miss the thousands of tourists and dozens of boats that inundate Tahiti, Moorea and Bora Bora. In the Austral Islands, off the beaten path, lies a different Polynesia well worth a couple of weeks of your cruising time.

— Cruising World

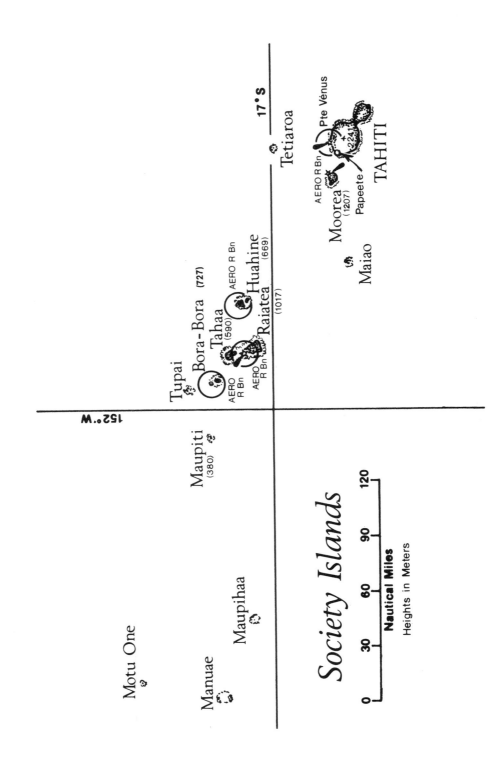

Society Islands

Nautical Miles
Heights in Meters

0   30   60   90   120

Motu One

Manuae

Maupihaa

Maupiti (380)

152°W

Tupai

Bora-Bora (727)

AERO R Bn

Tahaa (590)

AERO R Bn

Raiatea (1017)

AERO R Bn

Huahine (669)

Maiao

Moorea (1207)

Papeete

AERO R Bn

TAHITI

Pte Vénus

+2241

Tetiaroa

17°S

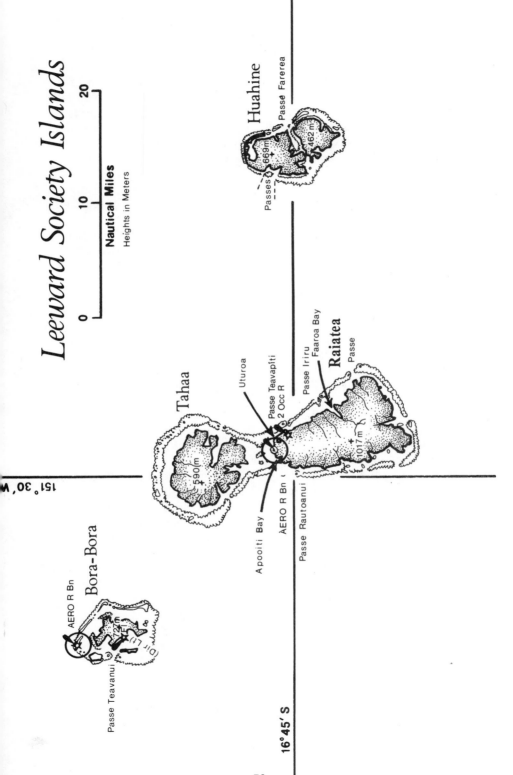

Leeward Society Islands

Nautical Miles
Heights in Meters

0   10   20

Bora-Bora

AERO R Bn

Passe Teavanui

727 m
Fl

Tahaa

590 m

Apooiti Bay

AERO R Bn

Passe Rautoanui

Uturoa

Passe Teavapiti
2 Occ R

Passe Iriru
Faaroa Bay

Raiatea

Passe

1017 m

Huahine

669 m

462 m

Passes

Passe Farerea

151°30' W

16°45' S

79

GARDEN ISLE OF THE SOCIETIES

Ninety-five miles northwest of Tahiti lies Huahine, the garden of the Society Islands. It is not one but two islands—Huahine Nui (Big Huahine) to the north of Huahine Iti (little Huahine). The two islands are connected by a natural isthmus which is awash at low tide, but a man-made bridge over it serves as a traffic connection.

Like most of the islands of the Society Group of French Polynesia, Huahine is a high island whose mountain peaks rise skyward 2300 feet. A coral barrier reef surrounds its 8-mile length and 5-mile width. Within the reef is the ever-entrancing jade green lagoon, the trademark of the South Seas islands.

Huahine is a laid-back agricultural community of about 3200 persons. It has an unspoiled beauty melding reefs and lagoon with coastal plains, deep-cut valleys and soaring mountain tops. Only about 500 of the island's population live in the main village of Fare. The others are spread throughout the rural countryside and the seven small villages hugging the coastal plain. A coastal road encompasses the smaller of the two islands, but does not go completely around the larger because of steep cliffs bordering Maro'e Bay. For the backpacker, though, a trail leads across the mountain, making a round-the-island traverse on foot possible.

The agricultural success of Huahine had not come without considerable industry on the part of the local people. While coconuts and taro are grown in abundance on the coastal plains, it is the development of reef agriculture that is unique. Techniques of atoll agriculture were borrowed from the island of Maupiti, 75 miles to the west. These were adapted to the motus (islands) on the reef and today Huahine is the principal supplier of melons to the tables of Papeete.

Huahine is still an unfound tourist mecca, not that you can't get there easily. Airplanes fly the route daily from Papeete and adjacent islands. It also has twice-weekly ship service which brings the local population out at 5:00 a.m., recreating an age-old ceremony of meeting the copra schooner.

Many Tahitians still ride the "schooner" even though the romance of sail has been replaced by the efficiency of diesel engines. Of course, fares are lower than flying, but there is a more deep-seated reason for traveling by ship. Given clean, reliable service, the overnight ride to Papeete gives the passengers a welcome chance to socialize with their neighbors. And, of course, there is always a guitar and singing to hasten the passage.

Huahine has long been a treasured port of call for overseas cruising yachts. Its relative isolation has left it with an aura of authentic Polynesia that is highly valued by the seafaring tourist. And the coastline of Huahine is deeply indented in many places offering secure and picturesque anchorages inside the barrier reef.

Along the north shore of Huahine Nui, lies an unusual inland lagoon called Fauna Nui. This lagoon, which has always been abundantly filled

with fish, plus the broader coastal plains surrounding the Maeva district, induced the early Polynesian population to concentrate there.

Today, ample evidence of this center of population exists in the ruins of basalt stone maraes and paved areas along the shoreline. Many of these religious sites have been restored through the efforts of the Tourist Bureau and the Bishop Museum of Honolulu. Included in these restorations is the great meeting house, Fare Poto'a, standing on stilts at the edge of the lagoon.

For a long time it was thought that the history of Huahine was solely that of the Maeva district whose stone maraes and pavements were able to defy the ravages of time. But in 1972, during new construction at the Bali Hai Hotel, wood and bone artifacts preserved for 1100 years in sand and mud were uncovered. Huahine, indeed, has an archaeologic history just now being uncovered.

— Pacific

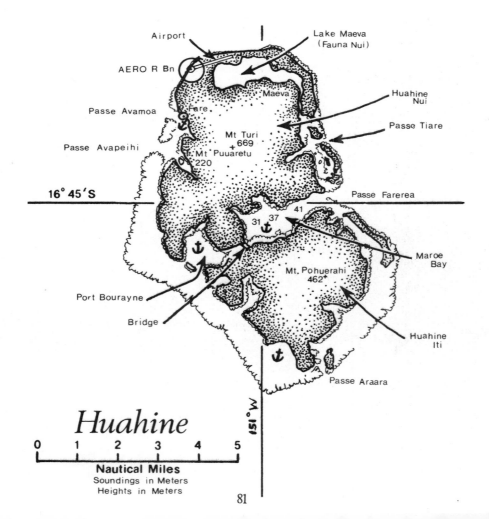

Huahine

0 1 2 3 4 5

Nautical Miles
Soundings in Meters
Heights in Meters

81

Cargo shed on wharf at Fare, Huahine

TAHITI'S CRUISING CENTER

It isn't even on Tahiti anymore, it is on the neighboring islands of Raitea in the leeward Societies. The old spell of tropical Tahiti as the prime cruising destination in French Polynesia is rapidly disappearing as urbanization of once-magic Papeete takes place. The Papeete quai is almost totally devoid of cruising boats and the romance of mooring at the doorsteps of such quaint South Seas establishments as Quinn's Bar, the Stuart Hotel or the old Vaima's Restaurant has faded into oblivion. the buildings have been bulldozed away to make room for more formidable and less friendly shoreline businesses.

But cruising yachts by their very mobility find solutions to such problems. They are now gravitating towards the leeward islands from whence all French Polynesia started—Raiatea and its smaller partner, Tahaa. Back in history, Raiatea was the spiritual center of the Society Islands. It was also the departure site for the remarkable canoe voyages that eventually peopled Rarotonga in the Cook Islands and later, New Zealand.

The attractions of Tahiti's leeward islands have grown through the years as more and more sailors found out about the good sailing in the sheltered waters inside the common reef. Most readers will recognize Raiatea as the home of The Moorings sailboat charter company that pioneered bareboat chartering in these islands about 10 years ago. Now there is a second charter agency here plus a full-service boatyard to handle the needs of not only the charter fleets, but overseas cruising boats as well—all without warping the personality of the scene.

The French boat rental company, ATM Yachts, operating also in Martinique and Guadaloupe, has installed a fleet of boats at Faaroa Bay, Raiatea. ATM's present fleet of seven bareboat yachts is planned to grow

to 20. Most of them will be French Jeanneau monohulls of 32 to 53 feet LOA. But the queens of the fleet are 47-foot cruising catamarans capable of accommodating 10 persons in great comfort. These cruising catamarans were designed and built by none other than Philippe Jeantot, France's premier multihull sailor. You don't have to be a multihull aficionado to quickly realize the benefits of a multihull platform for charter— no heeling, broad (very broad) deck space, separated living quarters, good performance and shallow draft. While you may not choose to own a catamaran back home for reasons of your own, chartering one along with friends for a cruise in the South Pacific can be a fun alternative.

Whether you select The Moorings or ATM Yachts for your charter, you have at your disposal the finest cruising grounds in the world. Within the common reef surrounding Raiatea and Tahaa Islands are bays of unbelievable beauty and tranquil waters. You can, in fact, circumnavigate Tahaa Island, staying entirely within the barrier reef and stopping at a different bay each night. And waiting for you just six hours away on an easy reach to the east, is the garden island of Huahine. There you can visit the colorful tropical village of Fare and sail inside its reef on the whole leeward coast enjoying additional isolated anchorages where you have the world to yourself.

And west of Tahaa, lies the glamour island of the Pacific, if not the whole world, James Michener's fictitious Bali Hai in the flesh—Bora Bora. It is but a five-hour reach in easy sailing. Here cruising yachts have been gathering for years at the famous Oa Oa Hotel and the Bora Bora Yacht Club. You can enjoy the comaraderie of world cruising boats or join the jet set tourists at such colorful hotels as the Bora Bora or Marara.

The latter was the headquarters for the filming crew and actors in the most recent version of the South Seas movie, "Hurricane."

There is a little islet almost centrally located between Raiatea and Tahaa. It is called Ile Toatautu and serves as a navigation aid because of its unique landmark—a single palm tree. More than one cartoonist has thought it original to create such a fantasy, but here it exists in real life and, next to Tahiti's Point Venus Lighthouse and Bora Bora's twin peaks, it is probably the most photographed object in the Society Islands. To the sailor, it is simply known as One Palm Tree Island, what else?

About a quarter-mile from Apooiti marina on Raiatea where The Moorings fleet is based, is the new Raiatea Carenage Services, a full service boatyard offering bottom and hull painting (Awlgrip), carpentry, electrical and engine work, rigging and spar work and a sail loft. This addition rounds out the attractions which now make Raiatea the new cruising center of the Society Islands.

One of the benefits of this new cruising center service will be to make it possible for cruisers to leave their yachts in relative security while they return home for business or other reasons. In the past, that could only be done at Papeete. It not only is away from the hustle and bustle of Papeete, but it has better storage facilities at reasonable rates.

None of the islands—Raiatea, Tahaa, Huahine nor Bora Bora, have yet been caught up in the urbanization chaos that is Papeete. Hopefully, they will continue to be spared as Moorea takes on the job of being the resort community for Tahiti.

Air access to the Society Islands from the United States has been improved with the addition of five-hour jet airplane service from Honolulu. There are often some very attractive domestic fares between the mainland and Hawaii making such a route worthwhile and the long haul from the mainland can be broken up with a visit to Polynesia USA while enroute to your South Pacific bareboat charter.

— Cruising World

Under sail on a Moorings charter boat, Raiatea

THE COOKS ARE STILL POLYNESIAN

The Cook Islands have been discovered more times than any other island group in the Pacific. First it was the Polynesians in their great canoe migrations of the 7th and 8th centuries. Then about 1300 A.D., Tahitians sailed via the Cooks to New Zealand and returned establishing the Polynesian-Maori culture and the initiative for today's close bonds between the Cook Islands and New Zealand. Even the Spanish looked in on the northern islands during the 16th and 17th century, but it was the islands' namesake, Capt. James Cook, who is credited in European eyes with discovering the islands in 1774.

The Cook Islands did not escape the *Bounty* mutiny incident. Bligh found Aitutake in 1789, and the mutineers of the *Bounty* called there the same year after seizing the ship in Tonga. The mutineers are believed to have introduced the first oranges and pumpkin seeds to Rarotonga.

Today the 15 Cook Islands, in particular Rarotonga, are being discovered by visitors flying aboard Hawaiian Airlines' new weekly service from Honolulu. Five hours out of the fast tourist lanes of Honolulu, visitors arrive in laid-back Rarotonga, a tranquil bit of paradise still existing in the South Seas.

One could hardly expect international jet service to all 15 of the Cook Islands. In fact, one would deplore the intrusion of jets into the tranquility of the outer islands, but that does not imply isolation. Air Rarotonga's fleet of small airplanes provides daily connections from Rarotonga to many of the outer islands and, where they don't fly, Silk and Boyd's trading ships carry passengers as of old, but in somewhat greater comfort.

Seventeen thousand persons, 98 percent Polynesian, populate the Cook Islands and 9300 of them live on the main island of Rarotonga. It is hardly a Honolulu (900,000 persons) or even a Papeete (100,000 persons). As a matter of interest, there are more Cook Islands' Maoris living in New Zealand than in the Cook Islands. This safety valve for population growth has enabled the Cooks to maintain their traditions and culture better than other island groups who have been forced to accept outside economic domination for survival. Best of all, Rarotonga's island skyline is not dominated by cloud-piercing concrete condominiums for here buildings can rise no higher than a coconut tree.

Rarotonga and other Southern Cook Islands of Atiu, Mauke, and Mangaia are insular Gardens of Eden supplying not only the local populace and restaurants with garden delights, but yielding significant export also. The fruit menu is almost endless topped by pawpaw, bananas, coconut, mangos, pineapple, starfruit, passionfruit, mandarins, and kumara. It is here that Nature's perverse artistry decided that an orange could be colored green and a lime colored orange.

Cook Islands agriculture is not limited to the usual South Sea island's produce, for its close connection with New Zealand has introduced into

the Cook's fertile soil a gamut of European vegetables. Beans, cabbages, lettuce, snow peas, chilis, peppers and the like are to be found in the markets and restaurants.

The culture of the Cook Islands is conservative in most ways. The people's dress is more Polynesian than on other Polynesian islands and their lifestyle holds strongly to traditional practices even though many Western trends are noticeable in Rarotonga. Drinking, rock music, and junk foods are restrained in this society that still gathers itself at family dining tables.

It is obvious that the church retains a strong influence over the lives of the people. If you had but one hour to spend on Rarotonga to mix with the Maoris, it would best be spent attending a service of the Cook Islands Christian Church. Just to hear the magnificent voices of the Islanders singing native and European hymns is all the justification you need to visit the Cook Islands.

If you had a second hour, it should be spent on the more obvious— attending a performance of one of the Cook Island's dance groups. They are held at Island Night feasts in many hotels and restaurants around Rarotonga (and some of the outer islands, as well). While the Cook Islanders dance the same energetic and pulse-quickening dances as do the Tahitians, they do it with less European showmanship. Cook Islands choreographers stick closer to the storylines of legends so that you can more easily imagine the past as your eyeballs dance to the present.

Should your tastes prefer Polynesian rock and roll entertainment, there is always the Banana Court located in the heart of "downtown" Rarotonga. With the passing of Quinn's Bar in Papeete in the late 1970s, Rarotonga's Banana Court took over as the legendary South Pacific waterfront watering hole. But today, it is jet tourists who mingle with the locals on the dance floor rather than the sailors of Jack London's day.

The Cook Islands fragile economy does not permit spending money on restoration of historic sites, yet they are there for the finding. Most famous is the great road of Toi or Ara-nui-o-Toi encircling most of Rarotonga. It was paved with coral slabs and traversed hill and valley. Although believed to have been built around 1050 A.D. by Toi, nobody today knows who Toi was or where he came from or went to. The road remains a hidden historic bonanza.

These are the last romantic islands of Polynesia where native peoples still smile, wave and call out greetings to passers-by with their delightful New Zealand accent.

— Pacific

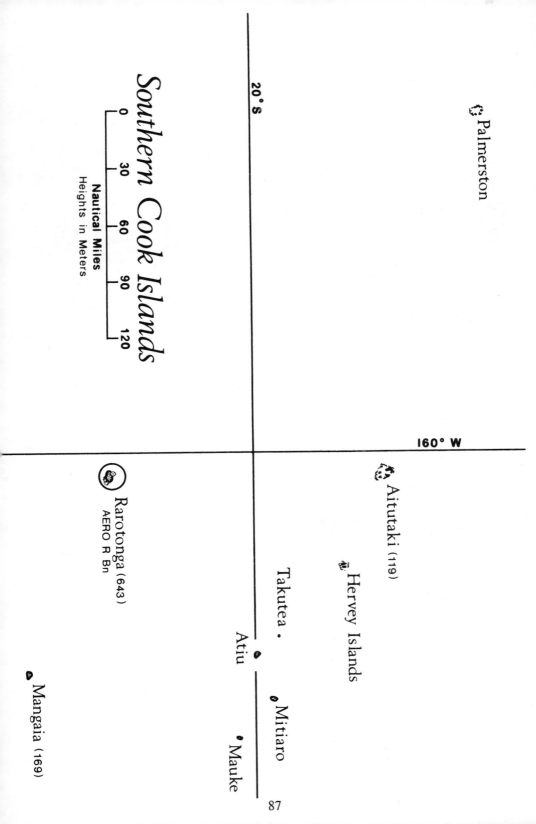

Southern Cook Islands

Nautical Miles
Heights in Meters

0   30   60   90   120

20° S

160° W

Palmerston

Aitutaki (119)

Hervey Islands

Takutea .

Atiu

Mitiaro

Mauke

Rarotonga (643)
AERO R Bn

Mangaia (169)

The famous Banana Court Bar along the waterfront at Rarotonga, Cook Islands

AITUTAKE—AN ALMOST ATOLL

Rarotonga, capital of the Cook Islands, was the cruisers favorite port of call in the Southern Cook Islands up until 1985, when work on harbor improvements commenced and cruisers had to be turned away for construction reasons. Then came Cyclone Sally in December 1986 to tear up old and new harbor works alike, delaying completion of Avatiu Harbor for several more years. The old welcome mat which had previously been out for cruisers (except during cyclone season), was then figuratively transferred to the Cook's second largest island—Aitutake, about 140 miles north.

Aitutake is an "almost" atoll having a magnificent barrier reef and an immense lagoon. The lagoon is triangular in shape, 7 NM across the base and 11 NM from top to bottom. Whereas the barrier reef is dotted with many small motus 10 to 12 feet in elevation, the central island of the lagoon (which prevents it from being called an atoll), rises to a height of over 400 feet and is incredibly fertile.

Your stay in Aitutake will be a real Polynesian experience made better by the fact that the people all speak English with a delightful Kiwi accent. The population is 95 percent pure Polynesian with that infectious need for a good time. Island Nights are held once a week at the two hotels (Rapae and the Aitutake Resort). There you will have all the hip-swinging dancing your eyes can handle as well as island feasting on pig, fish, breadfruit, pineapple and other locally grown goodies. There is no cover or entry charge for the entertainment and when you pay your bill, there is no tipping. Very civilized, I would say.

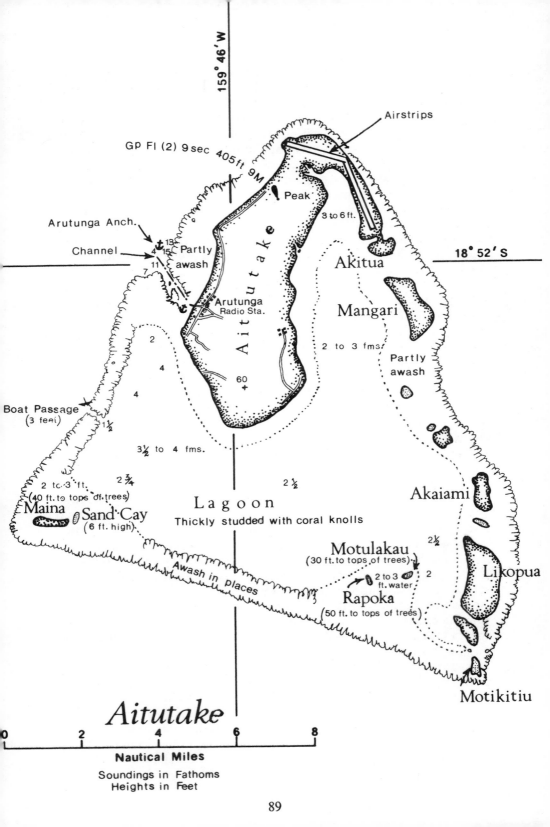

159° 46' W

Airstrips

Gp Fl (2) 9 sec 405 ft 9M

Peak

3 to 6 ft.

Arutunga Anch.

13

Channel

4 15 Partly
awash

11

7

Akitua

18° 52' S

Mangari

2 to 3 fms.

Arutunga
Radio Sta.

A
i
t
u
t
a
k
e

Partly
awash

2

4

4

60
+

Boat Passage
(3 feet)

1½

3½ to 4 fms.

2 ¾

2 ½

Akaiami

2 to 3 ft.
(40 ft. to tops of trees)

Maina

Sand Cay
(6 ft. high)

Lagoon
Thickly studded with coral knolls

2 ½

Motulakau
(30 ft. to tops of trees)

Likopua

Awash in places

2 to 3
ft. water

2

Rapoka
(50 ft. to tops of trees)

Motikitiu

Aitutake

0   2   4   6   8

Nautical Miles

Soundings in Fathoms
Heights in Feet

There is much to do on Aitutake outside of stuffing stomach and eyes. A tour around the main island and a hike up Mt. Maungapu (elev. 400 feet) will give you a bird's eye view of the entire reef-enclosed lagoon with all of its motus. Cars, motorcycles and mopeds are available. Take your dinghy into the lagoon and sail/motor around, being properly careful of coral heads. Board sailing is very popular in the lagoon. Two particularly interesting motus with good swimming and snorkeling are Akaiami, the former refueling stop for flying boats, and Motokitiu (One Foot Island). Swimming beaches are pretty sparse otherwise. Scuba diving is good right off the reef, but you should check with the local dive shops before jumping in. Since this is a resort island, you can rent all sorts of water recreation gear and have yourself a ball in these warm and clear waters. At the time of my visit last year, there was no ciguatera problem, but, again, always inquire in a strange lagoon.

Although you will have a feeling that you are discovering new land when you get to Aitutake, you will find that many have gone before you. Of course, the Maoris have been there since, probably, 1000 BC. The first European to arrive was our good friend Captain William Bligh, who stopped there on 11 April 1789, after departing Tahiti with the *Bounty* loaded with breadfruit trees on his way to Jamaica, or so he thought. Fletcher Christian, et al, had different ideas and 17 days later in the Tonga Islands, they appropriated the *Bounty* and the rest is history. In 1791, Captain Edward Edwards in *Pandora* went searching through these islands for the mutineers, and in 1792 Bligh paid his second visit to Aitutake.

European visits didn't stop after that. Charles Darwin on the *Beagle* visited Aitutake in 1835, and the first missionary from Europe arrived in 1839. Probably the largest group of foreign visitors were the U.S. Armed Forces who arrived during World War II and built the two long runways you will see at the north corner of this triangular almost-atoll. But don't give up the idea of being an explorer, that is what cruising is all about.

The weather at Aitutake fixes your visiting schedule as it does for the entire Southern Cooks Islands. The austral winter is the time to visit— May through October. Trades blow more consistently; humidity is lower; rainfall is less; and insects are no problem. During the austral summer, November through April, it is considerably warmer and more humid with the trades far less steady. This is also the South Pacific cyclone season and the Southern Cooks have been struck with cyclones (hurricanes) in many past years. Cyclone Sally in 1986 was the last to do significant damage and it sent storm-force winds against all the Southern Cooks including Suvarov, Palmerston, Aitutake, Rarotonga and Mangaia. At such times, one should be cruising elsewhere, like in New Zealand to the south or Micronesia to the north. Neither the Rarotonga nor Aitutake harbormasters will permit boats to stay overnight during the cyclone season, northing personal, just safety. If you foolishly should be in those waters and a cyclone approaches, don't go into a harbor for shelter. You are far safer at sea with plenty of searoom.

Aitutake's harbor is small and the entrance shoal, but navigable if your vessel draws less than 6 feet. The passage through the reef is about one-half mile long. Generally, there is an ebb tide through the channel and it may reach 3 or 4 knots in strength. On entering, the port side of the channel is marked with red stakes along the edge of the cut, so take them close aboard. You will also see some black stakes to starboard, but local knowledge says stay close to the red stakes. The bottom of the cut is sand and it has waves in it so you may touch bottom on occasion, but don't panic and turn out of the channel. If stuck, wait for help or a rising tide.

The anchorage itself is at the mouth of the man-made harbor. You can go into the harbor for provisions or fuel, but don't remain there. Find a clear location outside and anchor fore and aft to keep from swinging in the narrow space. If you plan on staying for a long time, like your full 31-day limit, think about setting four anchors for security.

Boats that are too large to enter the channel, can anchor outside on the reef to the north side of the channel entrance. The water is 40 to 60 feet deep with a mixed coral and sand bottom. Don't leave your anchored boat unattended on this reef (or on any other reef anchorage, for that matter).

Clearance into Aitutake is relatively simple. If you anchor outside, you will have to go to Customs to clear in. If you anchor inside the channel, Customs will come to you. Have the usual papers ready and you will be granted visitor permits for 31 days, renewable for another 31 days at a cost of NZ$25. There is a mooring fee of NZ$1.50 per day and a departure tax

Fish barbecue at "One Foot Island," Aitutake, Cook Islands

of NZ$20 per person. These are not great sums if you consider the current exchange rate of US$1=NZ$1.70. You will also notice when you go ashore that there are no dogs running around. There are different stories given for that, but I wouldn't bring my pet ashore under any circumstances.

The second place you should "clear in" is with Father Lane at the Catholic Mission. Father Lane is Hawaiian and has replaced Father George, who for many years was the cruisers' host. Father George's legendary logbooks are in Father Lane's custody and every cruiser should enter his piece of artwork.

Aitutake is not a good place to provision, since its small population (about 2000) does not require large stocks of food and other supplies. You can get the usual tinned goods of the South Pacific (mostly from New Zealand since this country is in "free" association with New Zealand) and you can get some fruits and vegetables. If you like cabbage, some of the world's best is grown on Aitutake. As far as reprovisioning is concerned, you should have filled up in Papeete, Rarotonga or Pago Pago.

You can get potable water here, but I recommend that every boat collect rainwater on board and not have to depend on land sources.

This can also be a mail stop, especially if you are going to hang around for a month or two. Daily air connections are made with Rarotonga, which has twice weekly connections with Hawaii and the U.S. Postal Service. If you are only having a short visit here, do not depend on the mail having arrived on a tight schedule. There is a hospital with resident doctors, but local capabilities are limited. Go to Rarotonga, Papeete or Pago Pago for major medical problems.

— Cruising World

SUVAROV—AN ISLAND PARK

Suvarov Atoll lies in the middle of the Cook Islands archipelago, pretty much in the path of boats cruising between Tahiti and American Samoa. For as long as written history has records, Suvarov has been the dream of those seeking a remote island on which to escape the clutches of civilization.

Cook Islanders came to Suvarov in search of pearls and to harvest the mundane coconut for copra. They found the atoll usable for short stays while they conducted their harvests but unsatisfactory for year-around living. And that is not surprising, for Suvarov has only about 100 acres of land on a half dozen islets that rise a mere 10 or 12 feet above sea level.

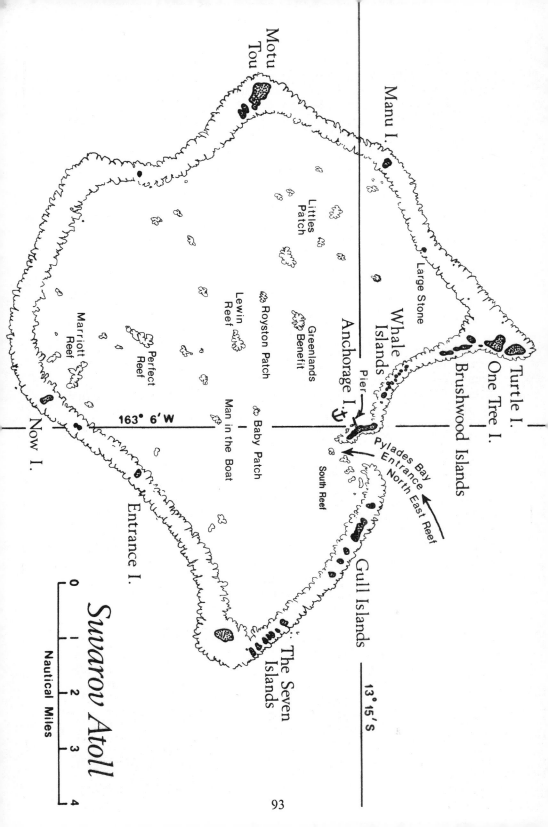

Suvarov Atoll

Motu Tou

Manu I.

Large Stone

Littles Patch

Whale Islands

Royston Patch

Greenlands Benefit

Lewin Reef

Marriott Reef

Perfect Reef

Pier

Anchorage I.

163° 6′ W

Man in the Boat

Baby Patch

South Reef

Turtle I.

One Tree I.

Brushwood Islands

Pylades Bay Entrance

North East Reef

13° 15′ S

Now I.

Entrance I.

Gull Islands

The Seven Islands

0   1   2   3   4

Nautical Miles

93

The 9- by 11-mile atoll suggests a large protected lagoon, but such is not the case. Except for the islets, the barrier reef is awash most of the time and the lagoon is laced with extensive coral patches and nasty coral heads. Only the northerly entrance is navigable and only adjacent Anchorage Islet offers security to the mariner.

Suvarov has had an almost magical attraction for many people but few have made it their home. American writer Robert Dean Frisbee took his four children to Suvarov in early 1941 and lived an idyllic life for most of a year before New Zealand coastwatchers settled there to pursue their mission during World War II. In February 1942, a rare hurricane stripped the islets bare of sustaining vegetation. Although none of the residents perished, Frisbee thought it overcrowded and took his family back to Manihiki.

The coastwatchers stayed until the end of the war and then departed, but they left behind a legacy of buildings, water catchments and a broken-down wharf. Probably more than any other element making up the atoll, the wharf symbolizes the frustration of man in seeking to domesticate Suvarov Atoll.

Anchorage Islet is surrounded by a broad fringing reef and in order to get supplies ashore, the coastwatchers built a coral block wharf out to the deep water. But winter gales and rare hurricanes quickly reduced the wharf to a line of rubble. Tom Neale, most famous of Suvarov's residents, rebuilt the wharf once only to have a gale demolish it shortly after completion.

Neale lived in Suvarov for many years starting in the 1950s with an occasional visit to Rarotonga for medical reasons. His book, "An Island to Oneself," gave readers the world over a chance to vicariously live the life of a hermit on a deserted island. Neale died in 1977, but by then Suvarov had become a maritime memorial for boats cruising the South Seas.

Cruising boats adopted Suvarov, and while there, clean up Anchorage Islet, maintain Neale's former home and feed the resident cats. Their reward is not only the self-satisfaction of paying tribute to a grand old man of the Pacific, but a meal or two of coconut crabs is a mighty fine treat.

Neale had brought two cats with him to Suvarov to control the coconut rat population, but well-meaning visitors later removed their progeny because they thought the poor things would starve to death. Then the rats multiplied like rats and overran the islet. A later boat brought in rabies-free cats from Tahiti and soon nature was in balance again.

Although Suvarov is not an official port of entry to the Cook Islands, officialdom had looked the other way as the occasional cruising boat stopped at Suvarov to clean it up and, occasionally, rescue one of its own kind that had come to grief on the inhospitable reef. Now, however, Suvarov is an official national park of the Cooks and has a resident administrator with family to welcome the arriving cruiser.

Dr. Tom Davis, former Prime Minister of the Cook Islands, visited Suvarov a few years ago and commented in Tom Neale's logbook that the

cruising folk, indeed, had made Suvarov a national park. That was a trib-tribute, not only to Tom Neale, but to all the cruising boats who have stopped there over the years.

— Pacific

Volcanic eruption of Kileauea on the big island of Hawaii, in the Hawaii Volcanoes National Park, lights up the sky.

A VISIT TO THE SANDWICH ISLES (HAWAIIAN ISLANDS)

It began as a hot spot in the earth's mantle 1000 fathoms below the surface of the ocean in the most isolated area of the Pacific Basin. The hot spot yielded a crack and molten magma from the earth's interior began flowing upward while at the same time the mammoth surface plate, that was also the bed of this mighty ocean, moved northwestward in a series of random-time jerks. Magma piled up in growing heaps on the ocean floor, then it penetrated the surface of the water and reached ever higher to produce volcanic mountains where nothing stood before. These were the beginnings of the Hawaiian Islands.

That started 25 million years ago and some of the firstborn islands have already eroded away and they are now visible only to the diver's eye. Others like Kure and Midway atolls at the far western end of the archipelago are next in line to oblivion. The inhabited islands at the eastern end of the chain are the youngest islands and, in fact, the island of Hawaii is still growing as Kilauea volcano continues to spew forth even more magma.

But even as geologic history was being made, other wonderful things were also happening. Flora, fauna and homo-sapiens found these isolated mounds and made them home. We do not know exactly how the indigenous flora and fauna arrived, but we know something about the arrival of man. They were Polynesians, most likely from the Marquesas, who sailed here in their giant double-hulled canoes about 1100 A.D.

Hawaii was the last and most northerly port of call of thousands of Polynesians who migrated from the Austro-Malaysia region of the Pacific. They roamed as far south as New Zealand and as far east as Easter Island, unwittingly creating an ethnic region now known as the Polynesian Triangle.

But their innocent paradise was to last for only a few centuries before the likes of Cook, Bouganville, LeMaire, LaPerouse, Roggeveen, Tasman, and other Europeans brought foreign culture to their lands. Since that time, the world has envied these islands where the sun always shines, the tradewinds cool and warm rains fall to create verdant foliage.

Contemporary Hawaii is a far cry from its Polynesian origin. It is populated by a remarkable mixture of races with the same goal—to live and let live. Its people can trace their roots not only to Pacific Rim countries, but to faraway Portugal, Germany, Poland and Russia.

Since islands form natural political barriers, each island in its earlier years was ruled by a hereditary chief. But eventually the strength of one island chief overcame the geologic division to form a royal kingdom that was eventually to become a part of the United States. That dynasty ruled for 103 years and the palace with its royal trappings still stands in downtown Honolulu.

But the world grew ever smaller and these islands were too strategically located to escape the notice of world powers. Hawaii was made a territory of the United States in 1898 and became a state in 1959. Coincidental with statehood, the jet airplane was born bringing the 50th state within five hours of the Mainland. It also brought Hawaii within 15 hours of the most remote population centers of the world. Thus was set in motion a train of events that was to make Hawaii with its attractive natural environment a playground for all people. The rainbow islands of Polynesia USA had entered the mainstream of a mobile world for all to enjoy.

Hawaii—The Orchid Isle

It is recommended to cruising boats from Mainland USA that they make their landfall at Hilo on the "Big Island." That not only makes easier subsequent passages to the other islands by sailing downwind, but it is a proper place to start a social and cultural tour of Hawaii. With your boat securely moored in Radio Bay inside Hilo Harbor, you can tour the quaint city of Hilo which is only now growing out of its early 1900s personality. You will find much of Hawaii's history on display at the Lyman Mission House Museum.

It is worth a couple of days around Hilo to get your introduction to Hawaii. Then rent a car for at least two days, one to go south along the coast visiting the Macadamia nut processing plant, orchid gardens and spec-

Photo by Hawaii Vistors Bureau

Aerial photo, Captain Cook Monument, Kona, Hawaii

tacular Kilauea Volcano. On the second day, drive north up the windward coast through the sugar cane fields and some spectacular coastline scenery. Stop at Waimea for lunch and a visit to the huge Parker Ranch, the second largest privately-owned cattle ranch in the United States.

Departing Hilo with your vessel, you can either go up the windward side directly to Maui or sail around South Point, the southernmost land in the United States. On the leeward coast you will find Kealakekua Bay, the place where Capt. Cook's days were ended. Overnight anchoring is prohibited, so be prepared to continue north at least to Kailua-Kona Roadstead where you can anchor out for your visit to the "Kona" Coast.

Kailua-Kona is Hawaii's premier tourist area with numerous luxury hotels and restaurants, but it is also noted for sportfishing, surfing and a good place to laze away days in the tropical sun. This is also the area where satisfying Kona coffee is grown and processed.

There is little to see along the coast as you take your departure north from Kailua-Kona (except a couple of good man-made harbors), but it is prudent to stay in the lee of the island all the way to Upolu Point before taking departure for Maui across blustery Alenuihaha Channel.

Lanai—The Pineapple Isle

Although your sights may be set on Maui and the wild whaling port of Lahaina, it is worthwhile to detour to Lanai along the way. Head straight for Menele Bay passing to either side of bombed out Kahoolawe Island. With luck you can get mooring space at Manele Bay for a couple of days

Pineapple being loaded on barge for trip to Honolulu cannery

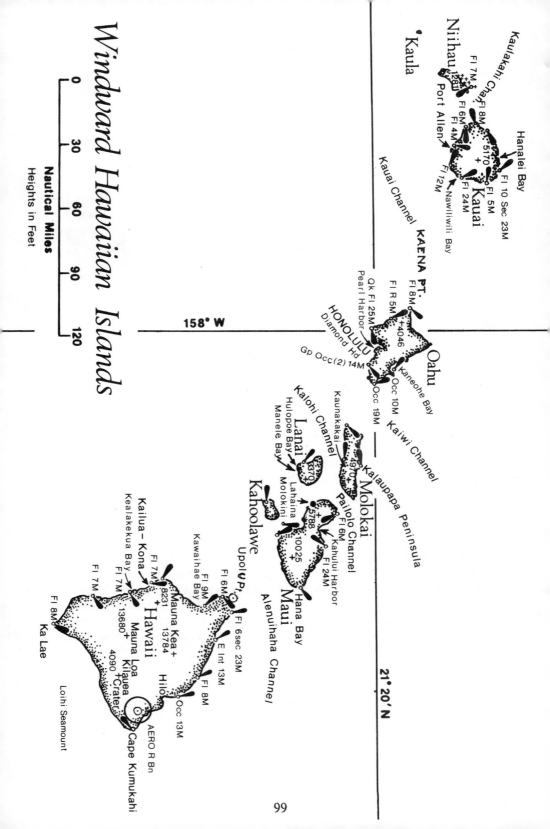

Windward Hawaiian Islands

Nautical Miles
Heights in Feet

0 30 60 90 120

158° W

21° 20' N

99

'Kaula

Niihau
Kaulakahi Cha.
Fl 8M
Fl 7M
Fl 6M
Fl 4M
Port Allen
Fl 12M
Nawiliwili Bay
Kauai Channel
KAENA PT.
Kauai
Hanalei Bay
Fl 10 Sec 23M
Fl 5M
5170
+
Fl 24M

Oahu
Pearl Harbor
Qk Fl 25M
Fl R 5M
Fl 8M
+4046
HONOLULU
Diamond Hd
Gp Occ(2) 14M
Occ 19M
Occ 10M
Kaneohe Bay
Kaiwi Channel

Kalohi Channel
Kaunakakai
Kaunakahakai
Molokai
4970
Kalaupapa Peninsula
Lanai
Hulopoe Bay
Manele Bay
8370
Molokini
Lahaina
Pailolo Channel
Fl 6M
5788
+
10025
+
Kahului Harbor
Fl 24M
Kaho'olawe
Upolu Pt.
Fl 6 sec 23M
E Int 13M
Fl 8M
Occ 13M
Maui
Hana Bay
Alenuihaha Channel

Kailua- Kona
Kealakekua Bay
Fl 7M
Fl 7M
Mauna Kea +
8231
13784
Kawaihae Bay
Fl 9M
Fl 6M
Fl 7M
+
Hawaii
Mauna Loa
13680
+
Kilauea
4090
+Crater
Hilo
AERO R Bn
Fl 7M
Fl 8M
Ka Lae
Cape Kumukahi
Loihi Seamount

giving you a chance to visit a real Hawaiian beach—Hulopoe Bay. This is a marine conservation area and the underwater scenery is superlative.

On a second day, hitch a ride up to the little village of Lanai for lunch at picturesque Lanai Lodge nestled in a forest of Norfolk pines. This quaint little town is home to most of the island's 2000 person population, all of whom make their living from the pineapple industry.

Photo Hana Bay, Maui

Maui—The Valley Isle

If there is any island that has an attraction for the cruising boat, it is Maui. Once the whaling capital of the Pacific, Maui has cashed in on its history to make itself a prime tourist attraction. The only problem with coming to Maui by boat is the lack of a harbor in which to leave it while you visit the Valley Isle. Lahaina's small harbor is taken up by charter boats with only enough room to accommodate dinghies from anchored boats. You will have to anchor in Lahaina Roads and take your dinghy ashore.

Anchoring here can be a challenge, even though it is in the lee of the island. The problem is twofold, a rock and coral bottom under a thin layer of sand and a sometimes strong current. Assess the capability of your anchor set before leaving the boat for hijinks ashore. If you have qualms about your boat's safety in the roadstead, move north to the vicinity of old Mala Wharf which is farther from town but has better holding ground.

Although Lahaina is the obvious attraction with its mainstreet Lahaina Yacht Club and historic Pioneer Inn, a car rental to drive to Kahului for a day would be well worthwhile. You might also want to drive up mighty Haleakala Mountain or take a drive out to Hana Bay (if you didn't stop there with your boat). The latter is a punishing one-day drive on a road that is only 52 miles long but takes 2½ hours to drive each way because of the curves and dozens of waterfalls.

Molokai—The Friendly Isle

From Lahaina, work your way up to the west end of Maui and take anchorage in beautiful little Honolua Bay. From there, sail to Molokai Island stopping first at Kaunakakai, which is a secure harbor and within walking distance of the little town. Here, again, it would be worthwhile to rent a car for a day of sightseeing on the Friendly Isle.

In one day you can visit spectacular Halawa Valley at the east end of the island and the dizzying Kalaupapa Overlook on the windward side. Kalaupapa is the isolated peninsula where Hawaii's first lepers were sent and later cared for by the famous Father Damien. If you make arrangements, you can ride a mule train down to the peninsula itself. Taking leave of Kaunakakai, sail west to isolated Lono Harbor for a short stay and then get ready for civilization as you head across Molokai Channel to Oahu.

Local home, Molokai

Oahu—The Gathering Place

If you are not ready to face Honolulu yet, set your course for Kaneohe Bay, a lovely windward bay protected by an offshore reef. Here you can be a guest of the Kaneohe Yacht Club, which occasionally has some slips available, but there is also anchoring nearby. You can get a limited membership and enjoy some fine Windward hospitality.

You will eventually have to stop at Honolulu, if for no other reason than to reprovision and repair before the long voyage home. The usual place to stop is at the Ala Wai Boat Harbor where you can be a guest of the Hawaii Yacht Club for two weeks and/or stay in the State harbor itself. Whichever you choose (at the season's peak, you may not have a choice), you are in the center of the Waikiki action and within walking

Ala Wai Boat Harbor, Honolulu

distance of all establishments where you may need to spend your money. Other places to stay are at Keehi Lagoon and (for the military) Rainbow Marina in Pearl Harbor.

Oahu is truly the Gathering Place and you will meet boats from around the world while you are there. Windsurfing and board surfing take place within eyesight of the harbor. There is much to see on Oahu and the bus service is unsurpassed. You really do not need to rent a car to enjoy the island. Such places as Bishop Museum, Arizona Memorial, Diamond Head and the fabulous North Shore are all on a bus line.

Waikiki coastline of Oahu, seen from Diamond Head

Hanalei Bay, Kauai. A summer retreat for boats cruising in Hawaii.
Heavy surf is prevalent during winter

Kauai—The Garden Isle

You can take your mainland departure from Oahu or make one more
highly recommended port of call and that is Hanalei Bay on the Garden
Isle. This remote bay on the north coast of Kauai has been used as a filming location for many South Sea movies and when you visit it, you will realize why it is so appropriate.

Kauai is a big island and not heavily populated. The best way to see it
is to rent a car for a day at the community of Princeville and take a drive
down to Port Allen at least, or maybe as far as Waimea Canyon, a remarkable mini-Grand Canyon. I can think of no better place in Hawaii
to close out your cruising log than Hanalei Bay.

— Cruising World

CHAPTER 4

ISLES MYSTERIOUS

"The graceful palm, the source of much sustenance and many other needs for the people of the islands, shielding a roof of curly, bare metal from the blazing sun, is a sight that is repeated endlessly in the South Pacific. The stark contrast in the scene neatly captures the essential ingredients in the story of the South Seas in two universal symbols. The sheltering palm conveys the feeling of the soothing environment, untroubled by the clashing diversities of a system spawned by harsher climes; the rusting tin roof (actually corrugated iron, to be precise) suggests the incongruities resulting from a monetary society parachuted into a communal culture that had evolved in the islands over centuries of isolation from a more competitive, mechanized world."
—Robert Trumbell, "Tin Roofs and Palm Trees"

Islands are by nature mysterious. They rise from the abyssal depths of the ocean to become specks of land in an endless expanse of water. What is on these pinnacles of marine mountains, isolated from the common haunts of man by boundless water? Is there animal, mineral or vegetable? Buried treasure? Lost seafarers? These marvels of nature born eons ago breed 20th century mystery and intrigue, just as they did in the days of Spanish caravels and English privateers.

Some islands like Howland, Palmyra and Rose Atoll are uninhabited for reasons not clear to the outside world. Are such islands so bereft of the necessities for life that they must forever be barren?—just geologic curiosities and navigational hazards? While others like Pitcairn, Johnston and Lord Howe are just as isolated, yet they are inhabited. Who are their inhabitants? Why are they there? What kind of a culture have they developed to offset the ravages of island fever?

And there is yet another group of islands whose value extends far beyond simple habitation—Mururoa, Kwajalein, Midway, et al. By government preeminence, these have been isolated from prying eyes—not Pacific Island governments, but governments from as faraway as Europe. Inside reefs closed to prying eyes, these foreign invaders of insular beauty despoil more of nature's great creations.

There is a mystery to islands that urges the cruisers to sail off the beaten path; to see for themselves what fortune each island holds. Out of the 10,000 islands in the Pacific Ocean, many are still cloaked in mystery awaiting the wandering cruiser to land and investigate. We can but penetrate the mysteries of a few.

The rest we leave for others.

IN THE WAKE OF THE BOUNTY MUTINEERS

Many sailors (Fletcher Christian was the first) think that Pitcairn is at the the end of the world. It really isn't. You will find Pitcairn to be an exciting landfall on the alternate Coconut Milk Run from the Galapagos to French Polynesia. This route takes you from the Galapagos to Easter Island, to Pitcairn, to Mangareva (Gambier Islands) and then to the Marquesas Islands.

Distances and typical sailing times are:

Galapagos to Easter	1945 NM	15 days
Easter to Pitcairn	1120 NM	12 days
Pitcairn to Mangareva	290 NM	3 days
Mangareva to Hiva Oa	830 NM	10 days

On a westbound passage, this is pretty much reaching and running sailing. It is different, though, if you are an Aussie or Kiwi headed the opposite direction. Eastbound, they stop at Rapa, a rarely visited French Polynesian island for which you need permission to visit and then on to Pitcairn, Easter and the Galpagos. The trick with the eastbound route is to stay well south of the French nuclear test site at Mururoa. Obviously, the eastbound routing is on the wind, but that is why we buy sailboats with Marconi rigs.

Photo by Mark Balsinger/Ocean Voyages, Inc.

Pitcairn Islanders returning the crew of the cargo schooner *Edna* to their vessel.

The numbers of cruising boats calling at Pitcairn is on the rise. During the years 1975 to 1977, there were only three boats per year. During the years 1983 to 1986, 14 boats per year called, half of them during the month of April.

Pitcairn is one of those islands without a protected anchorage. You can anchor in Bounty Bay (over the spot where the *Bounty* was burned) in 8 to 10 fathoms of water in a sand bottom with some rock. Alternative anchorages in variable weather are at Down Rope bight or Gudgeon harbor. If these alternatives won't work, then it will be necessary to stand off the island until the weather improves, which may be in a day or two.

The islanders are known for their canny weather predictions and they will advise you of expected changes in the wind necessitating a change of anchorage. Although it is possible to leave your boat unattended at anchor during the day in settled weather, you do not leave it unattended overnight at any time.

Pitcairners have learned to take care of their daily needs, but they live in dread of infectious diseases being brought to their island. Their very isolation has prevented them from developing immunity to all diseases, so do not plan on stopping there if you have an infectious disease aboard you boat. In June 1987, a passenger ship with infectious hepatitis aboard paid a call and the Pitcairners were torn between hospitality and survival. They resolved the situation by allowing passengers who had received gamma globulin innoculations to come ashore.

Do not plan on taking your own dinghy ashore. The Pitcairners will come out to your boat to pick you up, most likely in an outboard-powered inflatable "sportboat."

The traditional longboats are reserved for large ships. But even there, things are changing. The old wooden longboats formerly built on Pitcairn (one was 47 feet long with a 10-foot beam!) are all but gone. They are being replaced with aluminum boats made in New Zealand and England. The reason for this change is manifold—suitable trees no longer grow on Pitcairn; there are not enough men left on the island to handle the heavy wood boats; and, like everywhere else, technology must be served.

While the rest of the world is growing in population, Pitcairn has been shrinking. The December 1986 census showed a total population of 68, of these 20 were non-Pitcairners. There were 15 students enrolled in the school.

The loss of Islanders, whether temporary or permanent, is always a cause for concern among those who remain, particularly when they are part of the workforce or administration. Pitcairn's future lies in its young people and they can ill-afford to have a net population decrease, for there is a minimum number required for mutual community support. Apparently their numbers are still adequate provided cargo ships stop with outside supplies and passenger ships stop to assist their economy.

The Pitcairners are religious people and that is, undoubtedly, the secret of their survival on this beautiful, but isolated island. Writing in "Pitcairn

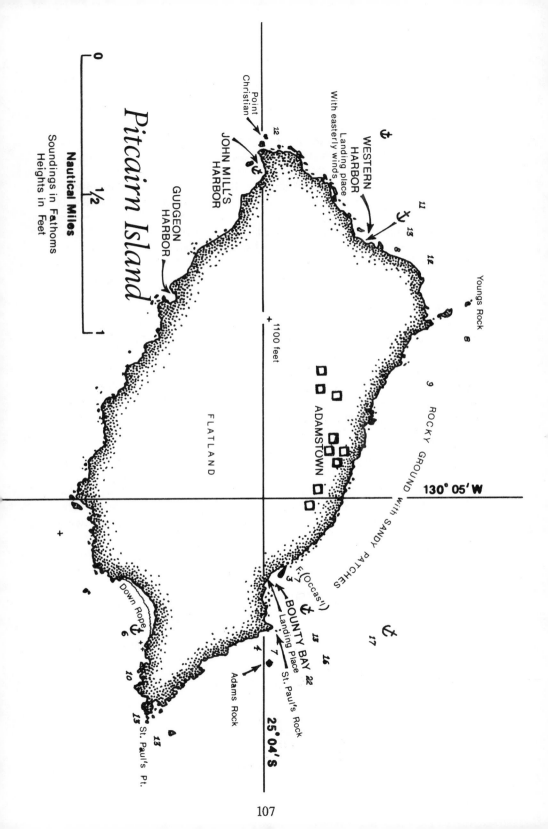

Miscellany," Pastor Oliver Stimpson said: "True, our island is a long way from other islands in the vast South Pacific Ocean—about half way between New Zealand and Panama. By shipping routes it takes a week or more to get to New Zealand.

"People often ask if we don't get desperately lonely living in such isolation? The answer is no. Everyone stays busy, carving curios, gardening, meeting ships, working at paid jobs or public works. What happens is that there are not enough hours in each day. The sun sets all too soon.

"Pitcairners are like an extended family. We need each other and rely on the distribution of talents to make life flow smoothly. We enjoy our island family. Sometimes you might wish to be removed from the 'rat race', to enjoy the calm and peace of such a little paradise. No taxes, water nor phone bills. No smog, no crime. No locks needed to keep burglars out. No fear of anything. The worst thing that can hurt you might be an occasional wasp, if you disturb its nest. Wouldn't you like to retire at night with your doors and windows open? We do.

"Our homes are far away from the noise of the bustling cities, but we are not lonely. We live here by choice. Our many friends in the outside world have been kind and generous. It has made life so much better here. We thank you."

The Pitcairner's income comes primarily from stamps, although at this time the stamp market is soft. Their secondary source of income is wood carvings. They no longer carve soley by hand for there is now electric power on the island. Trees that once were felled with axes and hand saws are now felled with the chain saws.

The wood used for the carvings is miro (me-ro), a reddish-black wood with an attractive grain. Around the turn of the century a wood carver from Europe taught them the skill, but the indigenous stand of miro trees had virtually disappeared by then, having been used for firewood. The enterprising carvers then went to Henderson Island, 100 miles northeast of Pitcairn, for miro wood and have been doing it ever since, except in 1983. That year the carvers harvested a small forest of miro wood on Pitcairn that had been planted in 1964, but that harvest finished the grove for another 20 years.

If you are willing to sail off the beaten track, the Pitcairner's new T-shirt says it best. The front reads: "Pitcairn Island—I've been there." The back reads: "But nobody said it would be easy."

— Cruising World

green
Sea Turtle

At Home with the Pitcairn Islanders

While their own blue water cruising boat swung at anchor near Guaymas, Mexico, Carl and Leona Wallace of La Jolla, California, flew to Tahiti to rendezvous with an Ocean Voyages charter boat for a long-awaited trip to Pitcairn Island. At Papeete, they boarded the 44-foot sloop *Tiare Moana* for a 10-day passage to Pitcairn and a 14-day stay on the island that was a "dream come true."

There is no way to get to Pitcairn Island other than by sea—Fletcher Christian had chosen it well. Although the *Bounty* mutineers wanted such isolation, their descendants are more wordly, according to the Wallaces, and would welcome better transportation. Isolation, per se, is not the problem. It is their income derived from the sale of artifacts and postage stamps to outsiders that creates the need. With fewer ships these days, there are also fewer visitors and the fragile economy suffers.

Besides a help to the economy, the Wallaces pointed out that better transportation would be a viable hedge against serious medical problems. As it stands now, an illness or injury requiring off-island medical treatment requires an emergency radio call to any ship in the vicinity to evacuate the patient. It may take days before a ship can be detoured to affect the pickup.

To the Pitcairners, an ideal solution would be a small airport on their island that would allow service to Mangareva, 290 miles away, and thence to Papeete and then the outside world. With such an airport, they believe that their economy would also prosper with more tourists, their bonds with children who go away to school would be strengthened and, certainly, medical emergencies could be handled more easily.

There is no such thing as a hotel on Pitcairn, so the Wallaces were the guests of Tom Christian, a descendant of Fletcher Christian. Tom had more than enough room for them as his wife, Betty, and their children were off-island visiting New Zealand. This, of course, meant that Tom would also do the cooking for his guests and Leona said he did a marvelous job. Each day Tom would take his Honda ATV to one or more of his gardens (the Islanders disperse their gardens as a hedge against any natural disaster) and bring back cabbages, tomatoes, pineapple, yams and oranges.

All of the men on Pitcairn are wood carvers and each has a carving shop, but no longer is the wood hand-carved. With electric service available daily (9–11 a.m. and 6–11 p.m.), power tools have taken over much of the work. Although the carvings have changed in style due to electric tools, they are still individually fashioned from miro wood reflecting the personality of the carver. Pitcairn's supply of carving wood comes from Henderson Island, 100 miles to the northeast. At least one trip a year is made for the purposes of gathering wood carving materials.

Although transportation is in a tenuous state, communications by radio is not. The island has a sophisticated radio station and is in daily contact with the outside world. Tom Christian is the chief radio officer and

one of four Islanders who pursue ham radio as a hobby (VR6TC). It was the latter fact that convinced Carl and Leona Wallace to go to Pitcairn for they are both ham operators themselves (WD6B and WA6OHB) and had talked with Tom on the air. They brought along a portable transceiver and with a simple antenna strung between trees, sent greetings to their North American friends from Pitcairn Island.

The "native" population of Pitcairn is 48 persons, although several are off-island at any one time for school, holiday or medical reasons. At the time of the Wallace's arrival, however, the population was more than doubled by a large contingent of visiting Norfolk islanders who are also descended from the celebrated *Bounty* mutineers.

Even though the present Pitcairn population is small, there is no evidence that they are going to give up this verdant island. It has been their home for seven generations and with improved transportation, they believe that more visitors will welcome the chance to see this famous Pacific outpost. No, adventure is not dead, but like the Wallaces, you have to make some effort to enjoy it.

— Pacific

Photo by Leona Wallace

Pitcairn Island craftsman carving a cane in his shed.

PALMYRA'S UNIQUE HISTORY

There are a few tropical islands in this world capable of habitation on which no one lives. Palmyra is one of them. Located 925 NM south of Honolulu, Palmyra is in the northern Line Islands archipelago. Most of the Line Islands are a part of the Republic of Kiribati, but the United States has claimed possession of Palmyra since 1859, formally annexing it in 1912. Palmyra today is a privately-owned island whose owners live in Hawaii.

Most people know of Palmyra because of a pair of bizarre murders that occurred in 1974 and which are not yet completely solved. A more romantic part of its history has to do with buried treasure. Historical accounts from the 1903 era reported that Spanish pirates had departed Callao, Peru, in 1816 with captured loot and were, themselves, hijacked by other pirates. The captors then headed west with their prize only to discover Palmyra the hard way—by running aground on its reef. In true pirate fashion, they buried the treasure and sailed off in small boats. None returned, so if you assume that the tale is true, you can also assume that the Callao treasure is still on this sunny atoll.

On the other hand, during World War II and for many years afterwards, the atoll was occupied by United States armed forces who made improvements to it such as dredging out the natural causeway that separated west and center lagoons in order to make a seaplane landing area. They also built a 6,000 foot airstrip complete with service buildings on Cooper Islet. Around the periphery of the atoll were placed pillboxes for defense, while farther inland a line of small coastal gun emplacements and command posts were installed. Roads, waterlines, and other items of a modern military infrastructure were built, mostly above ground for under the thin layer of sand was hard coral.

During all this construction, one could reasonably expect that the treasure would have been uncovered, but it was not. Or is it possible that the treasure was coincidently buried under one of the piles of sand heaved up by the Navy SeaBees as part of a defense revetment?

Palmyra's involvement with the military did not end with World War II. Atmospheric atom bomb tests over Christmas Island 360 miles to the southeast, involved U.S. Air Force operations on Palmyra into 1961. That, however, was the last serious occupation of this pretty tropical isle.

After the military left, there was only one major attempt to use the island again and that was as a copra plantation in 1979. Everything was right for this effort—sun, rain, well-drained soil, a good harbor, land facilities and I-Kiribati workers under an experienced plantation manager from Fanning Island. But with the low prices being paid for copra, even that enterprise was doomed to failure. The atoll was again abandoned and salt bush, land crabs and sooty terns took over.

About the same time that the copra venture was being pursued, a small shellfish harvesting industry was given a try. A small refrigerator ship was

brought in along with traps, fishing personnel and three dogs. It, too, was short-lived and when the workers departed, they left behind the ship as a derelict and the three dogs to forage for themselves. And therein lies an interesting tale.

The three dogs were male mongrels and subsisted on the atoll by their own resourcefulness, living off birds' eggs, meat from coconuts (probably opened by coconut crabs) and an occasional shark caught in shallow water. This was supplemented by handouts of Spam, hamburger and other protein from visiting yachts who also tended to their medical needs.

Long ago, someone named the dogs Army, Palmyra and Navy, with Army being their obvious leader. They were the welcoming committee for the occasional yacht, even to the extent of swimming out to the anchored boat if the crew was too slow in coming ashore. You might think that the dogs would have become wild in their survival environment, but that was not the case. Visitors were welcomed with wagging tails to go along with the barked greeting. but time has taken its toll on the dogs. By 1989, all three dogs had died. Some well-meaning cruiser will probably leave new dogs there (I don't know why), but they can never be the same as Army, Palmyra and Navy.

Several cruising yachts visit Palmyra each year for it is on the heavily traveled route between Hawaii and the South Pacific. Few islands with such a good harbor are also uninhabited and this makes an ideal place for yacht crews who want to stop and stretch their legs or make boat repairs. But the fresh water available on Palmyra may be one of its biggest attractions. Thanks to military construction, there is a 100,000 gallon fresh water tank (always full) which gives yacht crews the luxury of a long shower after weeks at sea.

Anchorage at Palmyra is within the lagoon, well protected in all directions from the seas and sheltered from the prevailing northeast winds.

Palmyra's three dogs—Army, Palmyra, and Navy—now long gone

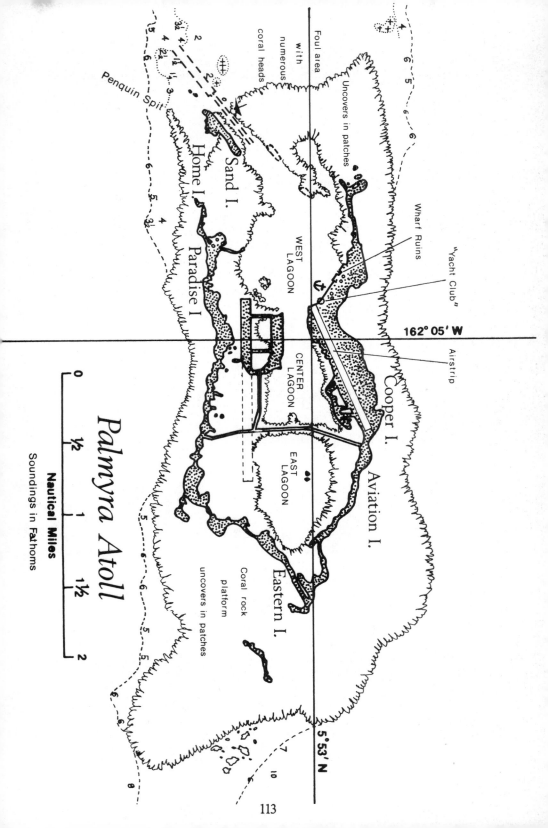

Palmyra Atoll

Foul area with numerous coral heads

Penquin Spit

Uncovers in patches

Wharf Ruins

"Yacht Club"

162° 05' W

Airstrip

Sand I.

Home I.

Paradise I.

WEST LAGOON

CENTER LAGOON

Cooper I.

Aviation I.

EAST LAGOON

Eastern I.

Coral rock platform uncovers in patches

5° 53' N

Nautical Miles

Soundings in Fathoms

0   ½   1   1½   2

113

The dredged channel into the harbor is long, narrow and straight, bordered by coral reefs on both sides but with safe depths of 20 feet or more. The best anchorage is near the old seaplane ramp but the bottom is coarse coral gravel so holding is not the best. For more security, you can tie a bow line to a coconut palm ashore and put out a stern anchor in deeper water to hold you off the beach just in case the prevailing wind does not prevail.

Palmyra remains somewhat of an enigma for it has all the resources of any other atoll of the Pacific but no permanent population. It will probably stay that way until a visionary comes along who not only has sound financing but an appreciation for the tropical environment which can reduce man-made buildings to dust and machinery to rust in a matter of a few years.

Now, though, the island is for sale. After having owned it for 67 years, its Honolulu owners have put it on the market. The price?—$33 million. The hooker? The present owners retain a 20 percent right to whatever buried treasure is found.

— Pacific

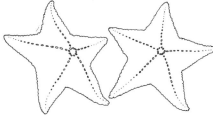

LIFTING THE VEIL AT JOHNSTON ATOLL

We approached mysterious Johnston Atoll in the dead of night, first seeing it glow in the sky at a distance of about 25 miles. By 3:00 a.m. we had found the entrance buoy and lowered the sails, drifting until daylight. Experience had told us not to attempt an entry to a strange harbor at night. At 5:30 a.m. dawn crept over the horizon and we saw the channel leading into the lagoon, well marked but only for daylight use.

Somehow we had expected to be shadowed on our approach and taken into protective custody as we approached the atoll, but, no, there seemed to be little interest in the fact that a strange vessel had intruded into their waters. The only life showing at this early hour was a couple of joggers, telling us that jogging at least was no mystery to this island.

It had not been our intention to stop at Johnston Atoll when we planned our cruise through Micronesia, nevertheless, we had procured charts of the atoll "just in case." That "just in case" materialized five months later when our crewman came down with a serious infection taking him off the watch list with 105° F temperature. The infection persisted as we sailed east from Howland Island and discretion told us to skip

Anchorage in the lagoon at Palmyra

Photo by U.S. Fish & Wildlife Service

Overgrown runway flat built for Amelia Earhart, Howland Island

Apartment barracks, Johnston Island

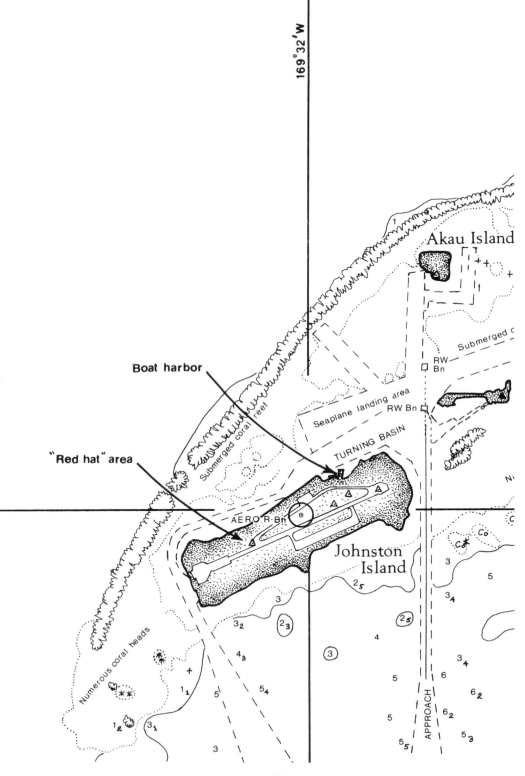

Boat harbor

"Red hat" area

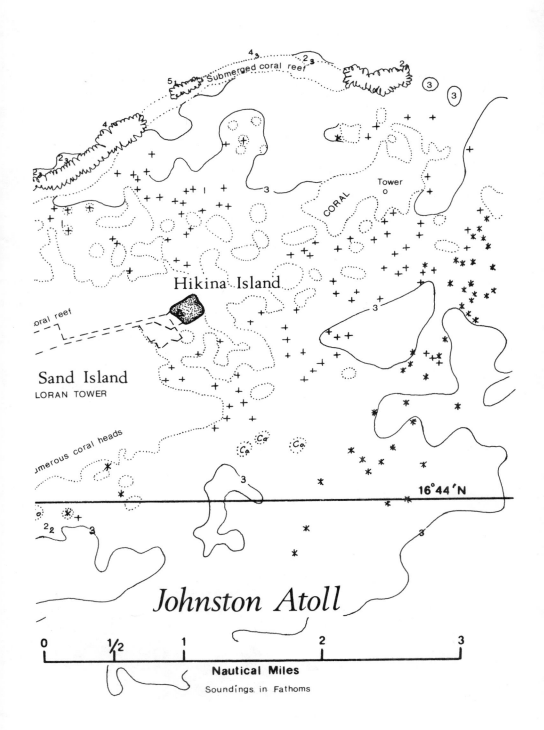

Submerged coral reef

CORAL

Tower

Hikina Island

coral reef

Sand Island

LORAN TOWER

numerous coral heads

Ca

Ca

Co

16°44'N

Johnston Atoll

0	½	1	2	3

Nautical Miles

Soundings in Fathoms

Christmas Island in favor of Johnston Atoll where better medical help would be available.

Now you don't just drop in on Johnston Atoll, it being closed to visitors at all times, but through the combined efforts of the 20 Meter Pacific Maritime Mobile Amateur Radio Net, the Coast Guard, and Tripler Army Hospital in Hawaii, a state of medical emergency was declared on board *Horizon* and permission was granted to make a stop at Mysterious Isle.

At daybreak we motored into the lagoon, heading for the small craft area where one person in a crowd waved directions to us from the shoreline. As we slid alongside the tire-fendered dock, intended more for landing craft than white-hulled cruising boats, eager hands took dock lines and secured the boat in place while medical personnel whisked our ailing crewman off to the dispensary.

The transfer over, we then faced Security which had papers to sign justifying our landing and absolved them of all responsibility while we were on the atoll. Formalities over, the atmosphere warmed considerably as the base commander welcomed us. We breathed easier then, feeling that we had reached friendly ground and were not trespassing on sacrosanct military soil.

But there were rules, and, to our surprise, they were aimed more at the safety of the individual than trying to protect any secrets of Mysterious Isle. There was first of all a gas mask and a lesson on how to use it. Then we were told of the "red hat" area which was off limits to all except Army personnel wearing red hats. Their duties take them within the fenced area at the downwind end of the island where chemical munitions are stored. We were just as happy to leave it alone.

Author's *Horizon* at small craft dock, Johnston Island

Finally we were given the "keys" to Johnston Island (Johnston Island is one of four islands in Johnston Atoll)—permission to use all of the personnel facilities (How wonderful that first fresh water shower felt!) and, if we needed mechanical or other help to prepare our boat for its departure, their staff was ready to assist. We had become official guests at Mysterious Isle and were about to see what few outsiders ever lay eyes on.

History records that Johnston Atoll, lying 715 miles west southwest of Honolulu, was first seen in 1796 by the American brig *Sally*. For the next 150 years, it was claimed off and on by the United States, Hawaii, and even a number of private companies who wanted the guano deposits there. It was, however, such an isolated and desolate spot, that it remained in obscurity until 1926 when the U.S. Department of Agriculture made it a bird refuge.

> "The atoll is unusual in that the main outer reef extends only about one-quarter of the way around its perimeter. A large portion of the atoll lies exposed to prevailing easterly weather conditions without benefit of barrier reef protection. Evidence suggests that subsidence and tilting of the reef platform to the southeast created this unusual condition."
>
> U.S. Army Corps of Engineers, "Johnston Atoll Chemical Agent Disposal System Environmental Impact Statement"

War clouds of the 1930s caused the Navy to take an interest in it as an unsinkable aircraft carrier and 1939 saw the construction of an airfield. What the Navy had at this point was really nothing more than a strategic location. Only 10 miles in total circumference, the atoll consisted of miniscule Johnston and Sand Islands and lots of reef. But Navy muscle changed all of that and coral was dredged and compacted to make 198 acres of usable land for the war effort.

Johnston's wartime role is little known and totally unheralded, but many fighter aircraft and anti-submarine airplanes operated from there, and it later became a refueling stop for aircraft being ferried to Pacific island war fronts. Johnston Island also refueled submarines making forays against Japanese shipping which was by then desperately trying to resupply their beleagured mid-Pacific island bases.

Following World War II, the atoll served a number of Defense Department masters but none so important as the Defense Nuclear Agency. It was here in the early 1960s that atmospheric nuclear weapon testing was conducted. To support that effort, the base was further expanded by coral dredging to a land area of 691 acres including the creation of two small islands on the reef, North and East Islands, of 25 and 18 acres, respectively.

The atmospheric test program was curtailed in 1963 when the Limited Test Ban Treaty brought atmospheric testing to a halt. The United States

then put Johnston Atoll on a standby basis in case the treaty was abrogated by the other parties to it.

Since that time, it has been maintained in a state of readiness by a crew of about 300 persons, mostly Holmes and Narver civilian personnel, but there is still action on the atoll. The Coast Guard operates a Loran C radio station on Sand Island; the Army stores chemical munitions here; and a few aviators and small boat sailors have found it a haven of refuge in rare emergencies.

All personnel live on Johnston Island, visiting the other islands only as maintenance schedules require. Recreation is the big thing here with fishing, scuba diving, and jogging taking the interest of many. Movies, bowling, basketball, tennis, golf and karate lessons all help pass the time in a climate that knows no seasons. Recreation and good food keep the empolyees in top physical condition and helps assure an alert mental attitude in spite of 715 miles of isolation from the nearest bright lights of civilization.

It took only a few days for the skilled medics of Johnston to solve the problem that had brought us to Mysterious Isle. With crew refreshed and fuel and stores topped off, we set our course for Honolulu and home. For an instant in time we had lifted the veil of mystery that surrounds Johnston Atoll, and we found the natives friendly.

— Pacific

HOWLAND—A REMOTE CORAL HEAP

There is no way to get to Howland Island except by boat, so when we planned our return sail from Abemama to Honolulu, we put Howland on our itinerary as a waypoint. By simply heading east, we would run down Howland in the course of a few days. It sounded easy, only 510 miles, but there were problems, for the route lay in the Intertropical Convergence Zone where the northeast and southeast tradewinds meet.

As we sailed east, we encountered light headwinds varying from east northeast to east southeast. Cloud cover ranged from full overcast to broken at best—not pretty tradewind clouds, but muddy-gray clouds without form. Progress was slow, an average day brought us only 70 miles closer to our way point. It was the east-flowing equatorial countercurrent that was our salvation. From it we got 24 to 36 miles per day of easting and that assured us we would eventually make our goal. We did on the seventh day out of Abemama.

120

U.S. Coast Guard and U.S. Fish and Wildlife Service landing party, Howland Island

Our first impression of Howland was one of bleakness. It is an uninhabited island of meager dimensions, just two-thirds of a square mile in area and shaped like an elongated kidney bean whose major axis is a mere mile and a half long. Howland rose quickly from the sea as it is only 18 to 20 feet high at its highest point, just a flat heap of coral and rubble without even a central depression to give it character. That feature is what made it attractive for use as an airfield in one of aviation's most adventurous events in history—Amelia Earhart's ill-fated around-the-world flight in 1937.

Howland Island came into the record books in 1822 when it was sighted by Captain Worth of the New Bedford whaler *Oeno*. He called it Worth Island. Other whalers subsequently visited it and it was Captain Netcher of the whaleship *Isabella* who renamed it Howland in 1842 and that is the name that stuck.

Howland became one of several central Pacific islands claimed by the United States under the Guano Act of 1856. Possession actually took place in 1857 when the Hawaiian schooner *Liholiho* arrived with a party of workers and equipment belonging to the American Guano Company of New York. Off and on for the next 35 years, guano companies mined valuable fertilizer created over centuries past by countless sea birds who had made this equatorial island their home. Then the island returned once more to its quiescent state.

The climate of Howland is warm and dry, being kept moderated by persistent cooling breezes from the ocean. Although it is in the Intertropical Convergence Zone known for its rain, warm air rising from the sandy flats of the island prevents the formation of clouds directly over

it. Only light nighttime showers offer any moisture to the sparse kou trees and the bunchgrass that preceded known man to this island.

An American scientific expedition visited the island in 1924 but it was not until 1935 that a serious settlement of the island was undertaken. It was not to be the first settlement, however, for archaeologists had already uncovered evidence of excavations, mounds, coral stone walls and footpaths which were there before the arrival of the whalers. These were probably built by Polynesian sailors blown off course between more hospitable islands and their stays were as short as they could make them.

The first serious "colonists" arrived at Howland in April 1935 to farm, study the environment, document the flora and fauna and prepared a landing field to expedite communications by air. Scientific and building crews came and went by ship and slowly the settlement to be known as ItascaTown grew. (Named after the U.S. Coat Guard cutter *Itasca*.) Building of the airstrip to support Amelia Earhart's flight started in January 1937 and was completed, such as it was, in a few months.

But Amelia didn't show. She had departed Lae, New Guinea, for Honolulu on July 2, 1937 with Howland Island as a refueling stop, but she never arrived at Howland. The mysterious disappearance of this famous aviation pioneer has created numerous theories on what happened, but that is best left for another story.

The colonists stayed on until the outbreak of World War II. A Japanese warship shelled the island on 18 December 1941 killing two colonists and the rest were removed from the island in February 1942. Today, Howland basks in the everpresent equatorial sunshine and it is administered by the U.S. Fish and Wildlife Service as a wildlife refuge. It is still remote and hostile to landings from the sea. But that is the way the birds like it.

— Pacific

Photo by U.S. Fish & Wildlife Service

Howland Island ruins of Itascatown. Amelia Earhart Lighthouse in distance

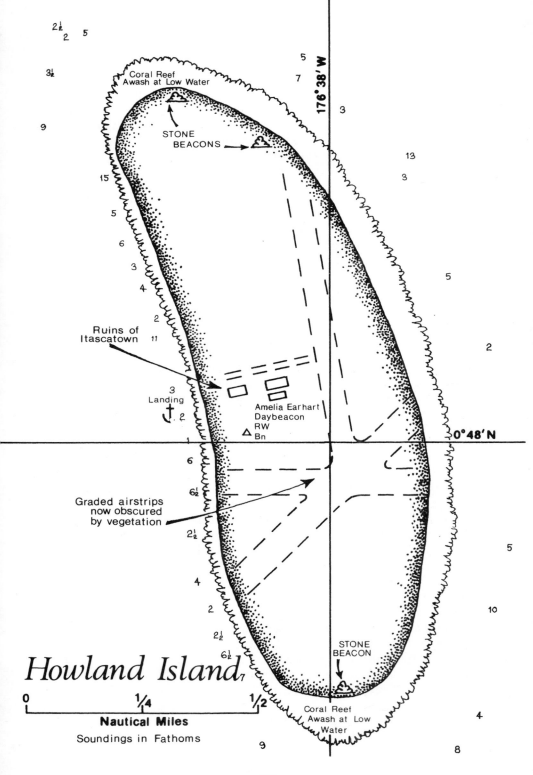

2½ 5
2

3½

9

15

5

6

3

4

2

Ruins of
Itascatown

11

3
Landing
2

1

6

6½

2½

4

2

2½

6½

Howland Island 7

Coral Reef
Awash at Low Water

STONE
BEACONS

176°38'W

5

7

3

13

3

5

2

0°48'N

Amelia Earhart
Daybeacon
RW
Bn

Graded airstrips
now obscured
by vegetation

STONE
BEACON

Coral Reef
Awash at Low
Water

5

10

5

4

9

8

0   1/4   1/2

Nautical Miles

Soundings in Fathoms

123

THE CASE OF THE MISSING AVIATOR

Even before the flames of World War II were to make the Pacific Ocean household words, the islands of Micronesia were the scene of an aviation drama. That was the mysterious disappearance of Amelia Earhart in her dramatic around-the-world flight in 1937. Taking off from Oakland, California, in a Lockheed 10 aircraft known as the Electra, Earhart hopped first to Miami, Florida, and thence to Brazil, across the Atlantic to Africa, then to India, Java, Australia and finally to Lae, New Guinea, where the mystery of "Lady Lindy's" disappearance begins.

Just who was this woman who brought the eyes of the world to the Pacific Ocean? Those of us with gray hair will remember her as a spirited yet shy 40-year-old, boyish-looking blonde woman who felt that women had a role in society well beyond the challenge of the home. She was a "woman's libber" way before her time.

Departing from Lae, New Guinea, her heavily loaded twin-engined Electra literally staggered off the runway at 10:00 a.m. on July 2, 1937, ostensibly headed for tiny Howland Island 2,370 miles to the east. The United States had hastily scraped a landing strip on this 1½-mile-long equatorial island and brought in refueling supplies so that the Electra could make its next 1,650-mile leg to Honolulu. The choice of Howland was itself a bit of pioneering effort in the building of airstrips on inhospitable islands which was to become so commonplace during World War II.

Earhart maintained sporadic radio contact with ground stations for 18 hours into the flight. The airplane flew slightly north of its planned flight path to enable it to overfly Nauru just before midnight. Nauru turned on all of its lights to serve as an airway beacon and Earhart responded by radio that she "could see the lights of Nauru." Then something went awry. Radio transmissions became confused. The U.S. Coast Guard cutter *Itasca* stationed at Howland could not establish contact with the airplane although they could receive her signals. The direction finding equipment put ashore at Howland was unable to home on the Electra. The last transmission heard from the airplane was, "We are on a line of position 157–337 (degrees). We will repeat this message on 6210 (kHz)." They waited listening on 6210, but Lady Lindy flew into oblivion.

The story, however, doesn't end there. Amelia Earhart was too much of a national hero to let vanish. A U.S. Navy search force consisting of the aircraft carrier *Lexington*, the battleship *Colorado* and four destroyers were dispatched to join two Coast Guard cutters and a Navy minesweeper in a search that was to eventually encompass 400,000 miles of the blue Pacific. Nothing turned up. Either the Electra had crashed at sea and sunk or had landed somewhere else. The search mission was terminated after 14 days. The Japanese search of "their" area turned up nothing, or so they said at the time.

Seven years passed with no further investigation of Earhart's disappearance but when World War II ended and the United States gained ac-

cess to the Marshall, Caroline and Marianas Islands, all sorts of clues began to take shape. Islanders and Japanese who had spent years in the islands recalled seeing an American woman with short blond hair and a male companion. An airplane crash was remembered happening around Mili Atoll and the crew, two Americans, were taken away to Jaluit and thence to Saipan. Less is known what happened to the airplane although many believe that it too, was shipped to Saipan.

Now, 50 years later, there is a plethora of theories as to what happened to Amelia Earhart. They range from simply lost at sea when the airplane's fuel ran out, to her having been involved with both United States and Japanese governments during the war years and later returned quietly but alive to the United States.

Spy missions were as intriguing then as they are today and they seem to dominate the theories. There are as many variations of them as there are investigators on the case. Most have one thing in common and that is Amelia Earhart and her navigator Fred Noonan were eventually incarcerated in Saipan's Garapan prison by the Japanese. There is no happy ending to these scenarios for witnesses reported that Noonan was decapitated and Earhart was either decapitated or died of dysentery. Eyewitness accounts, however, tended to be inconsistent because the cloud of time had descended. The recovery of bones, jaw fragments, blindfolds, and even a wedding ring stirred hope which later foundered as the investigators pressed for scientific proof.

Most extreme of the spy mission theories suggests that the Electra crash landed on Saipan's shores near the Japanese seaplane ramp at Tanapeg harbor and that the crew were immediately imprisoned. Proof of this was based on the recovery of a "Bendix" generator from a twin-engined aircraft wreckage that still existed in 1960. Expert examination of this evidence showed the airplane to be a Japanese Betty twin-engined bomber and the "Bendix" generator a Japanese clone.

Then there is the theory that Earhart and Noonan were still alive as late as 1965. This theory assumed that the Electra made a safe crash landing at some place (still in question) and that the Japanese who had followed the flight with great interest (and a certain amount of suspicion) had raced to the scene (which may have been Hull Island), beating the American Navy, picked up the fliers and airplane and quickly took them to Jaluit. The fliers were then taken to Japan and eventually became pawns in treaty negotiations after the fighting ceased.

Several spy flight scenarios involved targets ranging from Saipan to Truk and the Marshall Islands. To fly over this vast expanse of ocean would have required an airplane that was significantly faster and with a greater range than the standard Electra. Interestingly enough, there was just such a craft waiting in the hangar of Lockheed's Burbank, California plant. It was a souped-up Electra with supercharged engines, pressurized cabin, feathering propellers and a vastly extended range.

Now, 50 years later and after thousands of hours of investigation by

competent persons, the mystery of Amelia Earhart's disappearance remains. Was she lost at sea? Captured? A government pawn? You take your choice, but she did not reach Howland Island. That makes no difference, though, the legend of Amelia Earhart will never die.

— Pacific

UNCHARTED ISLANDS

One thing that sincerely bothers me about electronic navigation is that you can go from point A to point B without so much as looking at a chart. You can even make doglegs on your course and the receiver will signal you when you have arrived at selected waypoints. With such automated capabilities, I fear that the art of visual sighting may be lost and along with it many cruising boats.

I think of such shoals as Beveridge Reef (20° 00' S, 167° 50' W) which is near the rhumb line between Rarotonga, Cook Islands, and Vava'u, Tonga, and the Minerva Reefs (23° 56' S, 179° 06' W) which are near the rhumb line from Nuku'alofa, Tonga, to the Bay of Islands, New Zealand. Beveridge Reef is awash even at low tide while Minerva Reefs expose only 3 feet in places at low tide. Both reefs have claimed vessels without regard to race, creed or nationality even though they have been known for at least 200 years to lie in the general vicinity of their plotted positions. Of course, their plotted positions aren't all that reliable either. The Sailing Directions say such things as "The reef (Beveridge) has been reported to lie 4 miles southwestward and on another occasion 5 miles eastward of its charted position." That certainly doesn't inspire confidence in planning blind dogleg maneuvers around them.

Both reefs have been safely visited by cruising boats in the past. *Rigadoon* stopped at Minerva Reef several years ago and while anchored within the reef, enjoyed marvelous fishing and swimming. More recently, *Carioca* visited Beveridge Reef anchoring inside of it for fishing and swimming. Both boats reported that you have to use great care, first of all

in finding the reefs and second in locating the passes. Only eyeball navigation with the sun in the right place works in close quarters.

But now we have a report of an uncharted island which is not a reef or shoal, but almost as invisible. *Flying Lady* reportedly found uncharted land in the vicinity of Howland Island (0° 48′ N, 176° 38′ W). I know that it is uncharted because I studied every possible chart before I took *Horizon* there in 1982 and not even shoal water was reported in the vicinity. I have since studied bathymetric charts of the area and have found no seamounts anywhere near Howland that could rise to be a new island. Nevertheless, I shudder to think that if there is such an island, we might have come upon it in the middle of the night and become another statistic.

Flying Lady reported that the island was first sighted by sailing ships in the 1700s and again in 1860 but was erroneously logged as being south of the equator rather than north. It was *Flying Lady*'s mission in the vicinity of Howland Island that adds to the mystery. She had been chartered by an Amelia Earhart researcher who claims he had seen the island on a satellite photo of the area. That, of course, lent another theory to the disappearance of Amelia Earhart—she had mistakenly landed on the uncharted island. Although the researcher's book on his investigation has not been published, private correspondence relates that he has made a claim on the island and has named it after himself. Truly, the legend of Amelia Earhart will never die.

— Sea

FORBIDDEN ISLES OF PARADISE

There are several islands in the Pacific where cruising boats are not welcome for military, social, conservation or just plain security reasons. Whatever the reason, there is little need for cruising boats to challenge authority since these islands represent less than 3/10 of one percent of the total land area of Oceania. Cruising sailors have great freedom to move in the Pacific, but when they challenge authority, however well intended, that reflects badly on all cruisers. The usual result is a hardening of government attitudes toward cruisers and additional restrictions on their freedom.

The following Pacific islands are currently off-limits to cruising boats regardless of country of origin.

Under U.S. Jurisdiction

Hawaii—The island of Kahoolawe just south of Maui in the eastern Hawaiian Archipelago is under the jurisdiction of the U.S. Navy and access is forbidden at all times without the permission of Naval authorities. Kahoolawe is a target for ships and airplanes and should be given wide berth when transiting the area.

Niihau, the westernmost inhabited island of Hawaii, is privately owned. The 200 residents are native Hawaiians and the Hawaiian owners permit only relatives of residents to visit. In this way, a segment of Hawaiian culture can flourish with little contamination by the outside world. The only exception is a controlled-tour helicopter operation to an isolated emergency landing pad on Niihau.

Palmyra Atoll (5° 53' N, 162° 05' W)—This is a privately owned atoll and, technically, permission must be obtained from the owners to visit it.

Dinghy landing, Palmyra

In the past, there have been bad scenes resulting from both airplane and boat visits giving it a bad reputation. Cruising boats do visit it and many even engage in cleanup and maintenance of the informal "yacht club" on the beach.

Johnston Atoll (16° 44′ N, 169° 32′ W)—A U.S. nuclear defense standby test facility administered by the U.S. Air Force, Johnston is also used to store outdated chemical warfare products. It is also a National Wildlife Refuge. Waters within 3 miles constitute a prohibited area and no vessel without prior authorization may enter these waters. For cruising boats, only a bona fide emergency cleared ahead of time with the U.S. Coast Guard will permit access to this atoll. Even carrying persons of diplomatic influence is not a ticket to entry, as William F. Buckley Jr. points out in his book "Racing Through Paradise." Request for emergency entry of vessels or persons in distress should be made by any means possible to the Joint Rescue Coordination Center, Honolulu. They will make all necessary arrangements for a proper entry.

Midway Islands (28° 13′ N, 177° 24′ W)—This "almost atoll" surprisingly is not part of the state of Hawaii, although the islands are part of the Hawaiian Archipelago. Midway is a Defensive Sea Area administered by the U.S. Navy. Waters within 3 miles are off-limits and no vessel may enter these waters without prior authorization. Like Johnston Atoll, vessels or persons in distress at sea should contact the U.S. Coast Guard for emergency entry clearance. Non-emergency clearance must be obtained well beforehand through the Commander, 3rd Fleet, Pearl Harbor, Hawaii.

Wake Island (19° 18′N, 166° 38′ E)—This small atoll, a U.S. possession, is administered by the U.S. Air Force and is not off-limits to cruising boats in the sense that Johnston and Midway are. Wake Atoll simply has no facilities for visitors; only military and contract workers live there. At most, it should be considered only a temporary stop on passages between Hawaii and Japan. Although there is a lagoon, the passage is not deep enough for cruising boats to enter so you must anchor or pick up a mooring buoy on the reef. There are no supplies, but I am sure in a bona fide emergency, a boat could get provisions, fuel and water or make repairs. No prior permission is required for a stopover.

U.S. National Wildlife Refuges

The U.S. Fish and Wildlife Service administers a number of refuges in the Pacific known as Remote Island National Wildlife Refuges. They extend from Hawaii to Guam to American Samoa. Public access to these islands is severely restricted because of a history of abuse and the subsequent slow recovery of these vulnerable islands when disturbed.

Permission to land may be granted to those with a legitimate reason to visit any of these islands. You must secure permission ahead of time from the U.S. Fish and Wildlife Service in Honolulu. It is not as hard as you may think since these islands are remote and employees of the service do

not get to them as often as they would like. Therefore, if you can take a staff member along, you stand a good chance of getting clearance to visit. Beware that the very features that make the islands attractive as wildlife refuges also make them difficult to land on—surf and rocky shorelines. Approach with caution.

"Mere dots in the vast ocean, the remote mid-Pacific islands host breeding monk seals. turtles and millions of seabirds. They nest on rocky islands and islets among coral atolls.

The marine environment on the remote island refuges is largely undisturbed by commercial exploitation and consequently many species are unusually abundant. The relatively pristine nature of the nearshore waters and the importance of this habitat to seals, turtles and seabirds led to the inclusion of large bodies of protected lagoon and nearshore waters into the boundaries of various remote island refuges."

— U.S. Fish and Wildlife Service, "Hawaiian and Pacific Islands National Wildlife Refuges"

The following are Remote Island National Wildlife Refuges:

Hawaiian Islands—the northwestern portion of the Hawaiian Archipelago from 161° W to 176° W (Nihoa Island to, but not including Midway Island). Kure Island to the west of Midway is also restricted, but it is administered by the state of Hawaii and not the Fish and Wildlife Service.

Howland, Baker, and Jarvis Islands—These three span the equator south southwest of Hawaii.

Rose Atoll—The easternmost emergent land of the Samoan Archipelago is one of the smallest atolls in the world.

Under Republic of The Marshall Islands Jurisdiction

During the Trust Territory administration of the Pacific Islands by the United States, certain islands of the Marshall Group were used for military purposes and the following carry on to this date:

Kwajalein Atoll (8° 43′ N, 167° 44′ E)—A missile testing area, the waters within a 200-mile radius are subject to intermittent hazardous operations. Since all events are scheduled, vessels planning to enter this area should coordinate their movements beforehand with Kwajalein Atoll control via radio. On this atoll, the only restricted islands are those in use by the U.S. Army; the others are under the jurisdiction of the Republic of the Marshall Islands. Ebeye Island, for instance, is a port of entry to the Marshall Islands, but it has little attraction for cruisers.

Bikini Atoll (11° 30′ N, 165° 34′ E); **Eniwetok Atoll** (11° 30′ N, 162° 24′ E); **Rongelap Atoll** (11° 09′ N, 166° 54′ E)—Bikini and Eniwetok were used for early testing of nuclear weapons and have some degree of contamination left. Rongelap was never used for testing, but a wind reversal caused a heavy fallout from a mini-hydrogen bomb blast to pollute it. The indige-

enous peoples of these three atolls are still living on other atolls and when it is felt safe for them to return, then it would be safe for cruising boats to visit them.

Under French Jurisdiction

It is no secret that the French are continuing to conduct underground nuclear tests in the Tuamotu Archipelago. Although these tests take place at Mururoa (21° 50′ S, 138° 55′ W) and Fangataufa (22° 15′ S, 138° 45′ W) atolls, the French have cordoned off a huge restricted area in the Tuamotus: those waters south of 17° 20′ S and east of 145° 45′ W. That open-ended restriction taken from the Sailing Directions is rather nebulous. A more definitive restriction is found in the DMA Notice to Mariners which states: "Passage through the territorial sea between and within 12 miles of Mururoa and Fangatuaufa Atolls is temporarily prohibited."

During actual nuclear tests, the French navy patrols an extensive area of the eastern Tuamotus to warn off vessels on innocent passage and to discourage protest vessels. It should be noted that Hao Atoll (18° 15′ S, 140° 50′ W) is the principal supply base for nuclear tests and should, likewise, be avoided.

The Gambier Islands lie at the east end of the Tuamotus and fall within the open-ended restricted area. Cruising boats, however, have been able to visit them with proper clearance from Papeete and by avoiding the sensitive areas in their passage.

Whether you agree or disagree with the French right to test nuclear weapons at this site, it is not in the best interests of cruisers to challenge their authority in the area. Altogether, there are 76 atolls/islands in this archipelago and certainly the unrestricted ones can satisfy every cruising boat's needs.

When you arrive at a port of entry for a new island group, inquire if there are any islands in that group to be avoided for lawful reasons. These change from time to time, and the cruiser can get current information on the spot. It is wise to respect local authority when in a foreign land.

— Cruising World

NEW ZEALAND'S KERMADEC ISLANDS

The Kermadec Islands are a group of rocky islands lying 585 miles northeast of Auckland. The principal islands making up this group are:

Raoul (Sunday Island)	7200 acres
Macauley Island	760 acres
Herald Group	85 acres

The islands are all volcanic and in Raoul and Curtis islands signs of activity are still visible. Earthquakes occur at times and in 1870–1872 a small island was upheaved in Denham Bay, Raoul Island, which gave some shelter to vessels at anchor. Unfortunately, it disappeared again in 1877. A 1981 earthquake measured 6.8 on the Richter scale but no damage was incurred.

Raoul Island is thickly wooded and rises toward one end to a height of 1700 feet. The ground is very fertile and can support many forms of tropical and sub-tropical fruits. There are numerous large orange trees on Raoul which were grown from seeds given to the Bell family, which occupied the island for 36 years at the turn of the century. Wild cats, rats, and goats, however, prevent much extended growth. Fresh water is sometimes scarce, but rainwater is collected in three lakes near the center of the island and, being volcanic, steam sometimes issues from them.

There is no indigenous population on these islands. Archaeologists have established that Polynesians occupied the islands as early as 1000 A.D. and stayed for about 700 years. It is believed they were driven away by a major volcanic eruption. Today Raoul Island is home for five young New Zealanders who man a meteorology station for the New Zealand government.

The climate is mild, equable, and slightly warmer than that in the northern part of New Zealand. Extreme temperatures range between 48 and 82 degrees F. There is no frost and rainfall is plentiful but not excessive, averaging about 57 inches annually. Southwesterly and westerly winds prevail in the winter and northeasterly and easterly in the summer. There are strong gales in the winter. The tail ends of hurricane winds commencing in the southeast and backing to northeast have been experienced in January and February, but they are rare.

Visiting Raoul Island is an adventure in itself. There are no entry formalities other than to meet the personnel stationed there who are happy to see visitors. There are no boat landings, so you anchor out and try your luck in two locations. Boat Cove at the southwest extremity of the island can be used in good weather but there is considerable surge in the cove.

The best landing is at Fishing Rock on the north side of the island where there is a crane to lift personnel from the water up onto the landing. You will need the cooperation of Raoul personnel to effect a landing. If the wind is from the north, forget this landing. There is a depth of 13

feet in this area with good fine-sand holding ground but you are advised to leave a crewman aboard for safety.

— Unpublished Note

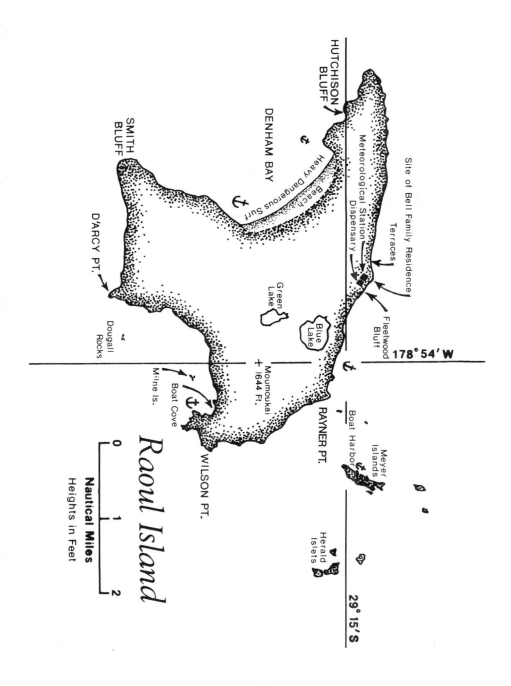

AUSTRALIA'S LORD HOWE ISLAND

While discussing off-the-beaten-path islands of cruising interest, Jerry and Rosemary Wilbur commented very favorably on Lord Howe Island. Lord Howe was a landfall on their return trip from Australia on *Tangent*, their Ranger 33.

This is not the easiest island to visit because it is in the boisterous Tasman Sea which doesn't always see eye-to-eye with the mariner. One story has it that an Australian yacht had tried unsuccessfully seven times to visit there on holidays and had been thwarted all seven times. It is not a navigation problem that makes it difficult to visit, but the only landing is on the west side through a coral reef and with any sea running there is no way in. *Tangent*, however, made it on the first try.

Lord Howe is about 300 miles off the east coast of Australia and somewhat over 400 miles from Sydney. It is a National Preserve of Australia. The 200-plus islanders who live on it are "natives" but their roots are in Australia. There was no indigenous population when the island was discovered in 1788.

Recently the island has been discovered by tourists and annually about 4000 of them find their way over by air from Australia. The island has a small airport but no seaport. The lagoon on the west side has been declared a marine sanctuary and further development has been banned. Approaching the island from the west, Jerry advises you to tack back and forth along the reef until a "native" comes out in a small boat and pilots you in through North Pass, that is if you have a shallow enough draft. Australian Chart 213 (Plans in the South West Pacific Ocean) shows about ½ fathom of water inside the lagoon but the 5-foot draft of the Ranger 33 posed no problem. One does not anchor in the lagoon but shackles to a heavy anchor chain laid north and south just inside the reef. It is about ¼ mile long and lies in 7 feet of water. Put out a stern anchor by dinghy to hold your boat away from the reef.

Lord Howe is a resort island, hence do not expect to get any great amount of bulk supplies there; they all have to be flown or lightered in. Fuel is available at the jetty in drums and fresh water can be obtained from a faucet on the jetty. At any one time there are about 250 tourists on the island, mostly Australians on a holiday. Guest houses abound and there are a few establishments where afternoon tea is served.

The attraction of Lord Howe Island is the natural beauty of its 5 square miles of land area. Mountains on the south end rise to about 2500 feet and they are covered with a luxuriant vegetation including palms and spectacular Norfolk pine trees. There is not a great deal of animal or bird life although birds abounded before rats were introduced by visiting ships. The qualified scuba diver can rent gear on Lord Howe and explore the beauty of the lagoon's barrier reef.

The urban section of Lord Howe is at the neck of the island on a gently

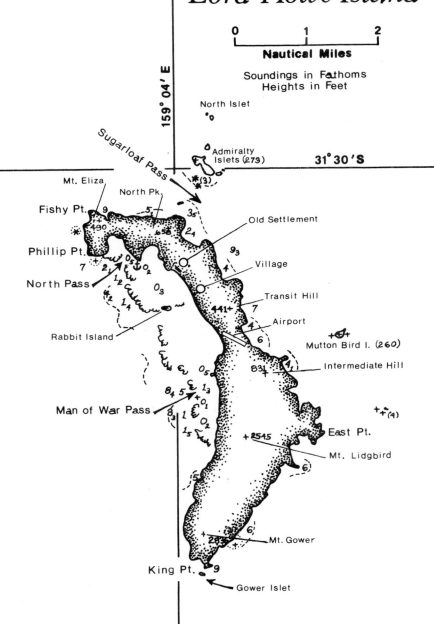

Lord Howe Island

0   1   2

Nautical Miles

Soundings in Fathoms
Heights in Feet

North Islet

Admiralty
Islets (273)

31° 30′ S

159° 04′ E

Sugarloaf Pass

Mt. Eliza

North Pk.

Fishy Pt.

Phillip Pt.

North Pass

Rabbit Island

Man of War Pass

Old Settlement

Village

Transit Hill

Airport

Mutton Bird I. (260)

Intermediate Hill

East Pt.

Mt. Lidgbird

Mt. Gower

King Pt.

Gower Islet

inclined slope rising from the beach at the lagoon to steep cliffs on the eastern shore. You will find the customhouse just off the beach and that is where you will clear vessel and crew in and out. If you have arrived from Australia, they will have received notification by radio of your impending arrival. If you are later headed to Australia, they will notify Sydney of your presence. The Lord Howe Island Board is located in Sydney.

Most boats crossing the Pacific to Australia visit Sydney because it is a good place for reprovisioning and laying over during the South Pacific hurricane season. Few visit Lord Howe en route, so it remains undiscovered by yachties. It, along with Norfolk Island to the north, would make interesting landfalls on passages between Australia and Fiji or New Caledonia.

— Sea

CHAPTER 5

MELANESIAN LANDFALLS

*" I wish I could tell you about the South Pacific. The way
it actually was. The endless ocean, the infinite specks of
coral we call islands. Coconut palms nodding gracefully
toward the ocean. But whenever I start to talk about the
South Pacific, people intervene. I try to tell somebody
what the steaming Hebrides were like, the first thing you
know I'm telling about the old Tonkinese woman who
used to sell human heads as souvenirs for fifty dollars!"*
—James Michener, "Tales of the South Pacific"

PORT-VILA — AN UNPOLISHED GEM

As a Pacific traveler, I have learned that the most interesting ports of
call are those that are hard to reach and, therefore, not yet discovered by
the jet-setting tourist. Such is Port-Vila, Vanuatu, an unpolished gem of a
seaport whose harbor was formed when the wall of an extinct crater was
breached by the sea. But that volcanic eruption eons ago may be nothing
compared to what is brewing politically in Vanuatu's capital at this moment.

To understand present day Port-Vila, one must harken back in time to
the arrival of the first Europeans and the beginning of trading enterprises. It began with the sandalwood trade to China and changed into
blackbirding when traders found they could make more money selling
human beings for contract labor on Fiji and Queensland sugar plantations than in harvesting sandalwood. This caused a drastic decline in the
Melanesian population while the numbers of British and French settlers
increased and land speculations ran rampant. Both the well-intentioned
British and French governments decried this ill-treatment of the islands,
but each country was so suspicious of the other that neither would back
away from an assumed responsibility to save the native population. The
only political solution to which they could agree was a joint protectorship
and thus was borne the awkward condominium government of the New
Hebrides, which was unlovingly referred to in the press as the pandemo-
nium government. It was administered simultaneously by Britain and
France during the period 1888 to 1980. So, when Vanuatu became independent in 1980, it already had the heritage of two European governments plus its own Melanesian traditions. If you think it is hard to separate from one colonial master, then think of the problems the ni-Vanuatu
faced in separating from two. Today's Port-Vila, in fact all of the Vanuatu
nation, is a blend of British, French and Melanesian cultures presenting
an interesting mix for the visitor as long as he doesn't get mixed up in tri-
partite local politics.

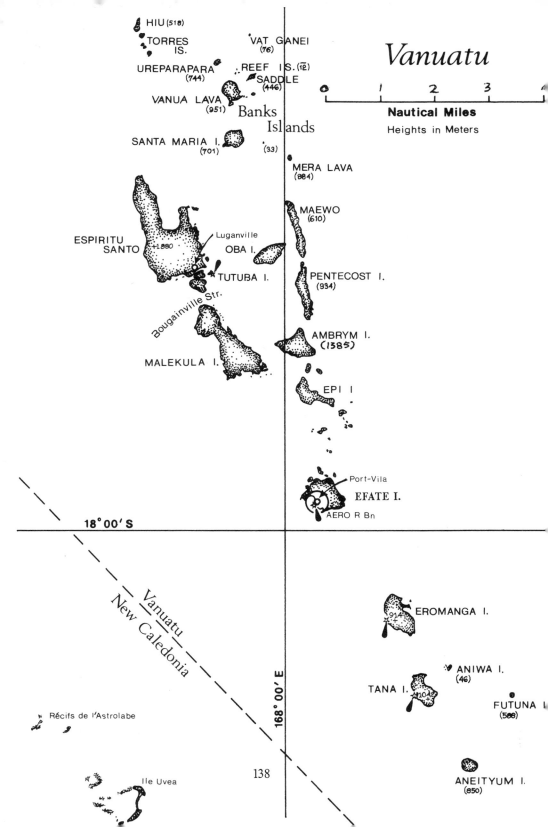

One of the rather foolish results of having the condominium
ment was leaving the people of Vanuatu with multiple langu
wasn't bad enough that the old New Hebrides had many tribal dia
the French and British imposed on them their European languag
business and government purposes, as well.

But the local people outsmarted their colonial governors in the end by
creating a form of Pidgin, mixing English with the local dialects. Originally it was only a spoken language but now it has been reduced to writing and is the *lingua franca* of Vanuatu. It is called Bislama. While difficult for outsiders to understand when spoken, it is not hard to decipher
when written. Here's a sample to try your hand at:

'Nambatu miting blong Representative Assembli hemi finis long
Desemba namba 7. Miting ia hemi stat long Novemba namba 29
wetem fofala kastom jif. Hemia hemi fas taem blong olgeta jif ia i
siadaon insaed long miting blong Assembli ia.'

Translated, it says:

'The second meeting of the Representative Assembly finished on December 7. The meeting started on November 29 with the four chiefs
present. This was the first time that the chiefs had been at a meeting
of the assembly.'

The hills surrounding Vila Harbor have constrained Port-Vila's business growth to a narrow crescent of land along the shoreline. Houses
have been pushed back up the hillsides by the relentless growth of the
business district. Now only stores, restaurants, harbor works and a few
traditional hotels occupy the main street in its sweeping spread along the
harbor.

To break the monotony of 20th century structures, the city fathers have
dedicated a strip of valuable waterfront property as a park for the pedes-
trian to enjoy. Now, if they would only plant some trees in it to break the
heat of the tropical sun, pedestrians would be able to pause and reflect on
the beauty that is Vila Harbor instead of running for shade in some
bistro.

At the opposing ends of this park that you will find "Old Vila." Abut-
ting it to the north is one of the best known hostelries of the South Seas—
the Hotel Rossi. Not a luxury hotel in any sense, as the broken bedspring
poking me in the back all night told me, but it is clean and neat with colonial tendencies and good service. Well-worn chairs on the veranda draw
a mix of guests at the end of the day for a beer, smoke and a smattering of
conversation.

But is is the sunset as seen from the Rossi open-air dining room that
forever lives in your memory. Gazing westward across the harbor, you
have a fantastic view of the setting sun. With one of the Rossi bar's famous fruit punches in hand and studied concentration, you can behold
the green flash phenomenon as the sun drops its upper limb below the
horizon.

The French heritage dominates Vila's restaurants of which there are many. None are large, overcrowded or even ostentatious, but they offer the cuisine of Paris in air-conditioned comfort. Such names as Le Rendezvous, Le Chalet, and Cafe de Paris tell you that this is the place to break bread and enjoy a bottle of wine.

At the south end of the waterfront park is the open air market where the produce of the island is offered for sale by the grower. Here, also, cottage industries offer clothing and handicrafts to the visitor. Like all tropical markets, Vila's market is colorful and social, the sellers being just as interested in conversation as they are in sales.

Looking across the harbor to what was the center of the volcano's caldera, you see what may be the treasure of Vila—Iririki Island. Once the residence of the British commissioner under the condominium government, it is now the site of a new international class resort with thatched roof bungalows for privacy and to give a feeling of the colonial trader's life. Vila's other resort hotels are located over the ridge behind town on shallow winding Erakor Lagoon. These are equally international in quality, but in a more rural setting.

In spite of its fine harbor, its profusion of traveler's accommodations and a hospitable people, there is trouble brewing in Port Vila. Nature herself, takes a mean swipe at Vila in the form of a cyclone every now and then, the last being in 1987 when Cyclone Uma battered the southern islands of Vanuatu. Vila suffered extensive damage, but is already back in operation welcoming tourists as before. But tourism itself was already far off its normal pace even before Uma showed up. If there is one thing that tourists don't like, it is political tension and, when the Vanuatu government began political negotiations with Cuba, Libya and Russia, large numbers of Australian, Kiwi and Yankee tourists bypassed these islands.

On top of the uncertainty of international intentions, Vanuatu's continuing internal political conflict makes tourists wary. There are so many beautiful islands to see in the South Pacific that visitors do not have to risk a valuable vacation in a potential trouble spot. But if you're diplomatic with people and careful with your associations, you may just have a delightful vacation in this land of Michener's beginnings.

— Pacific

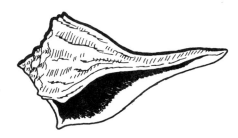

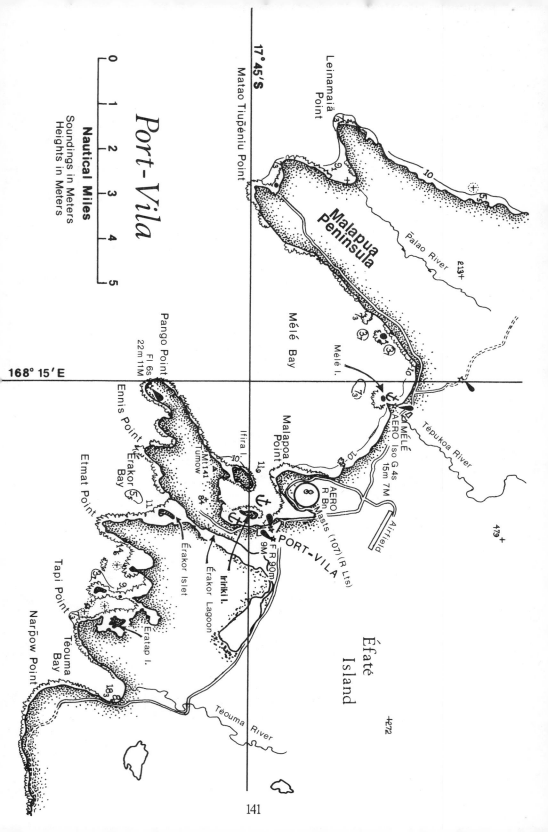

Port-Vila

Nautical Miles

Soundings in Meters
Heights in Meters

0 1 2 3 4 5

17° 45′ S

168° 15′ E

Matao Tiupēniu Point

Leinamaiä Point

Malapua Peninsula

Palao River

213+

Mélé Bay

Mélé I.

MÉLÉ
AERO Iso G 4s
15m 7M

Tépukoa River

Pango Point
Fl 6s
22m 11M

Ennis Point

Érakor Bay

Etmat Point

Mt141
Tumow

Ifira I.

Malapoa Point

AERO
R Bn

PORT-VILA
F R 90m
9M

AERO R Bn
Masts (107) (R Lts)

Airfield

473+

Éfaté Island

+272

Érakor Islet

Iririki I.

Érakor Lagoon

Tapi Point

Eratap I.

Teouma Bay

Narpow Point

Teouma River

141

Bismarck
Archipelago

KARAKAR I.

OTTILIEN Rf

WHIRLWIND
Rfs

VITU IS.

HANKOW Rf

UNEA I.

CROWN I

MADAN

TOLOKIWA I.

LONG I.

1655

UMBOI
I.

+4120

AERO
R Bn

AERO
R Bn

LAE

HUON

GULF

SOL

+3690

Papua
New Guinea

GULF OF
PAPUA

4095+

1715

PORT
MORESBY

10° 00′ S

2

EASTERN FIELDS

142

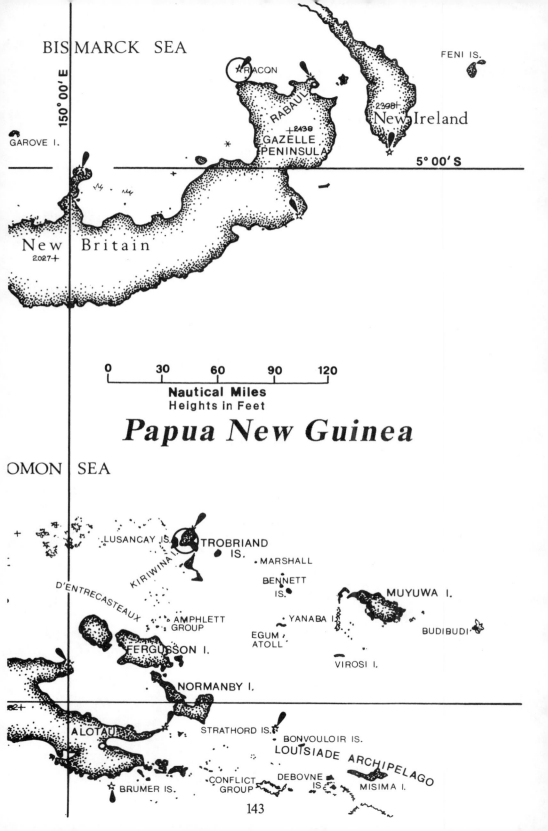

Papua New Guinea

Nautical Miles
Heights in Feet

BISMARCK SEA

150° 00' E

RACON

RABAUL

GAZELLE
PENINSULA

+2438

New Ireland

2398

FENI IS.

GAROVE I.

5° 00' S

New Britain

2027+

0   30   60   90   120

OMON SEA

LUSANCAY IS.

KIRIWINA I.

TROBRIAND
IS.

• MARSHALL

BENNETT
IS.

MUYUWA I.

D'ENTRECASTEAUX

AMPHLETT
GROUP

• YANABA I.

EGUM
ATOLL

BUDIBUDI

FERGUSSON I.

VIROSI I.

NORMANBY I.

ALOTAU

STRATHORD IS.

BONVOULOIR IS.

LOUISIADE ARCHIPELAGO

BRUMER IS.

CONFLICT
GROUP

DEBOYNE
IS

MISIMA I.

143

PNG'S PORT MORESBY

Port Moresby, Papua New Guinea's capital, was once a small neighborhood overlooking Moresby Harbor much like San Francisco overlooks a great harbor in the United States. Like San Francisco, the name became generic and now describes not a town by itself, but a sprawling complex of suburbs without boundaries extending into the foothills of the Owen Stanley Range.

Although Port Moresby is the capital of all Papua New Guinea, one still cannot communicate with the rest of the country by road. The entire island of New Guinea including Irian Jaya, is a series of forbidding mountain ranges preventing, to this day, the building of highways so necessary to the improvement of the welfare of the country. Port Moresby's nearest urban neighbor, the town of Popondetta, a mere 90 miles away as the crow flies (provided it flies high enough!), has no surface connection with Moresby except over the famous Kokoda Trail, something best left to adventurers. It is little wonder, then, that air transportation played such an early and vital role in the development of Papua New Guinea.

The beginnings of Port Moresby were found in a collection of tribal villages along the shoreline where food was plentiful and travel easy, compared with the mountain ranges. But the area had another attribute to attract the attention of European discoverers and that was its large well-protected harbor. It was this harbor that came to the attention of Captain John Moresby of the three-masted paddle steamer *HMS Basilisk* in 1873. He modestly named the outer harbor Moresby Harbor after himself and the inner reaches Fairfax Harbor after his father.

Koki Village market

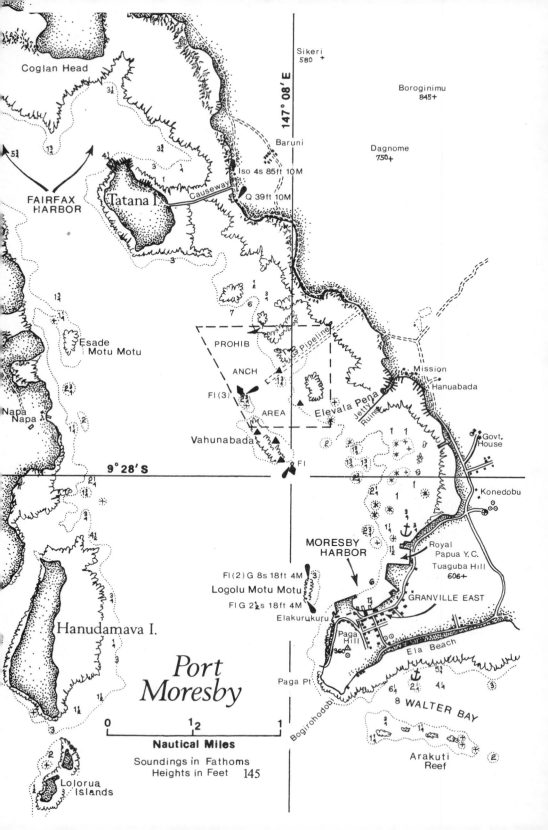

Coglan Head

Sikeri
580 +

Boroginimu
845+

147° 08' E

Baruni

Iso 4s 85ft 10M

Dagnome
750+

FAIRFAX
HARBOR

Causeway

Q 39ft 10M

Tatana I.

Esade
Motu Motu

PROHIB

Gas Pipeline

Mission

ANCH

Elevala Pena

Hanuabada

Napa
Napa

Fl(3)

AREA

Jetty
Ruins

Govt.
House

Vahunabada

9° 28' S

Fl

Konedobu

MORESBY
HARBOR

Royal
Papua Y. C.

Fl(2)G 8s 18ft 4M

Tuaguba Hill
606+

Logolu Motu Motu

GRANVILLE EAST

Fl G 2½s 18ft 4M

Hanudamava I.

Elakurukuru

Paga
Hill
360

Ela Beach

*Port
Moresby*

Paga Pt

8 WALTER BAY

Bogirohodobi

0   ½   1

Nautical Miles

Soundings in Fathoms
Heights in Feet   145

Arakuti
Reef

Lolorua
Islands

Capt. Moresby was the first European to extensively explore the New Guinea coastline. One other of his major achievements was the discovery of China Strait at the eastern tip of New Guinea which provided a shorter route for ships sailing between Australia and China.

At the time of Moresby's exploration, the collective population of the harbor's shoreline numbered, perhaps, 700-800 persons concentrated mostly around the area of present day Hanuabada—a native word meaning "great village." It was in this area that the London Missionary Society established its first mission in 1874 and the first government house was built nearby at Konedobu a year later. But when the pioneers of commerce and business chose to establish their enterprises, they selected the saddle between Paga and Tuaguba Hills on the peninsula forming the southern shore of Moresby Harbor. This is still the "city" of Port Moresby though its sibling suburbs stretch inland for miles.

An influx of expatriates followed the establishment of the British Protectorate over New Guinea in 1884 and the town of Port Moresby became the capital of the Province of New Guinea. In 1975, it took up its role as the present day capital of the independent country of Papua New Guinea.

Like most inner cities of this world, Moresby retains evidence of its past in its old buildings, some maintained with dignity while others are falling apart. Because the government has chosen to develop its cultural and administrative centers at the suburb of Waigani, away from its birthplace on the water, old Moresby has fallen on hard times.

Downtown Port Moresby still functions as a business and shopping center and that is about all. Street venders selling mostly betelnuts have taken over the public areas making it a less than desirable tourist attraction. Although there is one fine Travelodge Hotel in the downtown area, other accommodations are fading remnants of the past. Suitable restaurants for visitors do not exist and the streets are not recommended for visitors after nightfall.

Tourism is hardly a viable feature of present day Port Moresby though it's past has much to offer. Moresby's contribution to Papua New Guinea's tourism is only as a transient host for travelers going other places through Jackson's International Airport. Other interesting tourist destinations such as Madang, Rabaul, the Highlands and even Samarai have more to offer the visitor than Port Moresby and its suburbs.

If the tourist overlooks the decay of Port Moresby, the geologic wonders of the peninsula which attracted the early settlers are still there. The view of the busy harbor and waterfront from Paga Hill is inspiring; the saddle between Paga and Tuaguba Hills where the settlers developed "Granville East," is a blessing of nature; and Ela Beach is a recreational haven for those who love watersports in the comfort of a cooling southeast tradewind.

Like so many cities of the world, the good things in life at Port Moresby have escaped to the suburbs. Most of the history of Papua New Guinea lies in its old city center, dormant at present, but awaiting resurrection by

far-seeing leaders. For a tourist, Port Moresby is still the city in the saddle, not the one on the plateau.

— Pacific

Hanuabada Village, Port Moresby, Papua New Guinea

RABAUL—A TOWN WITH NINE LIVES

Few towns in the Pacific have survived as many tortures of nature and mankind as has lovely Rabaul on Papua New Guinea's New Britain Island. Maybe its because the town is still young and has the resilience of youth that it has been able to carry on in the face of adversity. Or, maybe it is the Tolai people who inhabit the Gazelle Peninsula on which it rests, for they are intelligent, hard working and proud people who respect their fertile land and farm it with enthusiasm. Whatever it is, Rabaul with its flower-lined streets is a delight to visit.

Rabaul was born of vulcanism. Cataclysmic eruptions of a volcano on the eastern tip of New Britain Island 3500 years ago and again 1400 years ago, produced magnificent Simpson Harbor and Blanche Bay along whose shores the town of Rabaul was founded. In 1937, another major eruption changed the geography of Simpson Harbor. As Tavurvur volcano erupted on one side of the Rabaul caldera, Mount Vulcan rose skyward on the other in a hail of pumice and lava rock that spelled death to 500 Tolais living in its shadow. In 1943 during the Japanese occupation, Matupit erupted and to this day continues to spew sulphurous fumes into the tropical atmosphere.

Everybody would like to believe that these eruptions were the last in this region where three of earth's structural plates meet—the Australian plate, the Bismarck plate and the Pacific plate. But these vast plates con-

tinue to grind against each other and earth tremors have become a way of life for the 40,000 citizens of Rabaul.

There has been an average of one eruption every 40 years and in late 1984, all signs pointed to another, possibly in the vicinity of the Matupit-Greet Harbor area. October 1984 became critical; seismic activity had risen to 35 times "normal," but then it subsided. Rabaul's evacuation plans were set aside and life returned to normal except for the Rabaul Vulcanological Laboratory where a 24-hour a day watch continues. Although everything is relatively quiet now on the seismic front in Rabaul, the fuse of disaster still sputters underground.

Nature alone has not been the only tormentor of Rabaul; modern man has done his share. Invading Japanese in World War II occupied Rabaul for three years. They had intended to give Rabaul a new life as an impregnable fortress, but that never came to pass for it was attacked by Allied bombers almost daily for the rest of the war.

To protect themselves from these attacks, the Japanese invaders built an elaborate system of tunnels in the surrounding hills. Hospitals, living quarters, storage rooms, workshops, bunkers and anti-aircraft guns went underground to avoid the rain of death. In the end, the entire surface city of Rabaul had been destroyed from the air; but there was no Allied invasion and the defenders' underground troops slowly wasted away as resupply became impossible. At the end of the war, the remaining Japanese troops who saw only anticraft defense were simply repatriated to their homeland having been an impotent part of the Imperial war machine.

The Gazelle Peninsula is a virtual museum of World War II relics. In Rabual itself is the former Japanese Naval Command's bunker, now an eery museum fitted out to give the visitor an idea of life underground. The floor of Simpson Harbor is a treasure trove of sunken Japanese ships while the surrounding hills are still riddled with most of the 360 miles of tunnels dug by the Japanese. Some distance outside of Rabaul is the most unique of all tunnels, a barge tunnel with five barges still in hiding. Nearby, a huge floating crane lies beached and useless, dragged there from Singapore by Japanese forces but abandoned after Allied air attacks began.

From the time New Britain was first seen by Europeans in the 1700s, there has been a tugging and pulling by many countries for the right to control this productive island. Until the start of World War I, it was the Germans who ran much of New Guinea for economic return. Then came the Australians, who administered it as a League of Nations Mandate until Japanese forces invaded in World War II. Following the Japanese defeat, the Australians returned to its adminstration until Papua New Guinea became an independent country in 1975.

Rabaul was the capital of all German New Guinea until 1899, when their headquarters were moved down the bay to Herbertshohe (now Kokopo). It was moved back to Rabaul in 1910 and remains the provin-

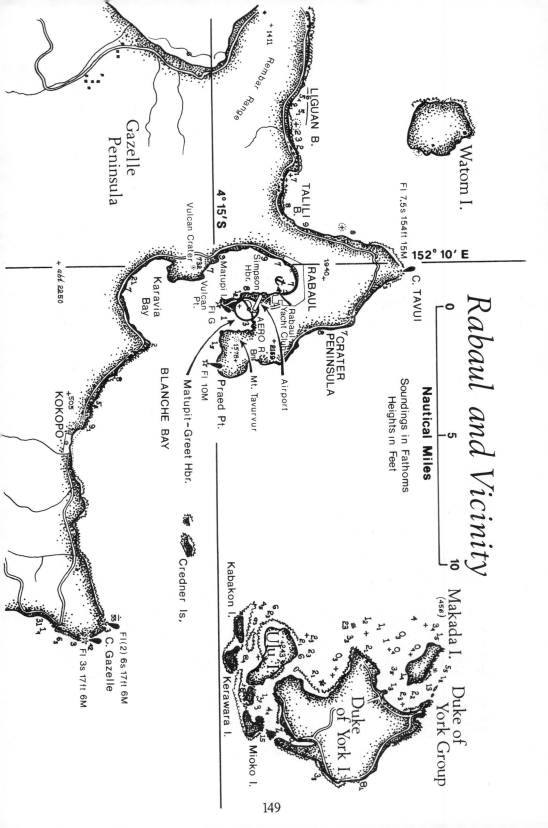

Rabaul and Vicinity

Nautical Miles

Soundings in Fathoms
Heights in Feet

0   5   10

Watom I.

Fl 7.5s 154ft 15M

C. TAVUI

152° 10′ E

LIGUAN B.

TALILI B.

Rembar Range

Gazelle Peninsula

4°15′S

+1411

+2250

Vulcan Crater

Karavia Bay

Vulcan Pt.

Matupi I.

Simpson Hbr.

RABAUL

Rabaul Yacht Club

AERO R.

Bn

CRATER PENINSULA

Airport

Mt. Tavurvur

Praed Pt.

Matupit–Greet Hbr.

Fl 10M

Fl G

BLANCHE BAY

KOKOPO

Credner Is.

C. Gazelle

Fl(2) 6s 17ft 6M

Fl 3s 17ft 6M

Makada I.
(456)

Duke of York Group

Kabakon I.

Ulu

Duke of York I.

Kerawara I.

Mioko I.

149

cial capital for Eastern New Britain—as long as the volcanoes behave. Should another major eruption occur, it is planned to move the administration and commercial activities of East New Britain back to Kokopo.

Boats arriving from the Solomon Islands to the southeast, will find Rabaul the best port of entry to Papua New Guinea. Visas are required and can be obtained at the Papua New Guinea Commission in Honiara, Solomon Islands.

Rabaul's Simpson Harbor is large, with literally miles of shoreline anchoring space, but you are advised to anchor off the Rabaul Yacht Club on the eastern shore, not only for convenience to town, but to get out of the swells sweeping the main harbor when the southeasterlies are strong. Do not anchor near the commercial wharves along the northern shore of the harbor for there are many World War II wrecks on the bottom that like to eat ground tackle.

One of these wrecks is a cargo ship sunk so close to the shoreline that it didn't completely submerge but remained upright with its weather deck exposed at low tide. To make the most of it, the town fathers had it filled with dirt and rubble and they now use it as a wharf. It's called the Wreck Wharf, what else?

The attractiveness of Rabaul to cruisers cannot be overemphasized. The anchorage off the yacht club is two short blocks from the town center. There is public transportation, but everything is within walking distance. Papua New Guinea was a trusteeship of Australia until 1975 and maintains many of the business and administrative practices common to Australia. Imported foodstuffs are mostly Australian, although Oriental

Workers unloading sugar cane, Rabaul, Papua New Guinea

products are making inroads into that monopoly. The currency is their own and not tied to any other country.

Burns-Philip South Seas Traders are still dominant in the area, operating several retail stores as well as a shipping line. Boats can get fuel by prior arrangement with the shipping manager's office at the head of the Burns-Philip wharf next to the yacht club.

The Rabaul Yacht Club offers honorary memberships to transient boats. Showers, beer, food and occasional movies are available, plus a nice lounge to relax in and get out of the tropical sun. Fresh water is available for your boat but it has a strong sulphurous odor. Collect rainwater to fill your tanks.

Boat provisions are readily obtainable from a variety of stores along Mango Avenue, which passes in front of the yacht club. Several banks can handle your financial needs.

The Rabaul produce market is one of the largest in the South Pacific, with an enormous variety of fruits, vegetables, melons and handicrafts. I have never seen as many varieties of bananas as here. Fresh produce is reasonable in price compared to canned foods in the stores. The market is clean, orderly and an excellent place to people watch. Many expatriates do their shopping here and you can easily strike up a conversation.

The industrial waterfront along Blanche Road features commercial wharfs where you can slip your boat, get any form of maintenance done or have special repairs made. It is not a yachting center, so don't expect anything but workboat hardware and paints. Rabaul, Madang and the Bellesana slipways on China Strait are the best places in Papua New Guinea to get work done.

If you come to Rabaul only to eat, drink and work on your boat, you are missing an interesting culture and history. In the foothills east of the harbor is a magnificent public orchid garden with an almost infinite variety of orchids and tropical flowering plants and trees. Several museums in the area are accessible by hired car. A guide can be useful if you are looking for historic and cultural spots immersed in the bush. If you have never seen where Nestle's chocolate begins life, there are many cocoa plantations along the way. Papua New Guinea is probably the most primitive of Pacific countries and since Rabaul has the most contact with Western civilizations, it is a good place to make your initial contact with its culture.

— Cruising World

FIJI'S PAST CAPTURED ON OVALAU

Ten miles to the east of Viti Levu, the capital island of Fiji, lies tiny Ovalau island, its 40 or so square miles of land dwarfed by its neighbor's 3700 sq. mi. But there was a time in history when tiny Ovalau Island politically dominated the Fijian archipelago and its main village of Levuka was headquarters for a flourishing world trade in copra and cotton.

Levuka town on Ovalu was the capital of the fledging Fijian state. Western traders had set up business there under the sheltering arm of the Tui Levuka who must have been a farsighted chief. But it was not only the traders presence that made Levuka a natural place for the new state capital, it was also its location on the windward side of the island with an extensive barrier reef far offshore to quiet the Pacific waves. The reef was unique in that it had two major passes—one to the north of Levuka and one to the south, allowing the big Fijian sailing canoes and the less maneuverable European sailing ships to enter through one pass and depart through the other. In between, they could anchor in peaceful waters.

Levuka made an ideal capital—the businesses were there (even a newspaper); shipping was easily handled and the tradewinds made living comfortable. But soon the coastal plain was filled with buildings and the mountains of the interior left no room for expansion. A new capital site had to be chosen. Suva was it, and in 1882 the British Colonial administration packed its bags and moved to its new home.

Levuka, however, has not lost its value to Fiji. Its very isolation from the modern world has given it a new lease on life as Fiji's window to the past. Walking the streets of Levuka is like having a time machine take you back to old Fiji when chiefs ruled, traders bought and sold and missionaries preached.

Ovalau Island's current population is about 6,500 persons with 1,700 living in Levuka town. Agriculture is the mainstay to the economy outside of the small local businesses and government offices in "downtown" Levuka. Although Levuka is still a Port of Entry to Fiji, its waterborne activity is limited to servicing the fishing fleet consisting of boats from Korea, Taiwan and Japan. The island is served from Nausori on Viti Levu by Fiji Air on a daily basis.

The main business section of Levuka runs along Beach Road while inland just one or two blocks, houses take over running right up to the steep sides of the interior mountains. Many are built on the slopes of the mountain necessitating long flights of stairs to reach them. For the ambitious visitor, these steps lead to a spectacular view of town and harbor.

But the real charm of old Levuka is found while walking along its saporific streets. There you will find the old Morris Hedstrom Ltd. building and the colonial-style buildings of the government at the wharf. A walk upstream along Tatoga Creek, whose headwaters form the town's drinking supply, brings you to a dam and a bathing pool where happy Fijian children have splashed for generations. Along the backstreets of

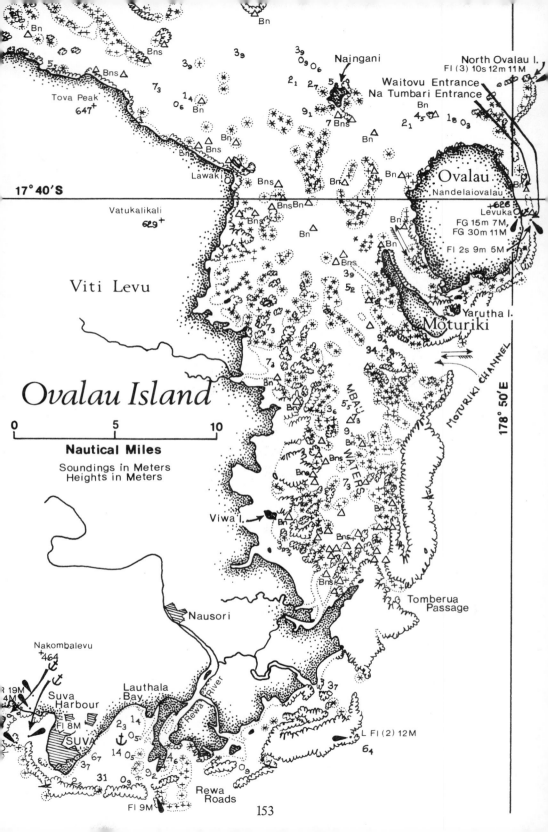

Bn

Bn
Bns

Tova Peak
647+

3_9 4_9

3_9 0_9 0_6 Naingani
2_1 2_7 5_4
9_1
7 Bns

North Ovalau I.
Fl (3) 10s 12m 11M

Waitovu Entrance
Na Tumbari Entrance
Bn
2_1 4_5 1_5 0_3

5_1 7_3
1_4 0_6 Bn

Bn Bns
Bn

Bns Bn

Bn Ovalau
Nandelaiovalau

17° 40′S

Vatukalikali
6_{29}+

Lawaki

Bns

Bns Bn Bn

Bns Bn

Bn

Bn Bns

Bn

Bn

+6_{26}
Levuka
FG 15m 7M
FG 30m 11M

Fl 2s 9m 5M

Viti Levu

3_9
5_2

Yarutha I.
Moturiki

3_4

7_3

7_3

Bn

Bn

Ovalau Island

MBAU WATERS

5_5
3_6
9_3 Bn
Bns
Bns

7_3

MOTURIKI CHANNEL

178° 50′E

0	5	10

Nautical Miles

Soundings in Meters
Heights in Meters

Viwa I.
Bn

3_3

Bns

Bns

Bn

Bns

Tomberua
Passage

7_9

Nausori

Nakombalevu
+464

R 19M
4M

Suva
Harbour

Fl 8M

SUVA

Lauthala
Bay

2_3 1_4
0_5

6_7
3_7 14 0_5
9_2
31 0_9

Rewa River

4_6

0_9

Rewa
Roads

Fl 9M

3_7

L Fl (2) 12M

6_4

153

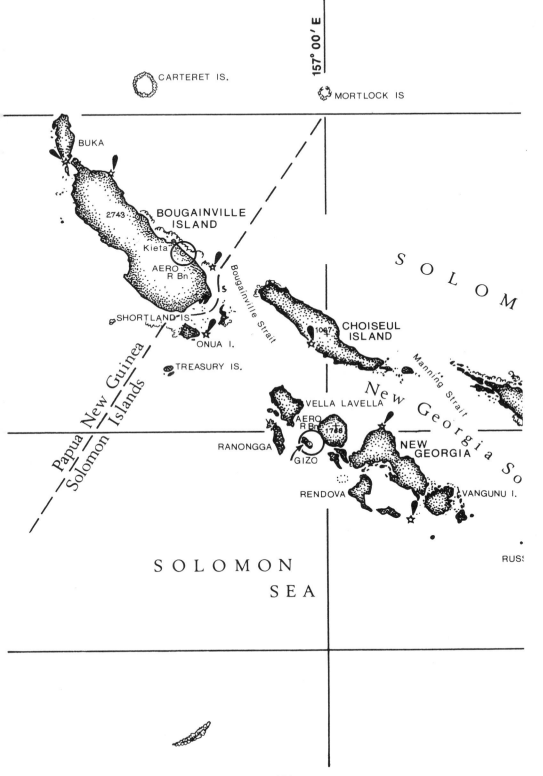

CARTERET IS.

MORTLOCK IS

157° 00′ E

BUKA

2743

BOUGAINVILLE
ISLAND

Kieta

AERO
R Bn

SOLOM

SHORTLAND IS.

Bougainville Strait

CHOISEUL
ISLAND

1067

ONUA I.

TREASURY IS.

Manning Strait

New Georgia So

VELLA LAVELLA

AERO
R Bn

1788

Papua New Guinea
Solomon Islands

RANONGGA

NEW
GEORGIA

GIZO

RENDOVA

VANGUNU I.

SOLOMON

SEA

RUSS

154

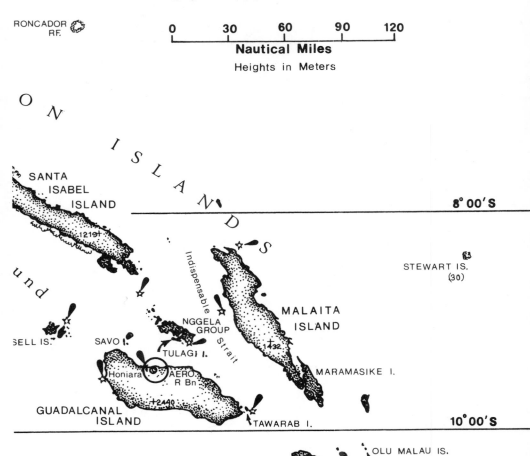

TASMAN IS
(30)

5°00'S

ONTONG
JAVA

Solomon Islands

RONCADOR RF.

0   30   60   90   120

Nautical Miles

Heights in Meters

O N   I S L A N D S

SANTA
ISABEL
ISLAND

8° 00'S

1219

STEWART IS.
(30)

und

Indispensable Strait

MALAITA
ISLAND

SELL IS.

NGGELA
GROUP

SAVO I.

TULAGI I.

132

Honiara   AERO.
          R Bn

MARAMASIKE I.

GUADALCANAL
ISLAND

2440

TAWARAB I.

10° 00'S

OLU MALAU IS.

1250

SAN CRISTOBAL I.

AERO.
R Bn

STA ANA
(158)

Levuka, you can feel the old Colonial atmosphere in building, street, store and hedge. A refreshing drink at the old Royal Hotel puts you right into the pages of Somerset Maugham. To savor the real history of Fiji, a short walk south on Beach Road brings you to Nasova and the monument commemorating the signing of the Deed of Cession with England in 1874. That is where modern Fiji began.

— Pacific

Laundry day in a stream near Levuka, Ovalau, Fiji

GIZO - SMALL, REMOTE AND BUSY

When your island is too small for both a town and an airport, what do you do? Why, put the airport on a neighbor island and treat the passengers to a refreshing boat ride along with the flight. Such is the situation at Gizo Island in the New Georgia Group of the Solomon Islands. The airport is on Nusatupe Island, a pleasant ten minute boat ride from the Solair terminal at Gizo. This wouldn't work for Honolulu, Guam or Papeete but Gizo is different. It is made up of people who worry less about the cosmetics of life than getting the business at hand done.

Take the Gizo Inn, for instance. It is a modest two-story wood frame building on the waterfront road. Its small lobby is large enough to get you registered and headed up the outside staircase to your room. The rooms are simple, functional and best of all, cooled with large ceiling fans.

Host and owner of this friendly inn is Charlie Siana Panakera, Member of Parliament, Minister for Tourism and a man whose literacy and English-language ability puts most Englishmen and Americans to shame. Charlie is all business during the day, but come the dinner hour, he will put you in touch with New Georgia's past. One of his most inter-

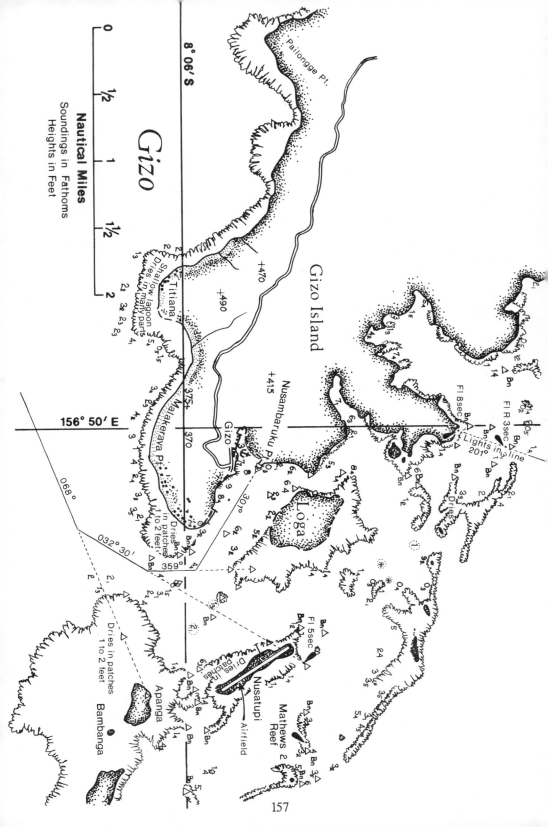

Gizo

Nautical Miles

Soundings in Fathoms
Heights in Feet

0   ½   1   1½   2

8°06'S

156° 50' E

Pailongge Pt.

Gizo Island

Titiana

Shallow lagoon
Dries in many parts

Malakereva Pt.

Dries
in patches
to 2 feet

+470

+490

+415

+375

370

Gizo

Nusambaruku Pt.

Loga

Lights in line
201°

Fl 8sec

Fl R 3sec

Dries

068°

032° 30'

359°

Dries in patches
1 to 2 feet

Apanga

Bambanga

Fl 5sec

Nusatupi

Airfield

Dries in patches

Mathews
Reef

157

Interisland trading boat at Gizo, Solomon Islands

esting stories tells of headhunter rituals which were commonplace before World War II. Much of this history comes from his 100-year old father sitting at another table in the restaurant who grew up in that bygone era.

Life in Gizo no longer centers around the prowess of war parties. Rather, the Islanders are now busy pursuing a modern day society fraught with profit and loss. At one end of Gizo town is a lumber mill slicing up logs harvested from surrounding islands. Necessary for the economy, yes, but devastating to the ecology of the hillsides. From an airplane, you see rivers dark with topsoil flowing into the ocean destroying land fertility and silting over productive sea beds. Furniture-making from local timber is another business helping the economy along. The factory is close to the waterfront which also supports yards building boats and giant dugout canoes.

Gizo is not so much an industrial center as it is a focal point of business. Freighters from Honiara discharge a variety of goods at Gizo, which is the District Center for the Western Province of the Solomon Islands. There it is warehoused and reshipped by small interisland boats to the myriad of islands which make up the province. This is a busy waterfront, for goods shipped out are paid for with incoming copra and timber from neighboring islands such as legendary Kolombangara. In turn, this trade generates the need for banks, shipping companies, trading houses and government.

Big business aside, there is also small business along the waterfront. Some of it is not even found in buildings, but on the streets where woodcarvers peddle their wares. My sailboat cruising friends have often remarked that it is here in the New Georgia Islands where the best woodcarvers do their work. I met one of these talented fellows, Fredrick Tonny

from Kohigo Island. His smile and his excellent work in ebony and kerosene woods caught my eye and a sale was made.

The waterfront in Gizo is colorful to say the least. A long row of buildings, some supported only by termite-ridden posts, set over the water's edge and serve as stores, homes and offices or all three. You can arrive at the front door by pickup truck and depart from the back door by dugout canoe. This is a convenient arrangement for a community whose main form of transportation is water. Each building has its own dugout canoe, no longer paddled, but propelled by a modern outboard motor. Sailing canoes disappeared long ago, for these islands are noted for light winds with long periods of calm. Like all the world, petroleum has become lord and master of the economy and Gizo serves as its distribution point for the Western Province.

While Gizo may be small and remote from population centers, it is remembered by visitors for the warm personalities and beaming smiles of its people and the refreshing airport boat ride.

— Pacific

NEW CALEDONIA — LAND OF ETERNAL SPRING

The French Overseas Territory of New Caledonia lies about 10 sailing days from Aukland or Brisbane and is a relatively little-visited South Seas destination. The reason being that boats taking the Coconut Milk Run from the United States or through the Panama Canal are usually destined to either return in a two-year time period or continue on in a circumnavigation. Aussies and Kiwis, however, use New Caledonia, Vanuatu and Fiji as prime destinations for six-month cruises during the austral winter. What is good for the Aussies and Kiwis is good for the cruising community.

New Caledonia consists of one (very) large island, La Grande Terre, and several smaller ones including the Loyalty Group on its eastern side. La Grand Terre is unique in being surrounded by the largest insular coral

159

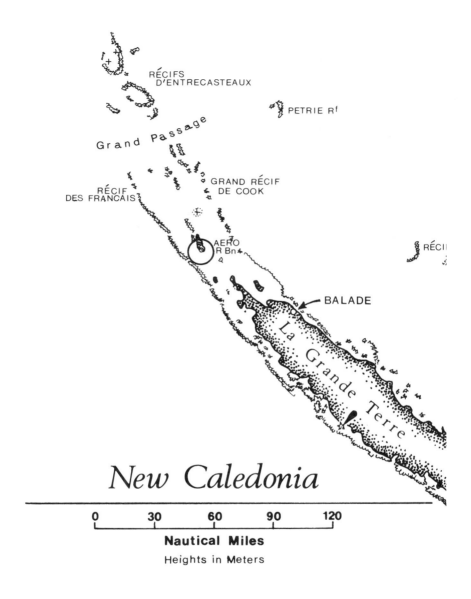

New Caledonia

| 0 | 30 | 60 | 90 | 120 |

Nautical Miles

Heights in Meters

reef in the world. The reef is well offshore and you can sail the lagoon along much of the island which is what Captain Cook did in his early explorations of these waters in 1774.

Lying just north of the Tropic of Capricorn, New Caledonia's weather is tropical with a humid, warm period from December to March and a cool and dry period from April to November. The southeast trades tend to

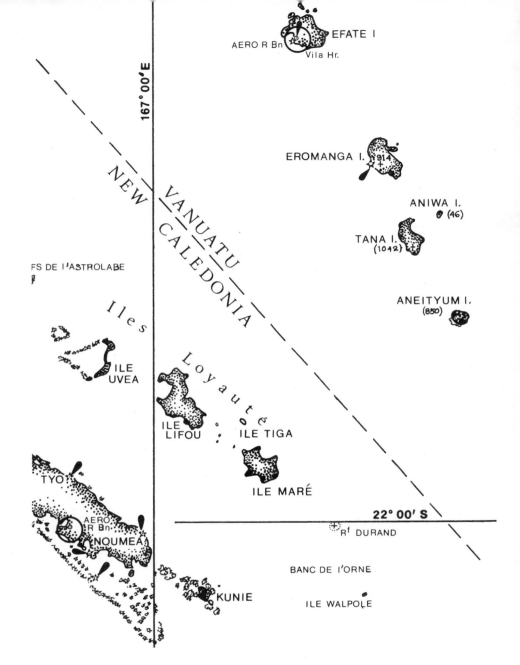

AERO R Bn
Vila Hr.

EFATE I

EROMANGA I. 914

ANIWA I.
(46)

TANA I.
(1042)

ANEITYUM I.
(850)

FS DE I'ASTROLABE

Iles

Loyauté

ILE
UVEA

ILE
LIFOU

ILE TIGA

ILE MARÉ

22° 00′ S

Rf DURAND

TYO

AERO
R Bn
NOUMEA

BANC DE I'ORNE

KUNIE

ILE WALPOLE

NEW

VANUATU

CALEDONIA

blow the year around, but they are stronger and more southerly during the austral winter. The west (leeward) side of the island is subject to daily cyclic onshore and offshore breezes because of the size of the island. The eastern (windward) side is blessed with the steady trades.

New Caledonia lies in the Southwest Pacific cyclone belt, whose season is nominally from December through April. Most years the cyclones cross

north of the islands but occasionally one will double back and head southeastward. Noumea has been little affected by cyclones in the past and with a well-sheltered harbor, is one of the better "hurricane holes" in the Southwestern Pacific.

There is only one Port of Entry to New Caledonia and that is Noumea on the southwest coast of la Grande Terre. Entry through the reef is made at Passe de Boulari under the watchful eye of le Phare Amedee-Amadee Lighthouse. This is a most unique structure having been built in 1865 of riveted steel prefabricated in France. It is 40 meters high and situated on Amadee islet, a popular holiday spot for Noumea boaters. Although the islet is quite crowded on weekends and holidays, it is worth a visit by cruising boats during the week.

New Caledonia has much simpler procedures for entering than French Polynesia, even though both are Overseas Territories of France. No visa is required for stays less than 30 days and there is no bond requirement. Your crew does need the usual onward airline ticket or the equivalent in money. Cruising boats can get their clearance at the end of the main wharf in Baie de la Moselle right in the center of town or they proceed directly to the yacht club—Cercle Nautique Caledonien in Baie de Pecheurs. The yacht club manager will call all necessary officials for the clearance.

There is no charge for time spent at the wharf; but it must be limited to essential business of clearance or provisioning. If you want to stay in the area longer, you can moor Tahiti-style farther along the quai out of the way of boats needing to carry out business at the wharf. Or, you can anchor out at many places in this large well-protected harbor. Wherever you stay, you are close to the center of Noumea and connecting bus service to many surrounding places of interest.

If you choose to stay at the yacht club, you can get seven days berthing gratis and after that you must pay trivial charges of 100 CFP per day for the first week, 200 CFP per day for the second week and 300 CFP per day for the third week. The club is modern with fine facilities including a bar and dining room. During the best cruising period, this is a popular place so don't expect to stay at the club for several weeks.

The town of Noumea has a population of about 60,000 persons, most of whom are French. As a result, Noumea has a delightful French atmosphere making it more akin to a Mediterranean French town than a South Seas Island. The French way of life can be very attractive, especially in a South Seas setting. Good wine, cheese and that delightful French bread enjoyed by all cruisers makes lunch ashore a real treat. If you are ashore at lunch time, don't expect to do anything but eat and drink for all stores close from 1000 to 1400 for a "siesta" period.

New Caledonia is the best place to resupply and make boat repairs between Suva and Australia although it is quite expensive. You will find the "peoples" market near the wharf well supplied with fruits, vegetables and fish. There are several boat chandleries in town and a "travel-lift"

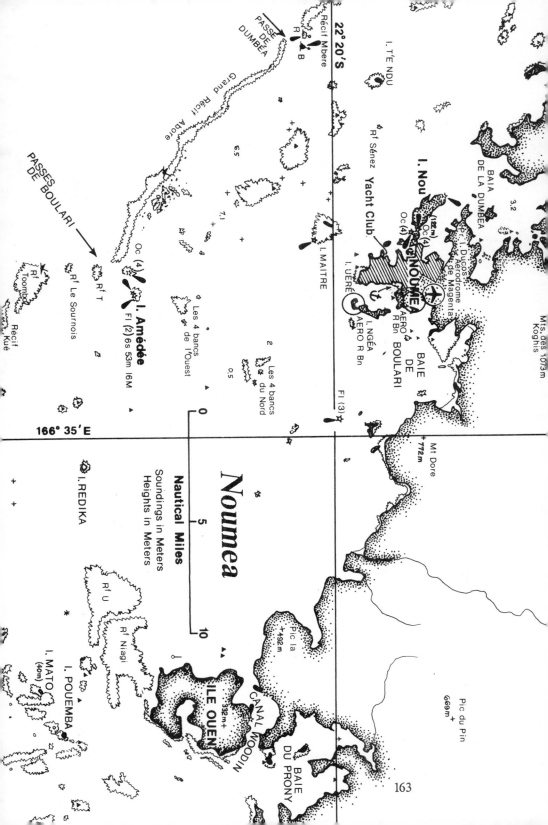

Noumea

Nautical Miles

Soundings in Meters
Heights in Meters

22° 20' S

166° 35' E

PASSE DE DUMBEA

PASSES DE BOULARI

Grand Récif Abore

Récif Mbere

R
B

I. TÉ NDU

Rf Sénez

Yacht Club

I. Nou

(12m)

Oc (4)
Oc (4)

NOUMEA

I. Ducos

T. Aérodrome
et de Magenta

BAIA DE LA DUMBEA

3.2

Mts. des 1073m Koghis

6.5

7.1

I. MAITRE

I. UÉRÉ

I. NGÉA
AERO R Bn

AERO R Bn

BAIE DE BOULARI

Oc (4)

I. Amédée
Fl (2) 6s 53m 16M

Rf T

Rf Le Sournois

Toombo
Rf
Récif
Kué

Les 4 bancs de l'Ouest

Les 4 bancs du Nord

2

0.5

0

5

10

Fl (3)

Mt Dore
772m

Pic du Pin
669m

I. REDIKA

Rf U

Rf Niagi

Pic Ia
492m

CANAL WOODIN

ILE OUEN

532m

BAIE DU PRONY

I. MATO
(40m)

I. POUEMBA

163

New Caledonia Yacht Club (Cercle Nautique Caledonian), Noumea, New Caledonia

haulout facility close to the yacht club. Remember, all French replacement hardware will be manufactured to the metric system. Shops for mechanical, electrical and electronic repairs are available as is a sailmaker and rigger. Neither you nor your boat need go unattended in this Land of Eternal Spring.

If you have been following the political news of New Caledonia, you know that there are some endemic problems to be solved. One strong indigenous Melanesian group called the Kanaks, wants total self rule. Most of the French and some of the Melanesians are happy with the contemporary French rule. Occasional confrontations take place between the Kanaks and the government, but usually on the east coast where most of the indigenous Melanesians live. It will not be very apparent to you, but there is a large contingent of French soldiers in New Caledonia. Since the Kanaks relate Caucasian to French, it is best to keep a low profile when traveling away from Noumea and wear your country's flag.

Although you can cruise inside the reef for hundreds of miles, the two most interesting cruising spots are the Ile de Pins at the southern tip of La Grande Terre and the Iles Loyautes 100 kms to the east. It will take you a long day's cruise south to the Ile de Pins and I would not recommend that you do it at night because of the coral reefs. When you do get there, head for Kuto Bay, which is the center of the resort activities and that is what

this island is all about. You can mix it up with the Noumeans on holiday and tourists on vacation or go it alone.

For the real South Seas Atmosphere, you must go on to the Iles Loyaute. Of the three main islands (Ouvea, Lifou and Mare), Ouvea has the best lagoon anchorage. The peoples of these islands are actually Polynesians having come originally from the Wallis Islands. Their politics are akin to the Kanaks along the eastern shore of La Grande Terre, so don't make political waves while there. The Loyalty Islands are not Ports of Entry, but you can get permission from Noumea to take your departure from them if you are headed for Port Vila or Suva.

It is not only the French atmosphere, the beauty of the islands and the winter weather that make New Caledonia so attractive, it is a rock hound's delight. One would suspect that from the geology of the land and the fact that minerals such as nickel, chrome and iron are found there, but the mineral most sought after is the jade from Ile Ouen. The Ouen jade is reputed to closely resemble the Nephrite of Siberia. There is only one term to describe this jade when it is cut and polished and that is "Magnifique."

So take a tip from the Aussies and Kiwis, add a few months to your South Pacific cruise and visit the Land of Eternal Spring. Yours will then be the unusual cruise.

— Cruising World

ISLE OF PINES OLD PRISON

At the southern tip of La Grande Terre, the principal island of New Caledonia, lies the Isle of Pines, or Kunie as the Melanesians call it. The island is not large, only 152 square kilometers; but it looms large in tourist advertising, enticing foreigners to come see the "Land of Eternal Spring."

The indomitable British Captain Cook was the first European to see these islands and he gave them the collective name New Caledonia. He also named Kunie the Isle of Pines since it, as well as La Grande Terre, was well-forested with the tall, columnar pine loosely called the New Caledonia pine, but more properly known as *araucaria cookii*. The tree has all but vanished as far as commerically economic stands are concerned.

It wasn't the only tree on the Isle of Pines to become endangered, though. In 1841, the assault on sandalwood forests began in an effort to satisfy an insatiable demand by the Chinese for this fragrant wood that had already disappeared from Hawaii, Fiji and the Marquesas Islands.

Old French Prison, Isle of Pines, New Caledonia

Now there is hardly a sandalwood tree to be found in all of New Caledonia and few in the entire Pacific.

The Isle of Pines figured heavily in the French decision to take possession of New Caledonia in the 1800s. As was so common in Pacific exploration by the Europeans, Britain and France were rivals in this area for trade and the privilege of converting the native population to Christrianity. But the French were doing poorly in both and when it became known that the British were planning a coaling station on the Isle of Pines, the French took decisive action. They raised the tricolor first at Balade, Grande Terre, on September 24, 1853, and then repeated the event five days later on the Isle of Pines. Now they were free to control trade throughout the islands and to press their missionary cause.

The Isle of Pines is a low island, only 262 meters above sea level, but it has some magnificent caves kept hidden from the visitor. These limestone caves are laced with stalactites and stalagmites and one cave is over three kilometers long. These caves, once the burial grounds of local people, are near the center of the island and a potential, though underdeveloped, tourist attraction.

The same can be said for the ruins of a 19th century penal colony that flourished from 1864 to 1897. One of France's early interests in New Caledonia, aside from just beating the British to it, was as a place far away from La Belle France where undesirable persons could be "transported" to rid the homeland of them. France already had French Guyana, but it wasn't large enough to handle all of the deportees. After the Franco-German War in 1872, thousands of socialists were rounded up in

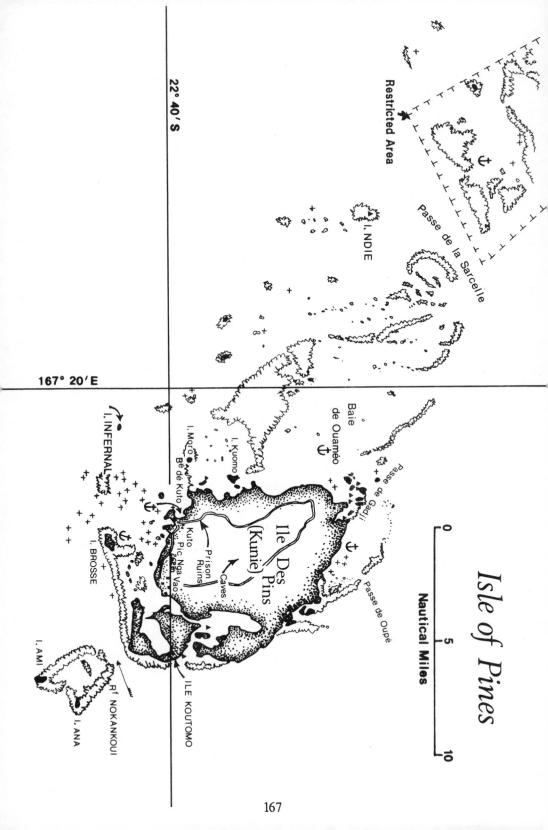

Isle of Pines

22° 40' S

167° 20' E

Restricted Area

Passe de la Sarcelle

I. NDIE

I. INFERNAL

Baie
de Ouaméo

I. Kuomo

I. Moro
Bé dé Kuto

Ile Des
Pins
(Kunie)

Kuto
Pic Nga Vao

Prison
Ruins

Caves

Passe de Gadji

I. BROSSE

I. AMI

I. ANA

Rf NOKANKOUI

ILE KOUTOMO

Passe de Oupé

Nautical Miles

0   5   10

France for transportation to New Caledonia and the prison colony on the Isle of Pines. Not long afterwards, shiploads of Arabs showed up following the 1871 Arab insurrection in Algeria. But the most ignominious group of internees on the Isle of Pines were about 700 indigenes from La Grande Terre, who were incarcerated there following a Kanak revolt in 1878. Now the crumbling prison walls are overgrown with wild bush, hidden from view of the curious visitor, nevertheless, a part of the history of New Caledonia.

Only about one percent of New Caledonia's current population lives on the Isle of Pines. The one population center of the island is at Vao where reside the island administration, Catholic church and school.

The Isle of Pines economy is basically an agrarian subsistence, one supplemented by a tenuous tourist trade. Although only a 45-minute flight from Noumea, few overseas tourists other than Japanese day-trippers find their way there. The remaining tourist trade seems mostly to be made up of New Caledonian colonists wanting to get away from Noumea for a few days. Admittedly, the island has some tempting beaches and certainly fine weather—even better than Noumea, but there is not much else. It isn't that resort operators haven't tried, for there are ample resort ruins to indicate better times, or at least more optimistic thinking.

The depressed Isle of Pines tourist economy may be laid to high prices—almost as high as Tahiti's, which are the highest in all the Pacific. Or, possibly, it is the poor exchange rate of the Australian and New Zealand dollars which were the source of much tourist income at one time. More than likely, it is the unsettled political situation in New Caldonia. Vacationers simply do not want to expose themselves to a country's internal problems while on vacation.

There are many signs of the Kanaks' desire for independence in the form of graffiti, if not violence. In the political scheme of things, the Isle of Pines has been designated a "reservation" and 92 percent of its population is Kanak. (The other outlying islands of New Caledonia also are "reservations.") The Kanaks of New Caledonia number about one-half of the total population and they want independence and are not willing to settle for the present pseudo-apartheid political arrangement. Until that is resolved, Kunie can only pine for tourists too afraid to go.

— Pacific

168

CHAPTER 6

MICRONESIA A LA AMERICA

*"The Micronesians themselves would have smiled at
all the fuss if they had known what was being written
about them. They had just passed through troubled but
exciting times and had emerged with their lives, their
land (regardless of whose flag flew over their islands),
and their social institutions rather well intact. Whatever
the future might hold for them, they had demonstrated
their ability to adapt to the unfamiliar and could do so
again and again if need be. Foreign nations would come
and go, but they would remain in the homeland that
their ancestors had settled centuries before Magellan had
first visited their shores. They would remain and survive,
as they had so often before."*
— Francis X. Hezel, "The First Taint of Civilization"

We had moved *Horizon's* home port to Hawaii to put us in a more
favorable location for future cruising in the Pacific as well as to enjoy the delights of living in the tropics. Albeit we were just at the northeast corner of
the Polynesian Triangle, but it did put us 2,000 miles closer to the other
islands making up the cruising grounds of the Pacific.

Polynesia had become very familiar to us from an earlier cruise we
made on what I call the Coconut Milk Run: the Marquesas, Tahiti,
Somoa, Tonga, New Zealand, Australs, Tuamotus and Hawaii. Most
cruising boats still follow that route because it is a spectacular introduction to Pacific cruising and can be done in two years' time. Some boats
even manage to make a stop in Fiji which gives them a touch of Melanesia. My writing research had also taken me by air to many other parts of
the Pacific, and the one area that seemed least traveled and in need of exploration by small boat was Micronesia.

Micronesia is made up of over 2,000 islands which collectively have
only 1,200 square miles of land area, or less than that of Rhode Island;
but what Micronesia lacks in land, it makes up in ocean, covering
4,000,000 square miles of the salty stuff. All of the islands of Micronesia
are west of the International Dateline in the Northern Hemisphere except
for the Gilbert Islands which span the equator. Guam, an American territory, is the largest of the islands and also the most populated, looking a
lot like a suburb of Los Angeles. Most of the islands, however, are true atolls—strings of pearls gracing the azure tropical waters.

Some islands of Micronesia are large atolls like mighty Kwajalein and
Ulithi that housed most of the United States fleet during World War II.

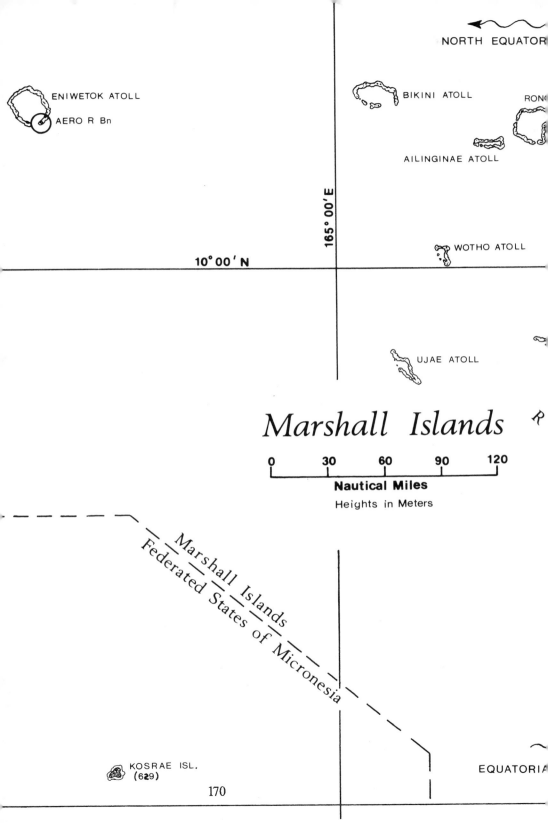

NORTH EQUATOR

ENIWETOK ATOLL

AERO R Bn

BIKINI ATOLL

RON

AILINGINAE ATOLL

165° 00′ E

WOTHO ATOLL

10° 00′ N

UJAE ATOLL

Marshall Islands   R

| 0 | 30 | 60 | 90 | 120 |

Nautical Miles

Heights in Meters

Marshall Islands
Federated States of Micronesia

KOSRAE ISL.
(629)

170

EQUATORIA

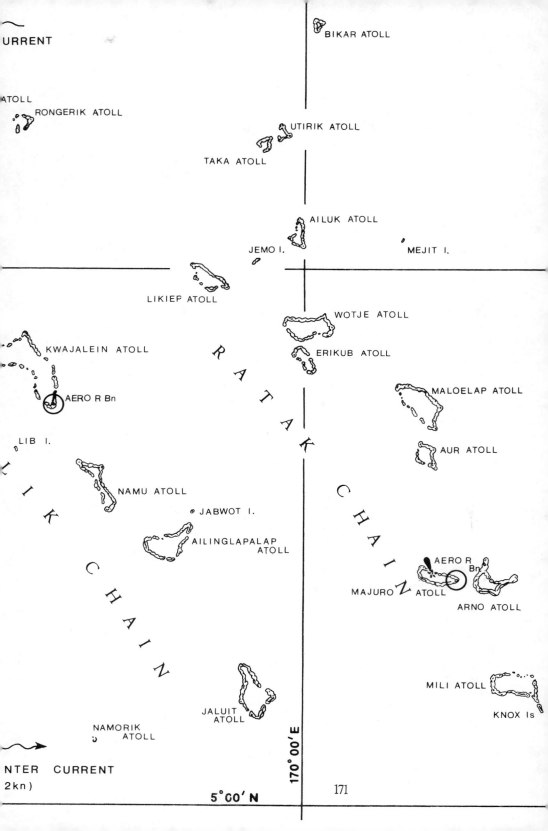

CURRENT

BIKAR ATOLL

ATOLL
RONGERIK ATOLL

UTIRIK ATOLL

TAKA ATOLL

AILUK ATOLL

JEMO I.   MEJIT I.

LIKIEP ATOLL

WOTJE ATOLL

KWAJALEIN ATOLL   ERIKUB ATOLL

MALOELAP ATOLL

AERO R Bn

LIB I.   AUR ATOLL

NAMU ATOLL

JABWOT I.

AILINGLAPALAP
ATOLL

AERO R
Bn

MAJURO ATOLL

ARNO ATOLL

MILI ATOLL

KNOX Is

JALUIT
ATOLL

NAMORIK
ATOLL

NTER CURRENT

2kn)

5°CO'N

170°00'E

171

R A T A K   C H A I N

R A L I K   C H A I N

Others are two-palmed spits of sand that give cartoonists so many inspirations, and a few are mountainous like Kosrae whose vibrant green slopes are covered with timber.

Natural resources are mostly sun, sand and water. Some, like Guam, Pohnpei, Yap, Babelthuap and Saipan are fertile enough for growing crops, but are grossly underdeveloped. A few—Nauru and Banaba are prime examples—are, or rather were, once rich in aged guano which is processed into phosphate-rich fertilizer for the rest of the world to use. By the early 1990s, Nauru, the last of the big phosphate producers, will have exhausted its supply of bird droppings and will then have to live off its considerable investments since the island has been devastated by mining. They are presently pressing the countries who mined and purchased their fertilizer—Australia, Britain and Japan—to return and change the moonscape back to a landscape. That will be quite a task.

Most of the countries of Micronesia, however, are on the dole. They were rudely introduced to the 20th century during World War II and have since been wards of either Great Britain or the United States. Nauru got its independence from Great Britain in 1968 and the Gilbert Islands in 1979; but the remainder of Micronesia, formerly called the Trust Territory of the Pacific Islands, remains associated with Uncle Sam—the Marshall Islands and Federated States of Micronesia in "Free Association," the Northern Marianas as a Commonwealth and Palau still as a "Trust" because they cannot resolve the differences in nuclear philosophy between their constitution and the proposed United States treaty of "Free Association."

The islands that made up the Trust Territory had known a succession of superpower rulers, none of whom seemed bent on improving the welfare of the indigenes as much as they sought to exploit them for their own purposes. First there was Spain in the 18th and 19th centuries, who ruled them with a religious fist. Then came Germany with its Teutonic business drive wanting copra, copra and more copra. Following Germany after World War I, came Japan who needed more land and food sources for its burgeoning home-island population and military outposts to secure its homelands. Belatedly, and somewhat reluctantly, the United States was forced by military reasons to take over the islands after World War II and has since ruled with benign neglect.

Life has not been good to the Micronesians under superpower rule but, like it or not, they are rapidly entering the 21st century. Before they became just another part of the Westernized world, we wanted to have a look and the Marshall Islands were the closest to our home port of Hawaii.

— Sea

CAPTAIN MARSHALL'S ISLANDS

The eastern end of Micronesia is anchored by the Marshall Islands, a group of 34 atolls lying in two parallel chains running from the southeast to the nothwest. Not suprisingly, the eastern chain is called the Ratak chain, meaning sunrise, and the western chain is called the Ralik chain, meaning sunset. The chains are only about 150 miles apart and early Marshallese soon found that by developing their navigational skills, they could sail canoes to neighboring islands thus enhancing their political unity as well as developing trade.

Out of this came the Marshallese sailing canoe (still seen in the out-islands) and the famous stick charts of the Marshalls. The emergence of the printed chart, compass and chronometer caused the demise of the old forms of navigation and present day stick charts are only a representative attempt to show what the early training charts looked like. "Operational" charts were created by each Marshallese navigator using his own interpretation of natural phenomena that would guide him between the islands.

Most Pacific island countries have only one or two ports of entry because they do not have enough international traffic to support more. The ports of entry to the Marshall Islands are at Ebeye Island in the Kwajalein Atoll and at Majuro Atoll.

Majuro Atoll

Majuro, with its population of 12,000 persons, is a typical atoll lying like a string of pearls on an aquamarine velvet base. As atolls go, it is of moderate size—24 miles long by 5 miles wide and nowhere does the land area measure more than 1,000 yards from lagoon to ocean. At one time, Majuro was composed of more than 75 islands but many of these have been fused together to give Majuro the longest road in the Trust Territory—30 miles of reasonably smooth sealed surface.

The urban area of Majuro is located at the eastern end of the atoll. There the three long islands of Darrit, Uliga and Dalap have been made into the business and government center of the Marshalls by filling in the gaps between them with graded coral. Nature has resented this restructuring of one of its beautiful creations, and in 1979 it sent rampaging waves across this end of the atoll, where passes no longer existed, causing severe damage to buildings, houses, roads and other man-made installations. Those left homeless lived in a tent city while reconstruction took place. Part of that tent city still exists in the shadow of the national government offices.

Main street of DUD (the unfortunate but descriptive acronym for Darrit-Uliga-Dalap) is a potpourri of corrugated iron shacks, wooden frame building and modern concrete structures. Absent are any traces of traditional Marshallese design or construction. Maintenance or preserva-

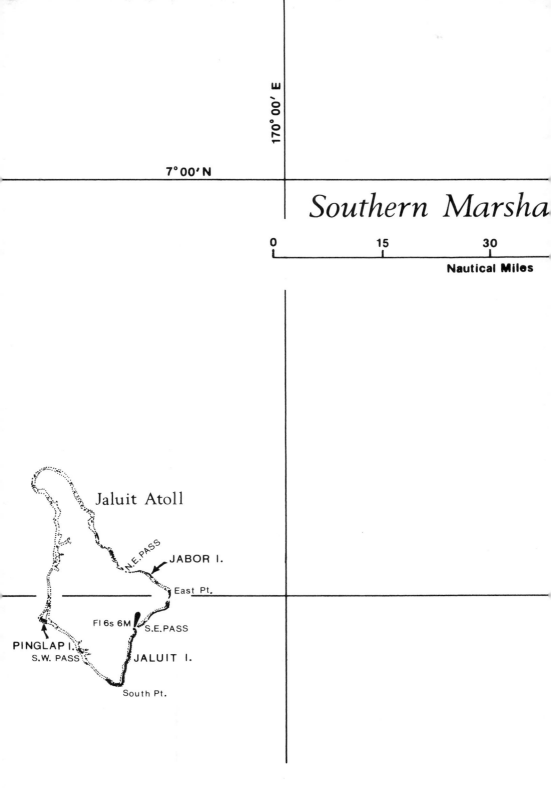

170° 00′ E

7° 00′ N

Southern Marsha

0   15   30

Nautical Miles

Jaluit Atoll

N.E.PASS

→ JABOR I.

East Pt.

Fl 6s 6M

S.E.PASS

PINGLAP I.

S.W. PASS

JALUIT I.

South Pt.

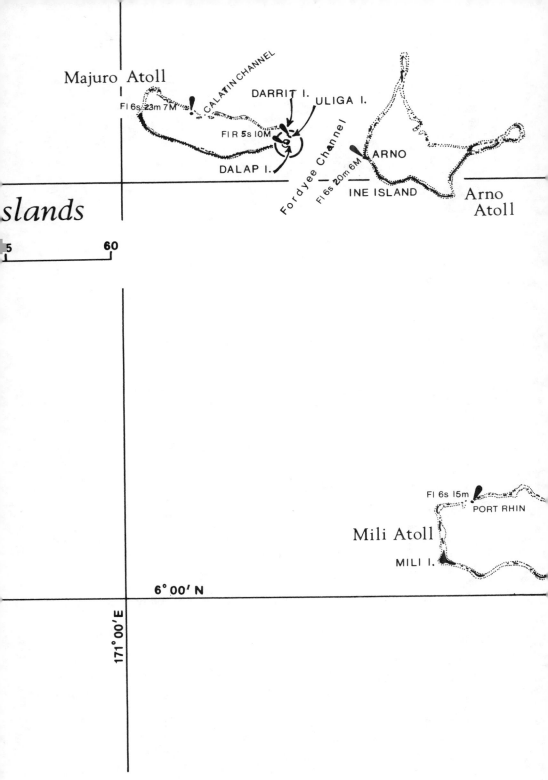

Majuro Atoll

Fl 6s 23m 7M

CALATIN CHANNEL

DARRIT I.

ULIGA I.

Fl R 5s 10M

DALAP I.

Fordyee Channel

Fl 6s 20m 6M

ARNO

INE ISLAND

Arno
Atoll

slands

5   60

Mili Atoll

Fl 6s 15m

PORT RHIN

MILI I.

6° 00′ N

171° 00′ E

Laundromat, Majuro, Marshall Islands

tion of buildings or machinery is not one of the Marshallese long suits and the town has an unfortunate rundown appearance. But that doesn't seem to bother the local population.

At the north end of DUD is suburbia with the small village of Rita forming the beginning of the 30-mile trans-Majuro highway. Rita is neatly maintained compared to the business area and it was fun to walk around and mingle with the local people who seemed to be mostly kids. These smiling youngsters are unwittingly part of a serious problem in Micronesia—rapidly growing population due to improved health care which has cut infant deaths and drastically extended life for more years. The number of mouths to feed long ago exceeded the ability of the land to feed them. Without Uncle Sam's help, starvation would be a way of life.

At Rita is an interesting memorial to the famous *Morning Star* missionary ship which first brought Christianity to the Marshalls. There were actually several *Morning Stars* and when old age or the reefs would claim a *Star*, another would be put into service. I am aware of four, although I don't know whether one exists today. The missionaries of the *Morning Star* and others have left their mark on the Marshallese who are very religious people, and children brought up in mission schools are a pleasure to meet.

Whether it has anything to do with religious precepts or is simply an attempt to emulate a Western business atmosphere, I don't know, but long trousers for men is a rule of dress. In this hot and humid climate even the thought of wearing long trousers is depressing; but I was forced into it by an unexpected incident. I headed for the government offices one day in a pair of very respectable shorts and an "aloha" shirt. Inside the building I was stopped by a security guard who advised me that I was "improperly dressed." I left immediately, embarassed and puzzled.

This same long trouser paradox exists in other parts of the Trust Territory but was not so evident in Kiribati. Having been brought up on the

English brand of colonialism, the I-Kiribati approve of walking shorts or their traditional lava lavas for all but the most formal of functions. Hail the I-Kiribati!

Going west on the trans-Majuro highway, you will pass the new seaport and industrial area housing the one big business in the Marshalls outside of government and the military at Kwajalein. It is the processing plant for reducing copra to coconut oil. The dock sheds are literally bursting at the seams with copra awaiting its turn at the presses attesting to the prolific nature of the coconut palm.

The trans-Majuro highway finally terminates in a rural area called Laura. We drove a rental car there for convenience, but you can bring your boat down the lagoon if you are careful about coral patches that almost fill the western end of the lagoon. Once you get there you will still need transportation of some kind to see the whole area.

Life in Laura is still *au naturel* compared to the rest of Majuro. There are sandy beaches, isolated houses (few thatched roofs) and only an occasional store selling Spam, canned tuna and bags of rice. We had almost despaired of finding any original handicrafts on Majuro but in Laura we found women making woven products in the shade of the palms. We had to invest in something, so we purchased a handmade sewing basket decorated with shells at $4—it seemed like a real bargain to us.

We were not unhappy to leave Majuro after a two-week sojourn. It is an island caught between a subsistence economy and an unknown future as a new country that someday will have to stand on its own. I don't think any boat should stay there very long—check in and leave for the outer islands. Nearby are Arno, Mili, Jaluit, Ebon and others which really are truer islands of Micronesia and not copies of rundown Americana. Our choice was Jaluit Atoll which, before World War II, was the headquarters of both German and Japanese overlords. It would give us a chance to see a bit more of the Marshall's history as we cruised farther west.

Japanese Radio Station from World War II, Jaluit Atoll, Marshall Islands

177

Jaluit Atoll

Two days later *Horizon* was anchored in the placid waters of Jaluit lagoon. We had come from South Seas mayhem to tropical tranquility. Jaluit is not the most rural of the Marshall Islands, but it is an order of magnitude more pleasant than Majuro. Jaluit is designated a political subcenter; but there is little evidence of bureaucracy in action.

Jaluit is a larger atoll than Majuro with about 265 square miles of lagoon area, 4 square miles of land and a population under 1,000 persons. The main island of Jabor is home for about 300 persons and the rest are spread around the other 85 islands surrounding the lagoon. This was once the center of commerce and government for the Marshalls, but it became just another atoll when Majuro was made the post-World War II government seat. What improvements had been made by the Japanese have since gone to ruin. Although useless now for their original functions, the old buildings have become homes for squatters.

The roads of Jabor are simply graded coral which is more than adequate for a town that you can walk completely around in 30 minutes. What roads there are sort of originate in the vicinity of the pier, which was broken up in a severe westerly storm a number of years ago, and never was rebuilt.

Electricity is furnished by an aging diesel generating plant that cuts off at 9:00 p.m. and starts blowing smoke rings again at 6:00 a.m.. Otherwise, there is no industry on the island and the only commerce is copra and one small general store.

Once you break through the reserve of the local people, they become friendly and solicitous. From the two Maryknoll sisters who have collectively spent more than 50 years on Jaluit tending a mission school, to the young lad who picked up my trail one day on a photo safari and presented me with five of the most beautiful cowrie shells I have seen, all seemed to enjoy life on this atoll far removed from its former position of importance.

The major building on Jabor is the high school to which students come from outlying islands and board there during the school year. It is the one modern structure contributed by the Americans and looks like it could weather a typhoon. The high school, together with the modest churches, is the social center of the island.

Jaluit is only 160 miles from Majuro, but it might as well be on the moon. Communications with the outside world appear to be essentially nil. No regular shipping, only an occasional light plane of Air Marshalls. Radio communications are limited to government business, which seemed to be very little. As a result, store goods are scarce, keeping people on a subsistence diet (which also minimizes litter). Even more essential things, such as medical aid and even a basic supply of medicines are lacking. With our ability to move around, a well-stocked larder, medicine supply and ham radio, I felt that *Horizon* was far better able to sustain it-

self than the people on land at Jaluit, but that didn't seem to bother them one iota.

We were more than pleased with our stay at Jaluit. It showed us a better side of the Marshall Islands—unhurried, friendly and with a cleaner environment in which to live. Now we were beginning to see Micronesia in its own image and not simply as fallout from Western civilization. Although it was with some reluctance that we left Jaluit, our enthusiasm for seeing Micronesia had been renewed and *Horizon* more willingly sailed westward to visit the high islands of Micronesia.

— Sea

Kids fishing near wreck of old boat engine, Jabor, Jaluit Atoll, Marshall Islands

EASTERN CAROLINE ISLANDS

Four hundred miles to the west of the Marshall Islands lies the eastern end of the far-flung Caroline Islands archipelago stretching 2,000 miles to the Philippines. These islands are a geologic mix of high islands and atolls; an ethnic mix of peoples with many languages and cultures; and they are divided politically into two new countries.

The new countries are the Republic of Palau (sometimes called Belau) in the far western Carolines and the Federated States of Micronesia (FSM) making up the remaining Caroline archipelago. Although the FSM may not be familiar to you as a political entity, the four states making it up are individually better known: Yap, the land of stone money; Truk, the Japanese Gibraltar of the Pacific during World War II; Pohnpei, the island of ancient stone ruins; and little Kosrae, the Garden Isle of Micronesia.

These countries are not completely severed from United States diplomatic military or economic assistance and this has a beneficial effect for cruising boats. It gives a single monetary system, the dollar; a common business language, English; unified entry regulations with special ease

179

for Americans; access to the low cost United States postal system; and, in the near future, satellite communications with the rest of the world.

Kosrae—A Garden Island

Kosrae is the farthest east of the FSM states and a particularly pleasant place to enter the new country because it provides a secure harbor in a lush setting of mangroves, coconut palms, banana trees and hillside timber stretching into the clouds. Everything is green and the only other dominating color is the silver glint of rainshowers that keep this island green. In truth, there is a surplus of water which the government is proposing to sell to Nauru which has money but no water.

The island of Kosrae, including the smaller islands on the reefs, measures 42 square miles in area and rises to a height of over 2,000 feet. We were able to see the island while 36 miles away at sea, urging us on to get there before nightfall. We made it in late afternoon, still in time to see the grandeur of the hills and to dodge the coral reefs at the harbor entrance.

Cruising boats anchor in the inner harbor adjacent to little Lelu Island which, with its 2,000 population, is the principal residential area for Kosrae's 5,500 population. Since human time began on Kosrae, Lelu has been the home of the ruling clans and the center of island commerce. It still is the center of island commerce; but the ruling clan is now the democratically elected government which has decided for reasons of space to build its capital across the harbor in the foothills of the main island of Ualan.

Although man has tried to make roads around and about this island, they are, so far, a miserable failure because of rain, mountain streams and small saltwater canals that intrude on the land from the lagoon. The native population in the past took the line of least resistance and opted for the canoe to take them and their goods to the market. They do not use sailing canoes, however, for there is no lagoon on which to sail or islands beyond the reef to visit. The canoes are either paddled or outboard motor-propelled along miles of freshwater canals or on the flat waters of the narrow lagoon surrounding the island complex.

Reflections in the Insaru lagoon, Lelu, Kosrae, Caroline Islands

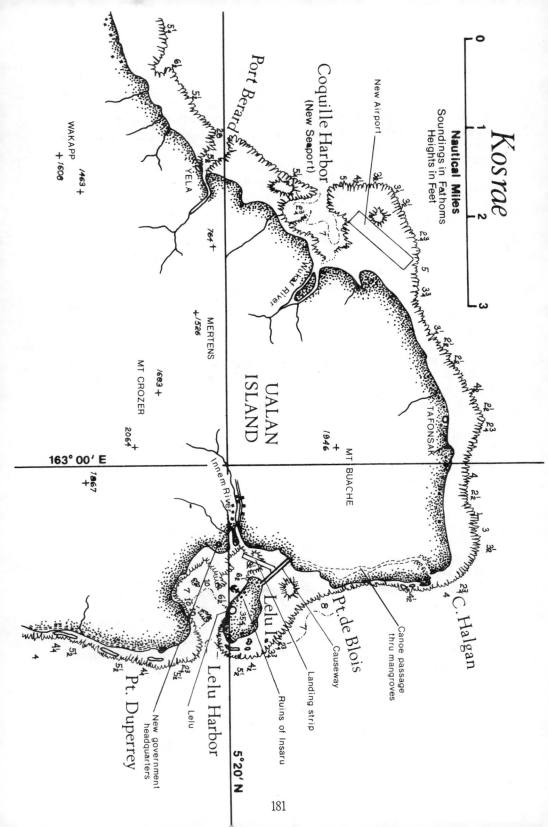

Kosrae

Nautical Miles

Soundings in Fathoms
Heights in Feet

New Airport

Port Berard

Coquille Harbor
(New Seaport)

WAKAPP
+ /608
/463 +

YELA

764 +

Wuxal River

MERTENS
+ /526

UALAN
ISLAND

MT CROZER
/683 +

2064 +

163° 00' E

/867 +

MT BUACHE
1946 +

TAFONSAK

C. Halgan

Canoe passage
thru mangroves

Causeway

Pt. de Blois

Landing strip

Ruins of Insaru

Lelu I.

Innem River

New government
headquarters

Lelu

Lelu Harbor

Pt. Duperrey

5° 20' N

181

Kosrae is often termed the Garden Isle of Micronesia because of its lush and vibrant growth. Any tropical plant will grow there and farming is more a matter of keeping the surrounding vegetation from encroaching on thriving gardens. But as easily as garden products can be grown, Kosrae has not developed agriculture as a business because it has no distribution system to market the products to other islands of Micronesia. We found one roadside stand that had a few bananas and limes for sale, but most fruits and vegetables were not in season for us. We did not lack for the produce that was in season however; Kosraeans are generous to a fault and kept us supplied with what produce was available from their gardens. Our main problem was one of transportation and learning something about the island's history.

One day we were approached by a local lad right at the shoreline where we landed our dinghy. He offered to show us the island in three steps: first the south shore; then the area called Insaru, Ruins of the Kings Residence; and on the third day, we would tour the north shore of the island and see the new seaport and jetport under construction.

The first day went well once we got the pickup truck fueled. On the second day it rained and we trudged through the muck and mire of the ruins, slipping dangerously on moss-covered rocks. On the third, we rode a vintage pickup truck whose fuel tank was a plastic jug in the front seat, which put an end to casual smoking.

On the third day we also got a $30 bill for our entrepreneur's services. This at first upset me. because now I had become accustomed to the handout generosity of the locals. Then I thought how resourceful this fellow was in cornering us, and we did get around the island, and he did give us a running commentary with no more than the usual tour guide's hokum. As I now review my photography from Kosrae, I realize how really useful this guide was to our seeing the Garden Isle.

To me, the rock ruins of Insaru were the highlight of our Kosrae visit. They are right in the heart of Lelu Island and so overgrown that a casual visitor would innocently pass by them. Insaru represents an early and very advanced civilization, somewhere around the 10th and 11th century, whose rulers not only ruled Kosrae but extended their rule as far west as Pohnpei. Unlike the ruins of Nan Madol at Pohnpei, Insaru is not being preserved and nature is fast reclaiming her own.

One of the big disappointments of cruising the Pacific is not finding tangible evidence of the pre-European history, for the peoples lived mostly in the open air and built what few buildings they did need out of biodegradable materials. The rock ruins of Insaru and Nan Madol, however, provide extensive hard evidence of early native culture and society.

Some of the rock construction techniques of the builder of Insaru must have rubbed off on their descendants, for Kosraeans today display considerable skill in building rock walls along the shoreline. These walls protect the land from wave erosion and also reclaim land from swampy areas. In a region where coastal lowlands are the preferred living area, walling

off the sea makes a lot of sense, besides giving the shoreline a neater appearance. I have seen it done nowhere else in the Pacific to the extent that it is done in Kosrae.

— Sea

Church at Lelu, Kosrae, Caroline Islands

Pohnpei—Land Of Stone Ruins

Horizon's next port of call in the Caroline Islands archipelago was the mountainous island of Pohnpei, a place where we had charter-sailed a few years back. We had enjoyed it so much that we wanted to go back with our own boat. The passage west from Kosrae took three days in light winds and under broken skies. There were frequent squalls dropping buckets of rain, and infrequent openings in the sky to get celestial observations so necessary in threading your way through the archipelago.

Pohnpei Island, which covers 129 square miles and rises to a height of 2,600 feet, is the principal island of Pohnpei State. The total population of the state is 22,000 persons and most of them live on Pohnpei itself with only a few hundred each on the eight atolls, making up the rest of the state. Pohnpei Island is surrounded by a barrier reef, although in some places the reef is so close in that it melds with the fringing reef of the shoreline. If you like basking in the sun on a white beach, this isn't the place to come, for there are no beaches. What isn't a fringing reef is overgrown with mangroves, some so large that they are made into beams for house construction.

The harbor at Kolonia, the principal town on Pohnpei, is one of the better ones in Micronesia. It is sheltered on three sides from wind and on all sides from the waves. What is colorfully referred to as the yacht harbor, is nothing more than the inner end of Sokehs Harbor, denied commercial use by the many coral reefs. A few local boats and the transient cruising yachts make use of it along with many canoes. The entrance into it from the outer commercial harbor is a torturous, weaving route through fields of coral, and first time cruisers are advised to get local knowledge before attempting the transit.

If you are looking for cruising objectives other than just seeing a new island, there are several in Pohnpei. The ruins of Spanish, German and Japanese buildings dating back to 1889 are one. The woodcarvers of Porakiet village are another. The growing and processing of gourmet pep-

183

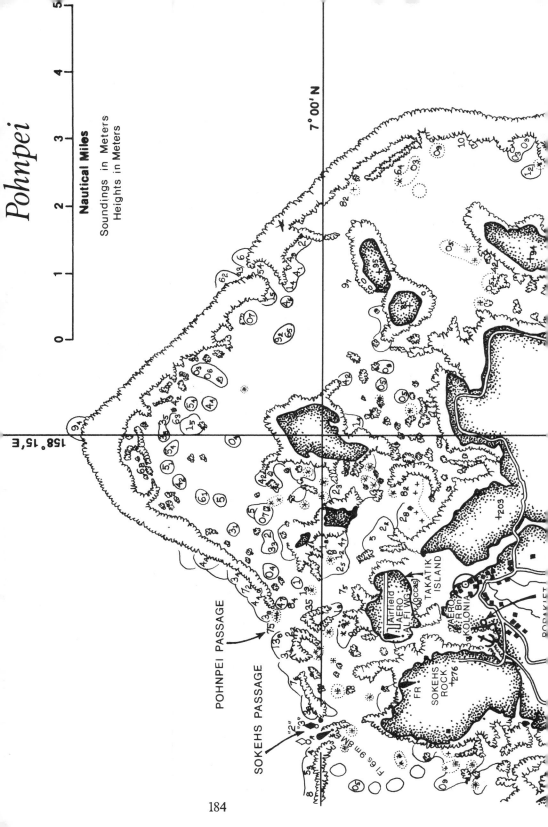

Pohnpei

Nautical Miles

Soundings in Meters
Heights in Meters

158°15'E

7°00'N

POHNPEI PASSAGE

SOKEHS PASSAGE

Fl 6s 9m 8M

"2"
"3"

FR. SOKEHS ROCK.
+276

TAKATIK ISLAND

Airfield
AERO
AL Fl WG
(GPcas)

AERO
R BN
KOLONIA

+203

184

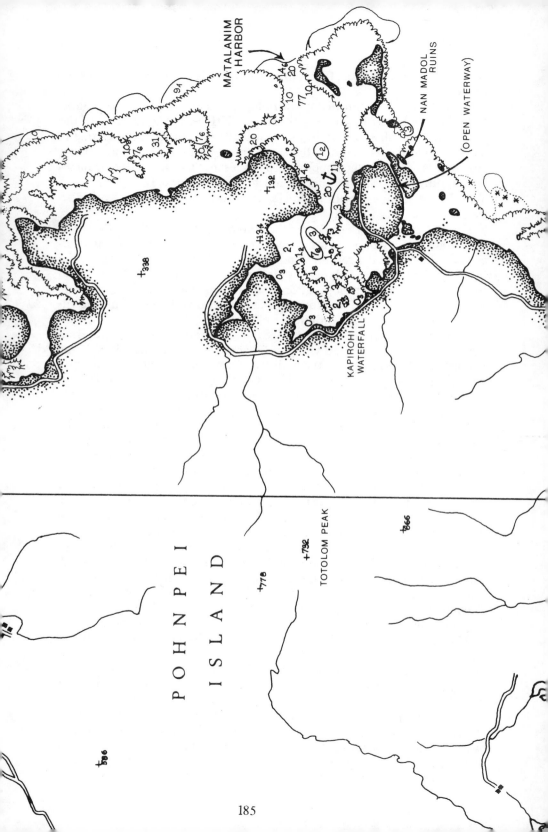

MATALANIM HARBOR

NAN MADOL RUINS

(OPEN WATERWAY)

KAPIROHI WATERFALL

POHNPEI ISLAND

TOTOLOM PEAK

+778

+792

+866

+586

+338

+434

+132

185

per is a third, but the most fascinating attraction is the ancient city of Nan Madol.

Most of the European history of Pohnpei is contained in and around Kolonia. The Spanish built Fort Alphonso XIII in 1899 and some of the rock walls are still standing in the center of town. In 1907, the Germans built a magnificent church in the same area, but the Japanese tore down most of it, leaving only the imposing bell tower standing. Only a few Japanese-era buildings are still standing, the most notable of these is the agricultural station. A Japanese-built hydroelectric plant on the Nanpil River also stands, but mostly in ruins.

The woodcarvers of Porakiet village are a bonanza to the collector of island artifacts. Woodcarving is uncommon in the islands of the eastern Carolines and the reason that it exists at all on Ponape is due to the overpopulation of the Polynesian atoll of Kapingamarangi, 300 miles to the south. To ease the population pressure on that atoll, many people were moved to Pohnpei and took up life in their own Polynesian-style village on the outskirts of Kolonia.

Porakiet bears all the color of Polynesia in contrast to the rather drab appearance of Micronesian villages. The houses have thatched roofs, the people wear lava-lavas and the men fish from sailing canoes. Breadfruit, coconut palms and bananas are cultivated for family use and the village is notably clean compared to its surroundings.

Today the woodcarvers of Porakiet fashion replicas of sharks, fish, turtles and other sea life out of tough red mangrove wood. Unlike the carvers of the Marquesas, the Kapingamarangis do not even use a chain saw for cutting down the mangrove trees; it is all done with hand tools.

Visiting the pepper fields is a touristy sort of thing, but if you have ever wondered where pepper comes from, it is just the thing to do. You need wheels for this, as the pepper fields are located on the western plateau of the Sokehs municipality. Along the side of the road, you will see acres of pepper vines being cared for by the owners of the fields. It is all a hand operation from planting to the plucking of the ripe berries that become the peppercorns. The processing of the berries takes place at the Agriculture Center in Kolonia, and the product is marketed through local stores with some exported. If you like a sprinkling of good pepper on your Bloody Mary or favorite green salad, you will want to take some Pohnpei pepper home with you.

The mighty and mysterious ruins of Nan Madol hold a special aura of intrigue, but they are not easy to get to. You can take your boat to Matalanim Harbor on the east side of the island and then visit the ruins by dinghy, or you can leave your boat at Sokehs Harbor and join a tourist tour by outboard motorboat which takes the lagoon passage to Nan Madol. The guide booklet "Nan Madol" suggests ". . . go at high tide, from 3 feet up, to reach the major islets by motorboat . . . a low tide is preferable when walking or wading. A Pohnpean canoe is ideal."

Waterfalls are the natural wonders of Pohnpei and two, in particular,

Ruins of ancient city of Nan Madol, Pohnpei Island, Caroline Islands

are outstanding. The two-step Nanpil waterfall drops a total of 110 feet out of the jungle-encrusted rocks only a few miles from Kolonia. A second waterfall is the great Kapirohi waterfall in the vicinity of Nan Madol. Here the visitor can jump from waterfall ledges into a pool of crystal-clear, cold mountain water. To the sailor who has been denied the simple pleasure of a freshwater bath for weeks at sea, nothing could be sweeter relaxation.

No trip to Pohnpei is complete without engaging in sakau drinking. Sakau is the Pohnpean equivalent of Fijian kava and is used for ceremonial events, but it is also a social drink where it is still served with great ceremony. Sakau juice is extracted from the washed roots of the shrub, *piper methysticum*, by pounding them on a flat "sakau" stone dedicated

Micronesia Cultural Center, Pohnpei Island, Caroline Islands

to this use. Some water is added to the slurry during pounding and the result is a muddy-appearing, earthy-tasting liquid that is served to the participants in coconut shells. The drink produces a mild "high" giving the lips and tongue a tingling sensation.

We were introduced to sakau on our first trip to Pohnpei, at the home of our guide. It was back in the bush and we had to walk the last several hundred yards along a dirt path. Unlike the formal dress of Kolonia, the women in the bush go about their work in topless dress but frown on picture taking. We joined the men under a low-sided hut whose roof of corrugated iron kept the rain off us while we were being indoctrinated to sakau. My wife Betty was an honored guest because women normally don't partake of sakau in these gatherings. There was little talk or animation, the root was pounded relentlessly and the coconut cup passed to guests and others as fast as it could be refilled. Drinking sakau becomes a test of your determination and all eyes follow the cup to your lips to see whether you are "one of them" or a squeamish outsider.

The one serious problem we found at Pohnpei Island was its huge size and our inability to conveniently get around. There is no public transportation so you have to resign yourself to renting a car for a couple days if you want to visit these places of special interest or to reprovision. It may strain your cruising budget, but it is essential to topping off your stay on this huge island.

When you get that car, don't expect that you will be driving far in comfort. The paved roads exist only in Kolonia and its suburbs. After that, it is graded coral with potholes that will swallow your vehicle, especially in the rainy season; but then if you had wanted freeways, you never would have left home.

— Sea

WESTERN CAROLINE ISLANDS

Dublon—Truk's Old Capital

Everyone knows that the capital of Truk State in the FSM is Moen Island and has been since 1945, but where was the capital before then? It was on neighboring Dublon Island.

Dublon Island has been known by other names throughout history. The Trukese called it Toloas until Manuel Dublon arrived on the scene in 1814. Its name was changed during the Japanese occupation to Natsu Shima, meaning Summer Island.

How long Trukese have lived in the vast Truk lagoon is not clear. Some say they came as long ago as the 13th Century. From where they came is also unclear. Their physical appearance suggests that they are a mixture of Polynesians from the south and Indonesians or Southwest Asians. There is no written history that far back and legends have been dimmed by the years.

Recorded history starts with the arrival of the Spanish in 1565. Another 250 years were to pass before the next European was to arrive, and that

189

Grating coconut, Dublon, Truk, Caroline Islands

was Manuel Dublon, after whom the Island was named. Spain took possession of all of the Caroline Islands but made no attempt to administer the Truk Islands. At the cessation of the Spanish-American War in 1898, Spain sold all of its Pacific interests not claimed by the United States, to the Germans who immediately expanded their copra business. They established a branch of the Jaluit Trading Co. (Marshall Islands) on Dublon Island to handle the Truk copra trade.

Dublon was not the largest island within the Truk lagoon nor was it the most populated. Dublon was simply an attractive island with plenty of coconuts, a deep water anchorage and easy access to passes through the encircling barrier reef. Germany's economic sacking of Truk was soon replaced by Japanese militarism. The Japanese developed Dublon to its peak, first as a source of food for its home islands and later as part of its ill-fated Pacific war machine.

Japan had acquired Germany's Pacific possessions in 1914 and likewise established their headquarters on Dublon. Later, in 1932, they added a military headquarters on Dublon in defiance of their mandate from the League of Nations. With the latter action, the outside world was summarily cut off from any knowledge of what was going on within the Truk Archipelago. An aura of mystery developed over these islands and, at the start of World War II, Truk was labeled the "Japanese Gibraltar of the Pacific." That was to be a misnomer since Truk turned out to be a paper tiger at best.

Activity in Dublon's life reached its peak early in 1943, when it was used as a Japanese submarine base, seaplane base, coastal defense base and an Army and Navy Command Post. There were approximately

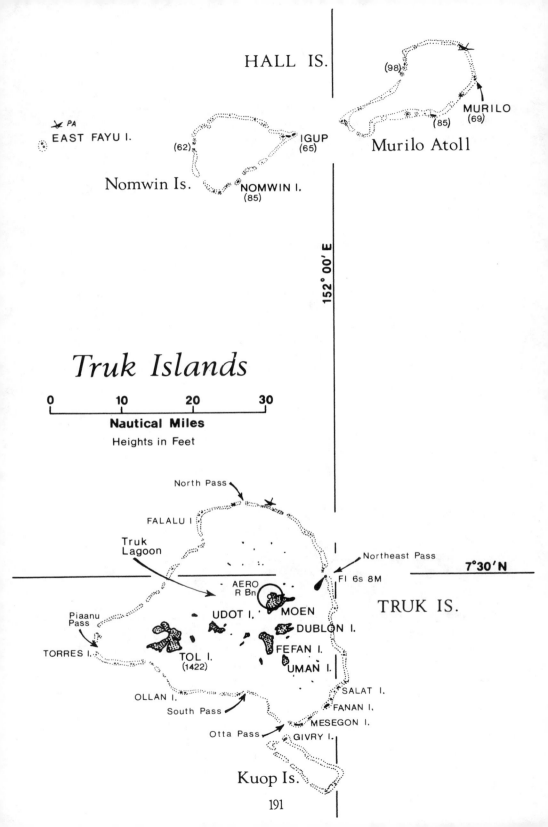

HALL IS.

(98)

MURILO
(69)

Murilo Atoll

(85)

PA
EAST FAYU I.

(62)

IGUP
(65)

NOMWIN I.
(85)

Nomwin Is.

152° 00′ E

Truk Islands

0   10   20   30

Nautical Miles

Heights in Feet

North Pass

FALALU I.

Truk
Lagoon

Northeast Pass

Fl 6s 8M

7°30′N

AERO
R Bn

MOEN

TRUK IS.

Piaanu
Pass

UDOT I.

DUBLON I.

TORRES I.

TOL I.
(1422)

FEFAN I.

UMAN I.

OLLAN I.

SALAT I.

South Pass

FANAN I.

MESEGON I.

Otta Pass

GIVRY I.

Kuop Is.

191

14,000 military personnel on the island at that time and several thousand civilians, mostly Japanese. After the American air attacks of February 1944, the military usefulness of all of the Truk Atoll ceased to exist and survivors spent most of their time attempting to assuage their hunger since supplies no longer came from Japan.

The surrender of Truk took place in September 1945 aboard the U.S. Cruiser *Portland* anchored in Eten Harbor off Dublon Town. Until the repatriation of the Japanese to their homeland was finally completed in December 1946, all Japanese prisoners of war lived on Dublon Island amidst the ravages of war.

Today Dublon is a sleepy backwater community of about 2,000 persons. It has no roads, only footpaths that can double for roads for an occasional pickup truck. Agriculture is its economic mainstay and fruits and vegetables as well as handicrafts find their way to market on nearby Moen Island. Dublon Town on the south shore has never been rebuilt. Only a single pier juts out into the waters of Eten Anchorage where lie the bulk of the coral-encrusted remains of the Japanese World War II fleet.

The lagoon is peaceful now. The tradewinds caress the palms and fish leap out of the water at dusk. Man-made riches of war have been replaced by nature's wonderous rags and Dublon is better for the passage of time.

— Pacific

Japanese seaplane ramp, Dublon, Truk, Caroline Islands

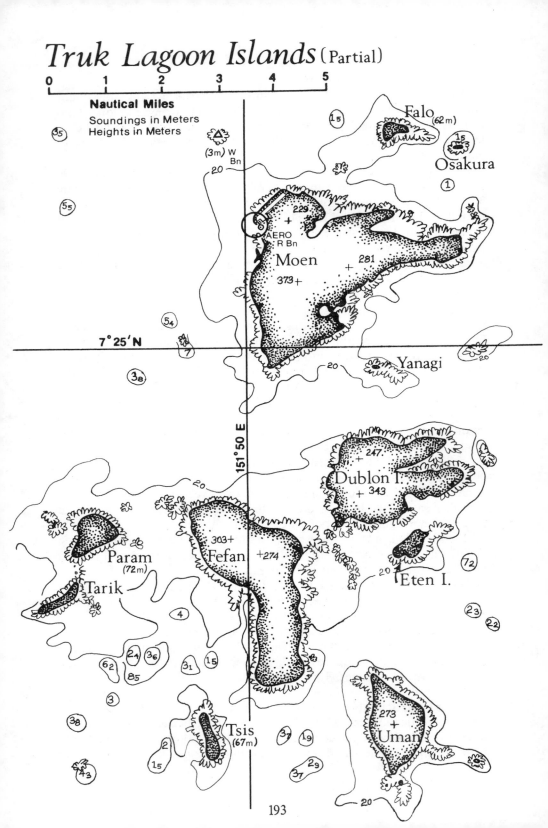

Truk Lagoon Islands (Partial)

0   1   2   3   4   5

Nautical Miles

Soundings in Meters
Heights in Meters

(3m) W
Bn
20

229

AERO
R Bn

Moen

281

373+

Falo (62 m)

Osakura
(1)

7°25′N

5₄

7

3₈

Yanagi
20

151°50 E

20

Dublon I.
247

343

Param
(72 m)

Fefan
303+

+274

Tarik

20

Eten I.
(72)

4

(23) (22)

2₄ 3₆
6₂
8₅

3₁ 1₅

3

38

Tsis
(67 m)

2

1₅

3₇ 1₉

2₉
3₇

Uman
273
+

20

Moen—Truk's New Beginning

Moen Island is not the largest island in the Truk lagoon, Tol is. Nor does it have the richest claim on history; for neighboring Dublon Island with its German and Japanese trading and military history is far better known, but today Moen Island is the capital of Truk State and the most populace island.

Things might have been different had there been fewer Japanese prisoners to repatriate at the end of WWII. As it was, there were some 38,000 Japanese and Korean prisoners of war who were being detained on Dublon Island in 1946 awaiting transportation home. That saturated Dublon's land area, so when the U.S. Navy had to set up a headquarters base, they chose neighboring Moen Island. There they built seaport and airport facilities, roads and buildings to support the occupation forces, leaving the other islands to return to their pre-Japanese rural atmosphere.

Moen would never be a quiet island again. Radios, trucks, motorcycles, airplanes, and a burgeoning population would see to that. Today Moen is home to 11,000 inhabitants—about one-third of the total population of Truk State. It has attracted more population than it can support. Trukese from the outer islands see Moen, with its relatively busy economy, as the place to come and make their fortune. While some do, many end up living in squalor and hopelessness, which is a sure road to crime.

This concentration of people has also had other bad effects. Poor sanitation caused by an inadequate waste system and bad personal habits, produced cholera epidemics in 1982 and 1983. Fortunately, these have now been controlled. Underemployed men took to drinking and that produced violence in both home life and on the streets of Moen. A declaration of prohibition reduced that to a tolerable problem. Today Moen is a relatively safe place to walk around and there are enough new cottage industries springing up to bode well for the future.

Moen Island is a beautiful work of nature but there is little man-made beauty on it. The majority of buildings are weathered wood and rusting metal separated by wrecked vehicles rapidly turning to rust. Mercifully, the rust is being camouflaged by lush tropical growth. Maintenance of buildings and equipment seems to be alien to the Trukese way of life, putting an added burden on new resources.

There are some notable exceptions such as the new construction of government buildings in the "saddle" of the island; the Intercontinental Hotel at the former Japanese seaplane base; some new businesses in the port area; and the Xavier High School sitting near the east end of the island.

Xavier High School is a unique remnant of World War II. Built as a radio communication center, it defied destruction because of its 1-meter thick reinforced concrete construction. Realizing that it would be tough to demolish, the American forces concentrated instead on the softer radio

targets which effectively put the communication center out of commission. After the war, the Jesuit Order purchased the building for $1000 and turned it into the leading high school of all the Trust Territory. They have maintained the World War II appearance of the building, making it a living museum.

Moen Island is the repository of many World War II relics, most of which are deteriorating rapidly for lack of care. The Japanese lighthouse that sits atop the knoll at the east end of the island is a treasure but has been vandalized and covered with graffiti of obscene nature.

Down the hill from the lighthouse are some rare 200mm naval rifles also turning to rust. Although war relics oft-times have little appeal to those who live among them and did not suffer their past, they nevertheless form part of history and are significant tourist attractions. The underwater wrecks of Truk lagoon are proof of that.

Now after 100 years of Spanish, German, Japanese and American rule, the Trukese have emerged as a self-governing state within the Federated States of Micronesia.

Today's hub of activity is the seaport area, central to business and merchandising activities. The port not only receives ships from foreign lands, but it is the transfer point for goods being shipped between islands of the state. Small boats ply the water of the lagoon bringing outer islanders and their produce to Moen. A half-mile north of the seaport is the jet airport with connections to several of the outer islands, to the other states of the FSM and to the outside world. While Truk may have been isolated from the rest of the world in its role as the "Gibraltar of the Pacific" during World War II, it is no longer.

Unloading bananas, Moen, Truk, Caroline Islands

Moen Island, sometimes called "Wena" in a local tongue, may have thought it was seeing the end of the world in the battle smoke of 1944. But such was not the case. The Japanese during their military occupation called it Haru Shimu, meaning Spring Island, but that was premature. Only in recent years has Moen found the spring of its ascendency into the 21st Century and what hopefully will be a peaceful world.

— Pacific

Yap—Land Of Stone Money

There has been growing interest in cruising the waters of the Western Pacific, especially by persons who are purchasing cruising boats in Taiwan, Hong Kong or China, with the intention of cruising home from those places. Not many years ago, practically all boats were shipped from the Orient, but that seems to be changing as people learn more about the possibilities of combining a boat delivery with cruising a very attractive area.

For those persons contemplating delivering a boat home from the Orient, make the most of your visit to Western Pacific waters by seeing the islands of Micronesia. One group I can highly recommend is Yap State in the Western Caroline Islands. These islands are 450 miles southwest of Guam and have two unique attractions going for them: they are the most primitive and unspoiled of all islands of the former Trust Territory and few boats visit them.

Yap is not so much a place as it is a peephole into a society that has somehow resisted the 20th century. Oh, there are the usual cars, TVs, refrigerators, beer and other accoutrements of the Western World—including an oversize government. These signs of the contemporary outside world seem constrained to the main village of Colonia which occupies but a few blocks of land around the harbor. Out in the bush, Yapese life goes on much the same as it has for centuries.

The Yapese are an enigma. They are able to pursue a traditional way of life in the face of electricity, telephones and jet airplanes. They show no signs of wanting to leap headlong into the 20th century with its man-

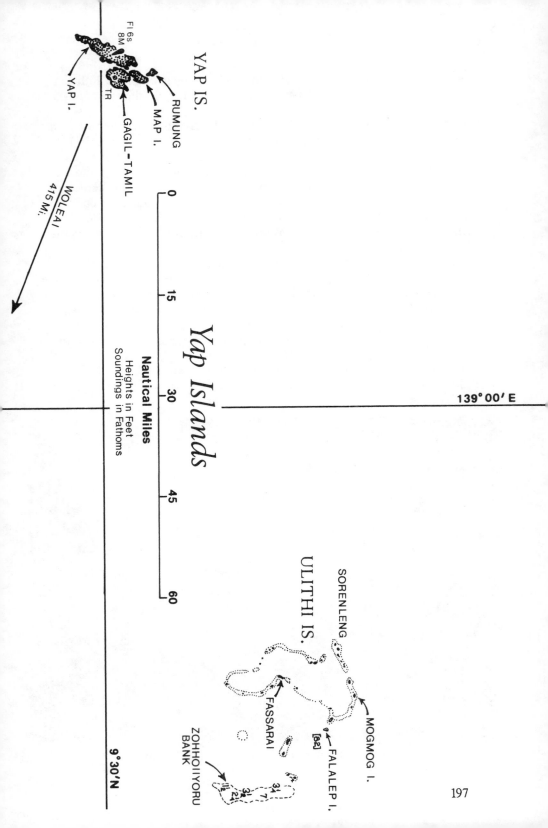

YAP IS.

Fl 6s
8M

RUMUNG

MAP I.

TR

GAGIL–TAMIL

YAP I.

WOLEAI
415 Mi.

0

15

30

45

60

Nautical Miles

Heights in Feet
Soundings in Fathoms

Yap Islands

139° 00′ E

9° 30′ N

ULITHI IS.

SORENLENG

FASSARAI

MOGMOG I.

[62]

FALALEP I.

ZOHHOIIYORU
BANK

197

made problems. Theirs is an attempt at blending the good of the 20th century into a culture that they have found could withstand the rigors of life on small tropical islands.

One can see in downtown Colonia the colorful "thu" (loin cloth) with its unique folds worn by Yapese men. Women still go about their housework and gardening in the topless dress of their ancestors, oblivious to the fact that they could be less comfortable, but more modern, in blouses designed for a temperate climate. While the administrative center of Colonia has drawn many rural people to its wage economy, the concentration of town dwellers is still not so great as to create the ills of condensed societies such as plague Moen Island in Truk and Ebeye in the Marshall Islands.

Although the main island of Yap is getting a 20th century infrastructure including running water, sewers, electricity, roads and a modern seaport, one has only to drive to the ends of the few roads and take off on foot to see the Yap of old. There are community houses with exquisite architecture but on a more modest scale; tended yards with pyramids of coconuts, clucking chickens and rooting pigs, neat piles of fire wood and the ever-shy and lovable children.

The main port of entry is Colonia (not to be confused with Kolonia, Pohnpei), located in the sheltered waters of a complex of four

This stone money wouldn't fit into the lady's purse

198

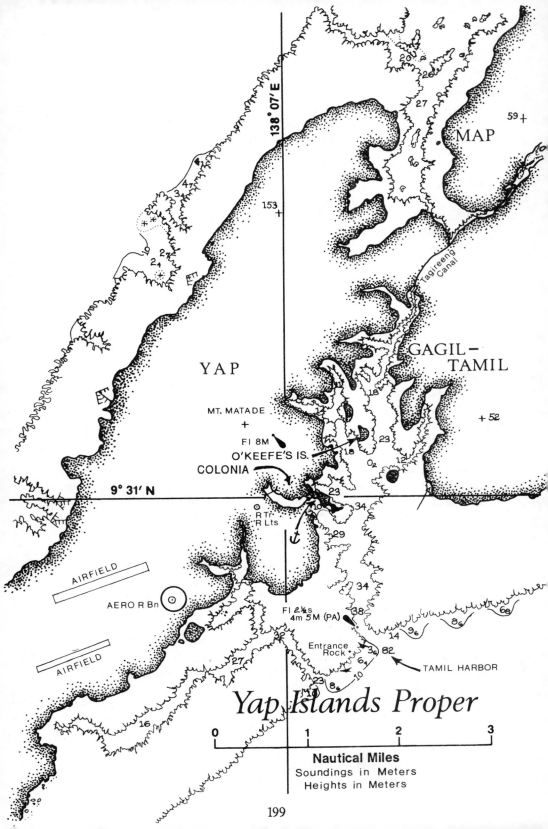

MAP

138° 07′ E

153

YAP

MT. MATADE
+

Fl 8M
O'KEEFE'S IS.

COLONIA

GAGIL-
TAMIL

+ 52

18

23

18

O₂

12

9° 31′ N

R Tr
R Lts

23

34

29

34

AIRFIELD

AERO R Bn

38

TAMIL HARBOR

AIRFIELD

Fl 2½s
4m 5M (PA)

Entrance
Rock

3

82

6

14

9

8

6

27

23

8

10

10

16

Yap Islands Proper

| 0 | 1 | 2 | 3 |

Nautical Miles
Soundings in Meters
Heights in Meters

"high-islands" simply called Yap Islands "proper." The remaining 140 or so islands of the state are all atolls. Like the Tuamotu Archipelago of French Polynesia, these atolls are only an overnight passage apart, making island-hopping an enticing reality.

Don't expect to find many of the conveniences of the Western world here. The roads are short and most transportation is by canoe, small boat or on foot along paths lined with red hibiscus. It is along these paths that you meet the real Yapese—those people who prefer their rural way of life to the "big city" of Colonia (population 5,500). When you are out in the bush, observe caution with your camera. The Yapese are not fond of candid photography and you should ask their permission before taking pictures.

Yapese are well-known in the Western Pacific for their use of betelnut, the fruit of the areca palm. It is not uncommon throughout the Pacific, but Yap apparently grows an excellent nut. Guam, Palau and Truk all buy the Yap betelnuts.

Betelnuts are about half the size of a small chicken egg, orange-green in color with a fibrous husk. The meat of the nut is laid on a leaf from the peppervine, sprinkled with burnt coral lime, then rolled up and put in the mouth for chewing. The reaction of the lime and betelnut produces a blood-red spittle which colors the lips like Revlon's best. It seems that everyone, from kids on the street to officials in the statehouse, chews betelnuts incessantly. It has a mild narcotic effect and is utterly devastating on tooth enamel.

There is also a social side to the betelnut that is most interesting. Personal betelnut supplies (nuts, pepper leaves and the lime shaker) are carried in a special basket woven of areca palm fronds. The lime shaker may simply be a salt shaker or it may be a small intricately-carved coconut shell. The basket's size and shape are somewhat indicative of the rank of the owner and more sacred than a woman's purse. Young people are taught never to reach into an elder's basket and it is considered ill-mannered to step over another person's betelnut basket.

A major relic of Yap's past is its stone money. The material is aragonite stone, which has a crystalline structure and the hardness of marble. The money is always circular (or as near circular as primitive stone masons could make it) and has a hole in the center to allow carrying it on a pole. Coins vary in size from six inches to 12 feet in diameter.

The raw material for these stone wheels was, surprisingly, not found on Yap but on the islands of Palau, some 300 miles distant. The effort required to quarry the stone, carve it into wheels and transport it to Yap is what gave the money its value. You might think that stone money was a difficult medium of exchange to handle, but it really wasn't. Stone money was rarely handled or moved from its place of "deposit." It was really a highly visible measure of an individual's wealth. No Swiss bank accounts here!

The aggressive approach to the 20th century seen in Palau, Pohnpei and the Marshall Islands is just not evident in Yap. Yap is laid back on

its ocean of blue with an innate capability to survive without outside help. Family ties are still in existence, the coconut remains king, taro is their staple food supplemented with yams, bananas, papaya and breadfruit, plus fish from the bountiful waters.

Yap's culture is at the same time conservative and permanent. One can see that in the carefully laid rock pathways leading to villages and the meticulous arrangement of rocks making up the platforms of community houses, men's houses and the residences themselves. The Yapese obviously do not expect to make major changes in their way of life for the foreseeable future.

If you enter Yap from the west, as you would in coming from the Orient, you will have no difficulty in making your first stop at one of the ports of entry, Colonia or Ulithi. If you enter from the east, coming perhaps from Truk State, then you have 500 miles to go to make the prescribed entry and you bypass such delightful atolls as Satawal and Lamotrek. There is no simple remedy for this eastern approach problem except to throw yourself on the mercy of the local chief of the atoll at which you stop and tell him of your dilemma. These people are seafarers themselves and would be sympathetic to your desire to avoid backtracking to windward. Whatever you do, have the all-important approved visitors' permits in hand before you enter the Federated States of Micronesia water.

— Cruising World

Community House, Map municipality, Yap, Federated States of Micronesia

Yap's Outer Islands

For the cruiser, Yap's outer islands can be the most interesting. Ulithi Atoll is the fourth largest in the world enclosing an area of 210 square miles. Its great depth (for an atoll) of over 200 feet allowed it to be used in the closing days of World War II as a staging base for almost the entire U.S. Fleet as it was preparing for the final attack on the Land of the Rising Sun. Surrounding this vast lagoon is a barrier reef on which 49 islets have formed with a miniscule land area of only 2 square miles.

The topography of Ulithi is similar to all atolls with the land rising only a few feet above the lagoon and the tops of the tallest coconut trees reaching a stately 80 feet above sea level. The only exception to this is the detached island of Falalop, whose ground level reaches 22 feet above sea level.

Before westernization, the islet of Mog Mog was the traditional home of the ruling chiefs of Ulithi. It was also the home of the best tattoo artists in the Yap Islands. More recently, the island of Falalop has become the administration center for Ulithi and its surrounding islands. Besides the administration offices, there is the high school for the outer islands.

The relationship of the people of the outer islands to those of Yap proper is most unusual. The outer islands in the Ulithi-Woleai area to the east are traditionally affiliated with Yap through three villages in the Gagil municipality, in a parent-child bond with the Yapese in the role of the parent. A chain of authority extends from Gagil to Ulithi to Woleai. In earlier days, large fleets of canoes made annual trips to Yap proper from the outer islands bearing tributes to the overlords. In return they were given even larger gifts of food and materials. This exchange continues to this day, but to a lesser extent and tends to be more symbolic than material.

Ulithians and Woleaians differ from the Yapese in a number of respects. They are generally lighter-skinned and look more like Polynesians and their language is more akin to Trukese. In dress, the outer islands men wear the same loin cloths as do Yapese men, but do not add the hibiscus bark to indicate manhood. Often loin cloths are woven of hibiscus or banana fibers. The outer island women wear brief skirts until they reach maturity, then they wear hibiscus or banana fiber fabrics made into wrap-around skirts similar to the lava-lava.

Unlike Yap society, class distinctions are not severe in the outer islands. Chieftainships are hereditary and are held in definite matrilineal lineage.

Seasonal typhoons are the most serious problems that face the outer islands. They can be destructive to food crops, housing and canoes. They also catch fishermen and other canoe traffic at sea, blowing them far away from their islands, if not outright causing loss of life. In recent years many outislanders have been evacuated to Yap proper for their survival during the onslaught of a typhoon.

The threat of typhoons (among other forms of pestilence) against which Yap magicians worked their feats of magic, was one of many ways by which Yapese maintained control over the outer islanders. Some outer islanders still believe that their traditional overlords from Yap are capable of bringing typhoons and pestilence. Ulithi is only 100 miles from Colonia, but it might as well be on another planet for here the veneer of the Western world is absent.

Another outer island of note is Satawal, far to the east, where the last of the true Micronesian navigators live. Mau Piailug, who taught the Hawaiians non-instrument navigation for the many successful voyages of the twin-hulled canoe *Hokule'a*, lives on this island. Along with navigational skills, the Satawalese are also known for splendid tattooing.

— Unpublished Note

Yapese boy wearing traditional red thu

CHAPTER 7

EQUATORIAL MICRONESIA

*"I had been speaking to a clever old native of the Gil-
bert Islands about aeroplanes and wireless. When I had
done, he pondered a little, then said, "Kurimbo, it is true
that the white man can fly; he can speak across the
ocean; in works of the body he is indeed greater than we,
but," his voice rang with pride, "he has no songs like
ours; no poets to equal the island singers."*

*The islander is a consummate poet. His songs are not
the mere barbaric babble of crude emotions that might
be expected from men of a culture labelled 'primitive';
they are clear-cut gems of diction, polished and
repolished with loving care, according to the canons of a
technique as exacting as it is beautiful."*

— *Sir Arthur Grimble, "Return to the Islands"*

Grade school geography clearly describes the steaming jungles of the
Amazon, the hot and arid Sahara desert and the Spice Islands of Indonesia that lie near the equator. Little is said of the beautiful atolls of the
Pacific, that span the equator just west of the International Date Line.
They are not well-known for few travelers indulge in the luxury of searching out isolated islands. These mid-Pacific atolls, the homes of two Pacific
nations, are ethnically Micronesian and, before World War II, were
colonies of Great Britain. They were not part of the mandated islands
ruled in secrecy by the Japanese between World Wars I and II, although they were invaded by Japan at the start of World War II.

Nauru is one of these mid-Pacific nations and resides in its entirety on
one lonely raised atoll lying just 30 miles from the equator. The other nation is the Republic of Kiribati (pronounced keer-ee-bas, "ti" is pronounced "s") made up of the Gilbert Islands, spanning the equator, plus
the Phoenix Islands, lying just south of the equator, and most of the Line
islands lying south of Hawaii. No other island nation has so many isolated islands spread over so much ocean as does Kiribati.

Nauru's Golden Guano

This atoll may appear to be little more than an isolated rock in a big
ocean; but it is probably the richest rock in the entire world. It is the tiny
island of Nauru in the Central Pacific, well off the beaten path, but nevertheless a unique port of call for boats cruising Micronesia. Nauru is located almost on the equator at 0°32' S, 166° 55' E.

Nauru's 8 square miles are the top of a seamount, a raised coral atoll
isolated from all other islands of the Pacific. Its nearest neighbors of

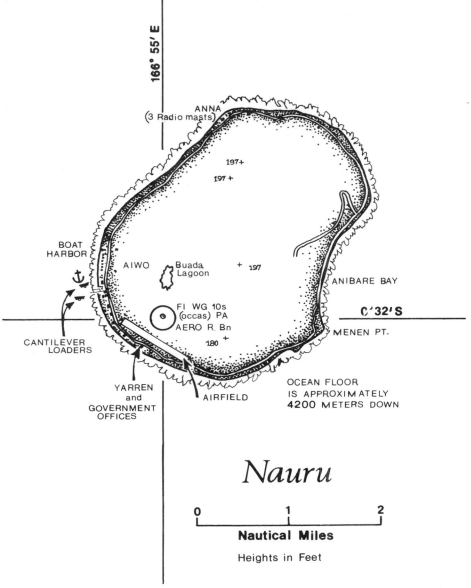

166° 55' E

ANNA
(3 Radio masts)

197+

197 +

BOAT
HARBOR

AIWO

Buada
Lagoon

+ 197

ANIBARE BAY

C'32'S

Fl WG 10s
(occas) PA
AERO R. Bn

CANTILEVER
LOADERS

180 +

MENEN PT.

YARREN
and
GOVERNMENT
OFFICES

AIRFIELD

OCEAN FLOOR
IS APPROXIMATELY
4200 METERS DOWN

Nauru

0   1   2

Nautical Miles

Heights in Feet

any consequence are 400 miles away. It is an independent nation whose native population has one of the purest bloodlines left in the Pacific. They also have the third highest per capita income in the world. The reason? Phosphate, a high-grade fertilizer generally acknowledged to be the droppings of sea birds accumulated over the centuries since the island was heaved up from the sea.

There are about 4,000 Nauruans living on this 8 square mile island with an additional 2,000 or so contract workers, mostly Gilbertese, Tuvaluans and Chinese who do the actual phosphate mining. Nauruans are the managers aided by Australian and British expatriates. The narrow fertile coastal rim of the island has been taken over by houses and workers'

quarters, plus all of the appurtenances necessary to run the phosphate business. There is virtually no agriculture left on this island.

Even if there still were adequate growing land available, rainfall is undependable and there are seasons and years of drought, which in the past, have made living precarious, even for the smaller pre-World War II population of 1,500 Nauruans. In drought years, fresh water is backhauled from Australia in the phosphate ships to supplement what is gathered in the island's rain-catchment systems. The state of Kosrae in the Federated States of Micronesia with its abundant rainfall has been bargaining with Nauru to become a water supplier for the future.

Little is known about Nauru in the tourist world because it was sheltered during the days of British Phosphate Company operation. Nauru gained its independence in 1968 and took over the phosphate business; but the Nauruans still shy away from publicity doing little to promote travel to their island.

Nauru's involvement in World War II was made at great sacrifice to the populace. Not only did they have to endure three years of starvation under Japanese occupation, but 1,200 of the men were shipped off to Truk atoll in the Caroline Islands as forced labor and only 500 returned. This has created an unusual age gap in the present Nauruan population. The Japanese also fortified Nauru with extensive coastal defenses and antiaircraft guns manned by 3,000 marines. This was all wasted effort for the island never figured in the Allied strategic drive across the Pacific.

Like Pitcairn, Easter and Niue islands, there is no ship harbor at Nauru. The anchorage on the leeward side of the island is easily recognizable by the huge cantilevered conveyors that load ships with phosphate. Although your chances of meeting another yacht here are minimal, you may share the anchorage with an itinerant fishing vessel. Small craft anchor just outside the fringing reef near the cantilevers and then dinghy ashore. (Leave a capable person on board your boat in case the ground tackle doesn't do its job.) When you take your dinghy into the barge harbor, it is best to lift it up onto the breakwater wall to prevent damage when the swells come in.

There are no buses or taxis on the island, so the best way to see Nauru is to rent a car, which can be arranged by telephone from the Nauru Phosphate Corporation offices just up from the landing. The NPC clubhouse is a good place to meet the expatriate managers and technicians and enjoy an Australian hamburger and a Foster's beer. There are two general stores nearby where you can buy provisions, provided that the supply ship from Australia has been there recently, but don't ask for water unless you are in dire need.

Like all Pacific Islanders, the Nauruans settled along the coastal plain of the island. A perimeter road takes you through many small, well-kept villages. There are no grass huts to see for the high income of the Nauruans has produced western-style houses with garages.

On the plateau of the island, 200 feet above sea level, lies Buada

Lagoon, a brackish lake of about 80 acres that for centuries has been used as a kind of fish trap. Nauruans caught fish off the reef and brought them to Buada for live keeping. More recently, they have tried aqua- culture techniques to grow fish in the lagoon, but without success. Now they go to the general stores for tinned protein. This lush inland lagoon is a place of tropical beauty.

The rest of the Nauruan plateau is dominated by open-surface phosphate mining where earth-moving equipment is creating a moonscape. The phosphate deposits are 50 feet deep in some places and, when removed, all that remains is a forest of coral pinnacles. The phosphate is transferred to ships via giant trucks, a railroad and, finally, by cantilevers. Nauru is one of the last phosphate-producing islands in the Pacific and it is being hauled away by ship at the rate of about two million tons per year. Sometime in the 1990s, all of the phosphate will have been exported and Nauru will be left without any natural economic resources.

While their island is being hauled away by the shipload, the Nauruans have handsome bank accounts to console them. The phosphate royalties are being put to work by the Nauruans through investments in other countries. One of the most recently announced, is a $500 million office-business-hotel complex in Honolulu.

Nauru is not the only phosphate island in the world, but it is the richest and one of the last still in business. For the cruiser who wants to see a different land and culture, this is the place.

— Cruising World

Cantilever #2 for loading phosphate, Nauru

THE GILBERT ISLANDS

The Gilbert Islands are the principal lands of the sprawling Republic of Kiribati that encompasses 1½ million square miles of central Pacific ocean. These are exciting islands, but few visitors see them because of their isolation. They are peopled with a native population that is every bit as friendly, fun-loving and warm-hearted as any in the Pacific.

All it takes to get to the Gilberts is some determined sailing in the Intertropical Convergence Zone better known as the doldrums. Not every boat is likely to see the Gilberts for the simple reason that sailing the doldrums is a difficult art far removed from leisurely reaching across the tradewinds of the higher latitudes. It took *Horizon* 11 days to sail the 945 miles from Pohnpei to Tarawa. Without the help of the equatorial countercurrent, it would have been even longer.

The Republic of Kiribati is made up of the Gilbert Islands, formerly a part of the British-Ellice Islands Colony; the sparsely-inhabited Phoenix Islands; and the Line Islands that stretch south across the equator below Hawaii. Practically the entire population of Kiribati, 56,500 persons, lives in the Gilbert group, with 40 percent of them living on the capital atoll of Tarawa.

Literally unknown to the world early in this century, the Gilbert Islands sprang into world focus during World War II when the Japanese invaded them early in 1942. They fortified the island of Betio on Tarawa atoll knowing that it was a desirable air base location for Americans to attack the Marshall Islands to the north. After the Japanese expansion southward had been stopped at Guadalcanal, American forces took aim at Tarawa. In November 1943, a great seaborne force comprising hundreds of ships and airplanes and thousands of Marines descended on Betio and history was made. Seventy-six hours after the initial landings, Betio was in American hands.

Today, the violence of war has been long forgotten and the rusting hulks of tanks, amtraks and landing craft along the shorelines are mute evidence of the past. On land, rusting Japanese coastal batteries point their guns aimlessly at peaceful skies and battered concrete bunkers mingle with rustling palm trees and the bright laundry of the native women.

Although World War II did not involve the Gilbertese as combatants, the early Gilbertese were known as fierce warriors themselves in the central Pacific. In their own way, they were more technically sophisticated in arms of war than the other peoples of the Pacific. They had no metal, so they made suits of armor using woven sennit (coconut husk twine) or manta ray skins. The heads were protected by skull caps of plaited sennit over which they wore helmets fashioned from the dried skins of inflated porcupine fish. Their swords and long spears were fashioned from well-seasoned coconut wood liberally imbedded with shark's teeth.

Marakei

Shallow
Abaiang
Lagoon
8
12
8
5
4
9

Central
Gilbert Islands

0   10   20   30

Nautical Miles

Soundings in Fathoms

L Fl 20s
9
11
Shallow
10
Lagoon
Tarawa
Passage
16
BETIO I.
Fl 8s
105ft 18M
EITA
BAIRIKI

7
5
Lagoon
5
Maiana
7
5

1° 00′ N

173° 00′ E

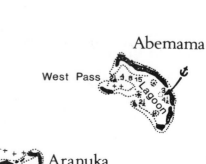
Abemama
West Pass
Lagoon
3
21
24

6   7
6
8   6
10
Kuria

10
Aranuka

209

Now all is peaceful on the islands and a democratic government rules the people. The seat of government is on the island of Bairiki in Tarawa atoll adjacent to the island of Betio. Betio has become the industrial/commercial island of Tararwa because of its harbor facilities, and Bairiki has become the government and economic center. That two islands share the business activities of Kiribati is not in itself unusual for space would dictate that. What is unusual is the islands are separated by about a mile of reef, mostly underwater. The ancient and colorful landing craft ferries that provided connections between the islands have been replaced by a long, sweeping bridge that joins neighbors. Gone is the colorful ride between islands when you could mingle with the natives for forty-five minutes, now it is a more business-like five minute ride in a bus or car.

With few exceptions, the Gilbert Islands are atolls with lagoons all exposed to the west making them less than the best anchorages in westerly blows which may come during the boreal winter. Sometimes the westerlies also blow during the summer as, for instance, when we were there in August. We had to keep an anchor watch for a couple of days until the winds died down; although they still continued to blow from the west in a most unseasonal fashion. If things had gotten really bad, we could have ducked into the small boat harbor and received adequate shelter, however, when I have good holding ground and plenty of swinging room as at Betio, I would rather be anchored out away from other boats.

Gilbertese like Americans and at one time even considered asking to become a colony of the United States. Their waters teem with migratory fish and the United States tuna fleet fishing under a recent treaty with the Republic frequent their waters in search of the migratory tuna.

Horizon's arrival in Tarawa was very timely for in a few days the I-Kiribati would again celebrate their independence day. With a few credentials as visiting American journalists, Betty and I were invited to join the official reviewing stand and then be invited guests to the Statehouse reception after the opening ceremonies. For this occasion, I was in long trousers and Betty in a colorful long frock, something out of the ordinary for cruising folk.

2-man canoe under sail, Tarawa, Gilbert Islands

From the grandstand we watched innumerable drill teams, police units, school groups and athletic teams march by in colorful dress and pay their respects to the president and flag. One hitch developed and that was when the flag was run up the pole upside down on the first try! After what I thought to be an embarrassingly long time, it was corrected. Upside down the flag has the ocean above the sky and I wondered if that portended rain or a tsunami, but the day remained sunny and calm.

After the formalities of Independence Day were completed, the celebration turned into a grand county fair. Contests prevailed on the soccer field ranging from footraces on the track around the periphery to log-heaving at the center. Later the national game of soccer took over with teams from many Tarawa islands competing. Outside the bounds of the athletic zone, entrepeneurs had set up their sales booths offering a wide variety of tempting foods which gave us a chance to sample home-cooked native dishes without offending the host if any didn't agree with our taste buds. Fish and bread were abundant, but my favorite was french fried breadfruit slices, something you can munch on as you walk along assessing other Gilbertese gastronomic temptations.

Canoe sailing is a popular sport in the Gilberts. Competitive sailing, fishing, traveling to other islands or just plain day-sailing are popular uses for the homemade canoes. The confidence which the I-Kiribati sailors have in their canoes is a constant souce of worry to the Marine Department, which has to search for them when they are overdue. Strong winds will carry the canoes across the wide lagoon to another island which has no contact with the urban area and then a search has to be started. Canoes also overturn in the rough waters with occasional loss of life; but that doesn't seem to deter these natural seamen of the equator.

We have visited many islands of the Pacific but none had as many sailing canoes as we saw in the Gilberts. The canoes are wood-planked and sewn together with synthetic cord—a concession to modern technology, but there the concession ends. Thwarts, outriggers and anything that works while the canoe is in motion are lashed together with sennit (coconut husk twine) which wears better than synthetic line. (That is, the twine wears and can easily be replaced instead of the twine wearing away the structural member which is difficult to replace. Darn clever these islanders.)

Tacking a canoe is an exercise in balance, for the crew has to stand up in the narrow hull and physically move the sail from one end of the canoe to the other. In this respect, the canoe hull is symmetrical fore and aft. The outrigger, incidentally, is just for balance and not flotation and it is always kept to windward. Sails are made of available materials. We saw one woven pandanus sail, many rice bag sails and a few sophisticated sails made of an unknown cloth, probably synthetic. What all the canoes had in common was a crew with a love of sailing.

The men of Kiribati are such natural sailors that German shipping lines sponsor the Marine Training School at Betio which turns I-Kiribati

youths into trained seamen. Surprisingly, although the school is primarily German-financed and its Captain and Executive Officer are German Merchant Marine officers, most of the training staff are English sea dogs recruited from the British Merchant Marine.

The school turns out about 200 seamen each year who immediately go to work for German shipping lines and end up seeing the world. Unfortunately, they also get very worldly, and conservative Kiribati doesn't look so good on their return. The lucky ones later may get jobs at home with the Kiribati Shipping Corporation or in the government's Marine Department. Others drift into the local economy somehow, while many just return to sea with some other country's ships. Like the World War I song said: "How can you keep them down on the farm after they've seen Paree?"

Trainees can choose from three sea-going specialties—deck hands, engine room mechanics or stewards. The academic courses are given in local classrooms at the Technical Institute and the "hands-on" courses are given at the Marine Training School itself. Experience at sea is given on cadet training ships which thread their way through the islands of Kiribati and, occasionally, make port in Samoa or Fiji. These are regular "copra runs" because the high cost of fuel prevents dedicated training voyages.

Merchant Marine Training School, Betio, Tarawa, Gilbert Islands

Layover In Abemama

We could have spent several more weeks in Tarawa enjoying the friendly people and their islands; but when you are cruising you tend to get itchy feet after you have taken in the major places of interest on an island. Besides, the skipper had his heart set on visiting Abemama ever since reading Robert Louis Stevenson's book "In the South Seas."

All of the islands of the Gilbert group are close together and pretty much oriented north and south making ideal tradewind sailing. A simple overnight sail past Abiang Island took us to Abemama, where we sailed directly into the lagoon's recommended anchorage area.

Stevenson was one of the first cruisers to write about the South Seas in his search for the ideal climate to aid his deteriorating health. Hawaii was one of his stops and Abemama another. Nothing remains of Stevenson's house on Abemama. A stone marker locates the site of the house, but I would defy any visitor to find that mark without the help of a local guide.

Easier to find is the grave of Tem Binoka, the famous chief in the Gilbert Islands who ruled from Abemama. Binoka has been termed a despotic king, but he and Stevenson became good friends. If you are wondering what became of Stevenson after six months on Abemama, he sailed on to Western Samoa and made it his final home and resting place.

With plain dumb luck (again) we had arrived at Abemama in time to see the festivities connected with a national holiday called Youth Day. It also assured us transportation on a special bus carrying youthful participants from up-island near where we had anchored at an abandoned copra wharf. Once in the main island village of Kariatebeke, we checked in with the District Officer, visited the rustic R.L.S. Hotel and spent the rest of the day watching Youth Day activities. In reality, we spent most of our time watching people for the Gilbertese are fascinating, as we found out earlier in Tarawa. Athletic contests were the order of the day, with soccer predominating for the boys and volleyball for the girls. Spectators either stayed in the shade of the palm trees or gathered under the roof of the open air meeting place called a "maneaba."

A maneaba is a building without walls used for town meetings at which political and social issues facing the communities are discussed. When not in use for this purpose, it is used for casual gatherings or simply shelter from the sun. Each village has at least one maneaba. Construction varies from thatched roofs supported by coconut logs with a coral floor, to an aluminum roof with concrete supports and platform. They all had one thing in common, they were clean. Maneabas are respected places in their society and no graffiti grows there.

It has been our experience that every Pacific island (except large administrative centers) will have a native volunteer host who has more than a casual interest in the overseas yachts stopping there. Most of the time your host has a wealth of local information to offer you. There is always an exchange of gifts in the way of hard goods and hard-to-get foodstuffs and the native's offering of handicrafts and local foods.

Abamama was no exception, except this time the head of the household was also a glutton for technical knowledge. He would take notes on the working details of such things as the depth sounder, whose rotating neon light fascinated him, and the ham radio, which must have looked like the 21st century to him. Besides meeting him in our daily forays to his island, he twice visited us in his canoe, each time bringing different members of his family, which seemed without bounds. Family planning was in need here and they obviously had not heard of it. Again our Polaroid camera was an icebreaker, for we took pictures of all the family members on *Horizon's* foredeck. This thrilled them, especially since we took enough pictures to give each of them a print for remembrances.

While the cost of instant picture film makes you sometimes think twice about taking so many pictures, the ease with which you weld new friendships is worth the cost of the film. If you don't believe it, wait until you are ready to leave. On our departure, the native family brought out bunches of freshly harvested coconuts still on the stem because that way they will last longer. The wife had fashioned for Betty a colorful pandanus fan made with unbelievably precise hand weaving. She apologized to me and our crew for not having had enough time to make one for each of us.

Our visit to Abemama reinforced our conviction that the out islands of an archipelago are far more interesting than the administrative centers. As much as we liked Tarawa—its cleanliness, friendly people and nice urban atmosphere—Abemama was a far more colorful and relaxing port of call. It ranks with the best we have found in the Pacific and, being English speaking, we felt right at home.

Although we still had a couple of more ports of call planned for our return trip to Hawaii, we felt smug that we had at last seen the true Micronesia, and we were glad that we had scheduled Kiribati last. We took home good memories of the people living on the equator.

— Sea

Over-lagoon guest house, PLS Hotel, Abamama, Gilbert Islands

KIRIBATI'S LINE ISLANDS

About 1,000 miles south of Hawaii lie the Line Islands, a chain of 12 atolls and reefs that spread 1,200 miles across the equator of the Central Pacific. Only three of the Line Islands are presently inhabited—Kiritimati (Christmas—note that pronouncing the "ti" in Kiritimati as an "s," makes it sound like Christmas), Tabuaeran (Fanning) and Teraina (Washington)—all of which belong to the Republic of Kiribati. One other island, Palmyra, is habitable, but no one lives there. Palmyra is a United States possession. The remainder of the Line Islands are uninhabitable atolls or reefs and none are of real interest to the cruising sailor.

Most of today's inhabitants of the entire Republic of Kiribati come from the Gilberts, since neither the Phoenix nor Line Islands had indigenous inhabitants. They collectively called themselves Gilbertese; but now refer to themselves as I-Kiribati.

The Line Islands fall geographically within the Polynesian triangle anchored at its corners by Hawaii, Easter Island, and New Zealand. The presence of I-Kiribati at Kiritimati, Tabuaeran, and Teraina Islands results in a Micronesian anomaly within the Polynesian triangle.

Archaeologists, in piecing history together, believe Tabuaeran was not occupied by man before the eleventh century A.D. Some stone ruins and fishhooks found on the atoll suggest that the first persons to set foot on this land were Tongans—or if not Tongans, at least Polynesians. The evidence does not indicate how long they stayed or why they left.

Turning copra on a sun-drying tray, Kiritimati (Christmas) Island, Kiribati, Line Islands

Sailing to the northern Line Islands of Kiritimati, Tabuaeran, Palmyra and Teraina requires careful navigation. Currents can be a nightmare for the navigator as the equatorial contercurrent flows east through this chain; it shifts north and south with the season and is never very steady. North of the countercurrent flows the North equatorial current, which is fairly steady, and south of it is the South equatorial current, which tends to be erratic in the vicinity of the islands. One day it can flow westerly at 2 knots and then disappear overnight. There are many wrecks in these islands attesting to the variability of the currents. Care has to be the navigator's watchword.

The best way to cruise the Line Islands is to start at Kiritimati and work your way northwest up the chain. That way you will be sailing off the wind all the way through the chain and have the current generally in your favor. Boats traveling north from the Samoas or Societies will find the Line Islands close enough on their routes to Hawaii to do one more stint of island-hopping before closing on Polynesia, USA. When you do depart Palmyra (or Teraina, a rarely visited island) for Hawaii, take your first tack to the east to gain enough easting to lay Hawaii on a starboard tack. If you don't, you will have to later make the tack anyway; but you will then be in areas of stronger northeast trades which will make it more difficult.

Police Chief, Christmas Island, Kiribati, Line Islands

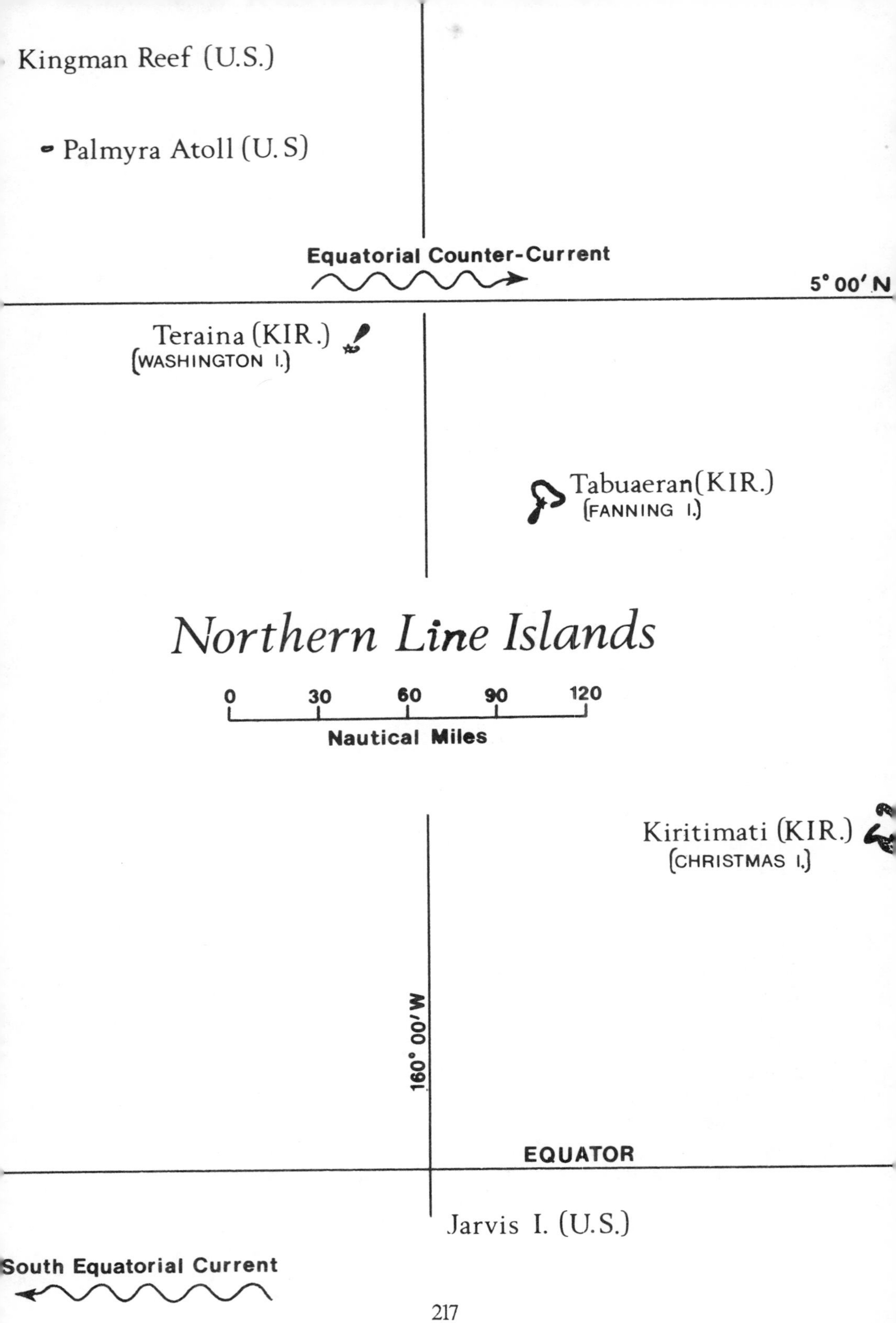

Kingman Reef (U.S.)

• Palmyra Atoll (U.S)

Equatorial Counter-Current

5° 00′ N

Teraina (KIR.)
(WASHINGTON I.)

Tabuaeran(KIR.)
(FANNING I.)

Northern Line Islands

```
0        30       60       90      120
|_____|_____|_____|_____|
         Nautical  Miles
```

Kiritimati (KIR.)
(CHRISTMAS I.)

160° 00′ W

EQUATOR

Jarvis I. (U.S.)

South Equatorial Current

Kiritimati

Best known of all the Line Islands is Kiritimati which is the Line Islands District Sub-Center for Administration for the Republic of Kiribati. It is a large atoll and has, in fact, the largest land area of all atolls in the world—140 square miles. Its lagoon is relatively small, measuring only 123 square miles in area. (Kwajalein Atoll in the Marshall Islands has the largest lagoon in the world, a colossal 839 square miles!) As an atoll Kiritimati is low—nominal elevation is 12 feet with the highest hill reaching an awesome 43 feet in height.

Located in the equatorial dry zone, Kiritimati receives only 34 inches of rainfall a year and in some years it gets as little as seven inches, not enough to support much agriculture. Recently a significant store of underground water has been found to exist which may greatly alter the future of this atoll. The relative humidity of 70 percent is relieved by the relatively constant and cooling east wind. Being on the southern edge of the Intertropical Convergence Zone, cloud cover averages about 50 percent on an annual basis.

The 1,000 people on Kiritimati are mainly Gilbertese working on contract to the Kiribati Government. They live widely spread out on this large island, although they cluster to some extent around the villages of London and Banana and an area known as Paris.

The potential wealth of Kiritimati lies in its fishing resources, both commercial and sport. One jet flight a week from Honolulu, Hawaii, usually brings 20 or so sportfishermen down to try the exceptional lagoon fishing and also deep sea fishing in the surrounding ocean. The same airplane carries back frozen milkfish and lobsters for the tables of Honolulu.

One of the lesser-known attractions at Kiritimati is its sea bird population. The atoll has been proclaimed an international bird sanctuary and is inhabited by millions of boobies, terns, tropicbirds, frigate birds, shearwaters and the like. There are an estimated 18 species living on the atoll, many of which are using it as a stopover in migratory flights. During the 1982/83 El Niño event, almost the total bird population, then estimated at 17 million, abandoned the atoll because of the drought and the disappearance of small fish in the vicinity. Most have since returned.

So what is there at Kiritimati to entice a cruising yacht to stop? Other than it being the only possible mail stop in the Line Islands, it would have to be to see another and quite different atoll. Among the sights on Christmas are the Japanese satellite tracking station; numerous brackish interior lagoons where milkfish and shrimp are farmed; and the abandoned facilities from the atmospheric nuclear tests of the 1960s. You can also see several wrecked boats and ships attesting to the need for accurate navigation in these waters.

Winds in the vicinity of Kiritimati tend northeastward from November to May and southeastward from June to October with occasional squalls from both the north and south. North to west winds occasionally occur between March and June. Offshore currents set westerly at rates that vary

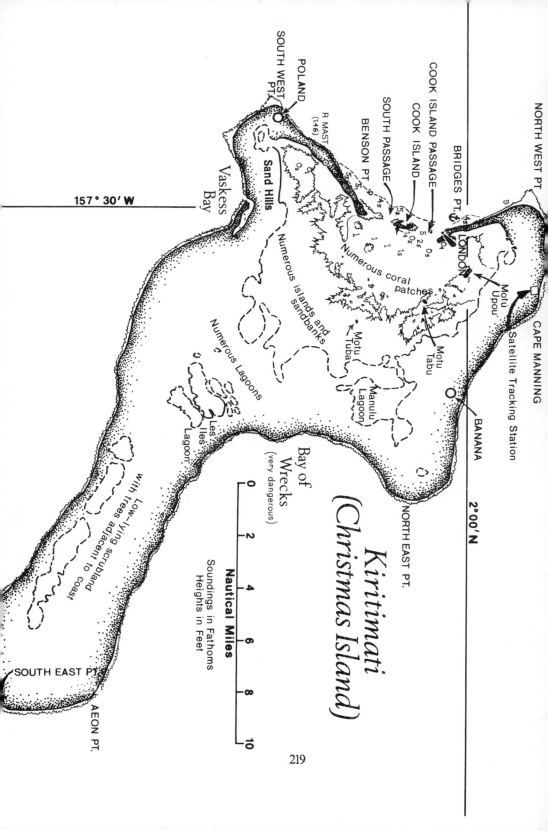

Kiritimati (Christmas Island)

NORTH WEST PT.

CAPE MANNING

2°00′N

NORTH EAST PT.

BRIDGES PT.

COOK ISLAND PASSAGE

COOK ISLAND

SOUTH PASSAGE

BENSON PT.

POLAND

SOUTH WEST PT.

R MAST (146)

Sand Hills

Vaskess Bay

157° 30′ W

Numerous islands and sandbanks

Numerous Lagoons

Numerous coral patches

LONDON

Motu Upou

Satellite Tracking Station

Motu Tabu

Motu Tuba

Manulu Lagoon

BANANA

Les Iles Lagoon

with trees adjacent to coast

Low-lying scrubland

SOUTH EAST PT.

AEON PT.

Bay of Wrecks
(very dangerous)

0 2 4 6 8 10

Nautical Miles

Soundings in Fathoms
Heights in Feet

219

between 10 to 60 miles per day necessitating careful navigation throughout the Line Islands. The surf is the least in September and October and heaviest from November to April. Between November and March, northwesterly swells frequently cause breakers to form across the lagoon entrance making passage hazardous to impossible.

Anchorage can be taken on the reef outside of Bridges Point, which can be rolly and absolutely impossible if swells are coming in from the north or west. You can take your dinghy around Bridges Point into a shallow bight off the village of London, where you are protected from the prevailing winds and there you land on the beach. An outboard motor is a real asset for this venture. You can row a hard bottom dinghy in with nominal effort but an inflatable without an outboard would be impossible.

Charts and sailing directions say that boats drawing less than 6 feet can find their way into the lagoon via the channels between the village of London and Cook Island, taking proper precautions to go on one side or the other of Cochrane Reef. Shifting sands and silt causes this passage to move about, so don't rely solely on the charts. The snaking channel through the coral is unmarked and, once inside, the land and reefs become a lee shore. You can anchor just to the east of London Wharf in water a couple of fathoms deep or it may be possible to tie up to the wharf if it is clear.

Although it may be possible to snake your way into the lagoon, I would recommend against trying to do so. One steel-hulled yacht had made its way into the lagoon before we had arrived. In stiff trade winds, its anchor rode parted, allowing it to drift outwards towards the pass where ocean swells picked it up and cast it onto the reef. There it still lies.

Kiritimati is an official Port of Entry to Kiribati unlike neighboring Tabuaeran which is a limited Port of Entry. At Kiritimati, you can get permission to cruise all the islands of Kiribati under the same conditions as if you entered at Tarawa. If you are staying for only a few days, the paperwork is less formidable. There is an inbound clearance fee of A$4.00 if you go ashore for it. If the officials have to come out to your boat at anchor on the Bridges Port shallows, they will charge an additional A$20.00 because they have to charter a small boat to get out there.

All government offices are within walking distance of the London landing as are the largest store, post office and fresh water supply. Rental cars and motorcycles are the only way to get around on this large island, although there is free bus service between London, the Captain Cook Hotel and the airport near Banana. If you decide to cross the neck of the island, take a guide along as the roads are not marked.

— Unpublished Note

220

Tabuaeran (Fanning Atoll)

Take an atoll whose barrier reef separates a cobalt-blue ocean from a jade-green lagoon. Cover it with majestic palm trees, exotic pandanus and brilliant red hibiscus. Add to it an English-speaking brown-skinned people and you have Tabuaeran (Fanning) atoll in the Line Islands.

Tabuaeran, situated 1,050 NM south of Honolulu and only 230 NM from the equator, is about 10 miles long by 7 miles wide, with a narrow rim of land, 100 to 1,500 yards wide almost completely surrounding the lagoon. The land gives way in only three places, two for shallow canoe passes and one deep channel for trading ships. Except at the ship pass, the lagoon is shallow and studded with coral heads that break the surface at low tide. In the sunlight, the lagoon casts its reflection onto trade-wind clouds hovering overhead, coloring them a pastel green. Experienced mariners usually can spot an atoll's location before they can see the land by noting the color of the clouds.

Tabuaeran's nearness to the equator gives it a warm, humid climate. The mean high temperature is 83°F, and it never drops below 70°F; the humidity stands at 80 to 85 percent, and faithful trade winds blow, mak-

Gilbertese dancer performing "Dance of the Frigate Bird" in the church maneba, Fanning Atoll

ing it very comfortable. Air conditioning requires only plenty of windows and a ceiling fan at most. S.G. Ross, a British medical officer with Cable and Wireless, Ltd., wrote in "The Medical Journal of Australia," "It would probably be difficult to find another place in the tropics where the climatic environment is more ideal for a (European) than at Fanning Island."

The recorded history of Tabuaeran starts with the arrival on June 11, 1798, of the American trading schooner *Betsey*, commanded by Captain Edmund Fanning. It was the prerogative of Western Hemisphere explorers to name islands they discovered any way they saw fit. Fanning understandably named the atoll after himself, "Fanning's Islands" for there are three of them. A half century later it was realized that those three islands were actually the top rim of a single vanished volcano. Today, such islands are called islets or motus.

> "The landing we found perfectly smooth, and effected by resting the bows of the boat on a small sandy beach, at the starboard hand, as we passed into the bay. On the south island, and nearby a grove of coconut trees, whose fruit then layed strewed around, covering the ground from one to three feet deep, and seemed to have ripened and thus fallen for many years past, our boat's crew . . . very quickly loaded her from the upper course of those nuts which had fallen last . . . I employed myself in taking a kind of fish, much like a striped bass. Of these there were great quantities continually crowding against the boat, so that it was an easy matter to take and spear them. . . The sharks here are very numerous, and while the boat was on her passage into the bay, before she entered the pass, they became so exceedingly ravenous around her, and so voracious withal, as frequently to dart at, and seize upon her rudder and the oars, leaving theron many marks of their sharp teeth and powerful jaws . . . When the boat was loaded, accompanied by an officer, the steward going along, we took a stroll into the interior for a few minutes, among the upland grass and groves of various kinds of trees, without being able to discover any of the valuable bread-fruit tree. At the barren spots, the birds, boobies, knoddies, and the like, were quietly sitting on their nests, so fearless and gentle, as to be easily taken by hand . . . "
>
> — From "Voyages Round the World; with Selected Sketches of Voyages to the South Seas, North and South Pacific Oceans, China, etc., performed under the command and agency of the author," Edmund Fanning, 1838

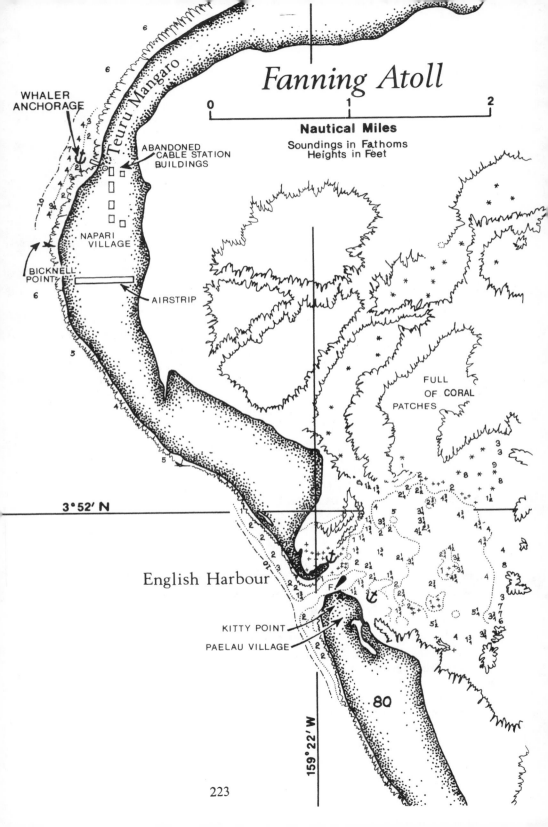

Fanning Atoll

WHALER
ANCHORAGE

Teuru Mangaro

ABANDONED
CABLE STATION
BUILDINGS

NAPARI
VILLAGE

BICKNELL
POINT

AIRSTRIP

0   1   2

Nautical Miles
Soundings in Fathoms
Heights in Feet

FULL
OF CORAL
PATCHES

3°52′ N

English Harbour

KITTY POINT
PAELAU VILLAGE

80

159°22′ W

223

The name was later simplified to Fanning Island (although the discovery had technically made it an atoll also) and was known as such until 1979, when the Gilbert Islands colony received its independence from Great Britain and also became a part of the Republic of Kiribati. At that time Fanning was renamed Tabuaeran, meaning "holy island" in Gilbertese. Simultaneously, Christmas Island, to the southeast, orginally named by Captain Cook, became Kiritimati—phonetic spelling for "Christmas" in Gilbertese. Washington Island, to the northwest, also named by Fanning, was renamed Teraina, "island with a lake."

Fanning was more than a trading captain. He was a discoverer and patriot who believed the fledgling United States should explore further and take possession of uncharted islands in the Pacific. His influence and sincerity eventually convinced President Martin Van Buren to authorize a National Exploring Expedition to scour the waters of the South Seas. This expedition was led by Lieutenant Charles Wilkes of the U.S. Navy in 1838—too late for Fanning to join because of his advanced age.

Post-discovery settlement of Tabuaeran found 10 or 12 Sandwich Islanders (Hawaiians) living along the beach in 1832. The first permanent settlement occurred in 1860, when John English set about to manufacture coconut oil there. He first brought in Cook Islanders from Manihiki and Rakahanga, but they were soon replaced by Gilbertese. The Cook Islanders call this atoll Tabuaeangi, "heavenly footprint," because of its shape.

English's venture proved very successful and by 1862, he was able to ship 44,000 gallons of precious coconut oil to Honolulu. The island was now of commercial interest, and in 1888 Great Britain formally annexed it, making it part of the far-flung Gilbert and Ellice Islands Colony with administrative headquarters at Tarawa, in the Gilberts.

Copra has been the mainstay of Tabuaeran's economy, but the island also had its fling at contemporary high technology. It was the site of a relay station for the British-owned Cable and Wireless Company's trans-Pacific undersea cable that ran from Bamfield, British Columbia to Suva, Fiji. The cable was laid in 1902, and it was a most remarkable technological achievement. The Bamfield-Fanning link, measuring 3,450 miles in length some places, was laid to a depth of 3,400 fathoms—almost 4 miles. The cable station remained operational at the little village of Napari until 1963, when a more modern coaxial cable system was laid that dispensed with the need for surface relay stations.

Local facilities for the cable station included an ocean wharf at Whalers Anchorage (since demolished by wave action), several multi-story concrete buildings which housed offices, shops, garages, and a power station, and a number of two-story houses for the expatriate workers. In spite of high humidity, intense tropical sun, and termites, these buildings are in a good state of repair.

The management of the British cable station imported a number of Chinese nationals to work at the facility. A 1946 census showed there were 170 Gilbertese, 27 Chinese, 20 Europeans, and 7 persons of mixed

Making sennit, Fanning Atoll

descent living on the atoll. When the cable station shut down in 1963, the Europeans and Chinese departed, leaving behind the Gilbertese and those of mixed parentage.

One of the latter is Willie Yee Ong, an elected official representing Tabuaeran in the Kiribati Parliament. Although Ong has no legal or appointive powers in his home district comprising Tabuaeran atoll, by sheer force of personality he makes things happen; he is the person the village elders look to for guidance in solving major local problems.

But Ong has problems of his own—such as when he needs to attend Parliament meetings 1,670 NM away in Tarawa. Air service to Tabuaeran is nonexistent, and ships call only infrequently. For one trip to Tarawa, Ong chartered a private yacht to take him to Kiritimati where he caught the weekly Hawaiian Airlines flight to Honolulu. From there he took Continental Air Micronesia to Majuro, in the Marshall Islands, where he caught an Air Nauru flight to Tarawa. This routine is very demanding on his time (as well as that of legislators from Kiritimati and Teraina atolls who do the same), and takes considerable money from the slim national treasury.

It is this very isolation, however, that makes Tabuaeran such an attrac-

tive place to visit. The best way to get there is by sailboat. Sailing weather from Honolulu is good, and the 1,050 NM passage takes only seven or eight days down and eleven or twelve back to Honolulu.

Tabuaeran's location in the equatorial ocean countercurrent and also in the atmosphere's intertropical convergence zone brought yet another fling at high technology. In 1967, the University of Hawaii, in cooperation with the U.S. government, established an ocean-atmosphere research station in the old cable station buildings.

It had long been suspected that much of the world's weather is controlled by the interaction between the warm ocean waters and the air in the region of the equator. The theory was proven when years of painstaking data-gathering at Tabuaeran and other equatorial stations recorded the most unusual and dynamic weather change in recorded history. This was the famous El Niño disturbance of 1982 and 1983 that affected the entire Pacific from Australia to Peru and Tahiti to Hawaii.

Federal funds for the project eventually disappeared. University employees returned to Honolulu, and local support personnel went back to cutting copra. Now, most of the cable station buildings are again empty, with only a few rooms in use for a school, a library, and a dispensary. Some of the buildings house idle vehicles and machinery.

Napari villagers still entertain hopes of bringing the buildings back to full use by moving the government offices from Paelau village at English Harbor to the cable station site. Such a move is dependent on establishing regular airline service at the dirt airstrip at Napari; but with the present state of the nation's economy, this is not apt to happen soon.

The population of Tabuaeran is limited by government edict with respect to immigration, and everyone works or attends school. One resident who was faced with the population limit edict was Pastor Joe. Joe Murdock was assigned to Tabuaeran as pastor of the Protestant church; but when his time came to be transferred he did not want to leave. His replacement had arrived, however, so Pastor Joe had to leave or find himself another job. He chose the latter, and became a fisherman.

The estimated 250 persons who live on the atoll are all I-Kiribati except for a storekeeper named Allen Rush, who is a Canadian expatriate. Rush sailed his 23-foot boat single-handed to Tabuaeran several years ago, and liked it so well that he stayed on as assistant plantation manager for the Fanning Island Plantation Company, a Burns-Philip enterprise no longer in business.

Most of today's Tabuaerans came from the islands of Beru, Nonouti, and Onotoa in the southern Gilberts. To relieve overcrowding on these islands, men could volunteer to take their families to the Line Islands, which had living space, natural foods aplenty, and jobs.

Almost all of the people of Tabuaeran live in Paelau village at English Harbor or at Napari village across the pass and 3½ miles north at the old cable station. Paelau, the larger of the two villages, contains the present government offices, two churches (Protestant and Catholic), the major school

Beachmaster, Fanning Atoll

buildings, and Allen Rush's store. English Harbor makes it the center of commerce, for only there can ships anchor inside the lagoon to discharge cargo.

Copra is harvested on all three motus that make up the atoll. There are about 60 copra cutters, but only enough land transport to take half of them to and from the groves. Consequently, there are always some unemployed workers.

There are other jobs besides copra-cutting, however. Men too old for this demanding task take on other jobs such as fishing and boat-repairing, which require skill but no physical endurance. The business of government takes a few more males for the positions of policeman, customs officer, government treasurer, health aide, postmaster, and teacher. The only women holding community jobs are a schoolteacher and the school's headmistress. The children of Tabuaeran are robust and active, and trained to take care of themselves.

Entertainment in a society such as Tabuaeran's is what you make it, and in this the two churches play a dominant role. Both the Protestant and the Catholic churches sponsor volleyball, dancing, singing, feasting, and of course, devotional services. They have an unwritten agreement not to compete against each other; schedules are coordinated, and representatives of each church are invited to participate in the other's events.

With no city council, chamber of commerce, or parks and recreations department, it falls to the churches to organize holiday festivities—religious or national. During one Easter holiday period when *Horizon* was there, the Catholic church sponsored a dance competition without prizes

so that no one person or group was singled out as better than another. Between dances, village orators would solemnly speak their pieces in Gilbertese. Some speeches were amusing, causing much laughter; others were inspirational and rewarded by hand—or leg—clapping. A good orator is considered a person of much talent and commands great respect.

Gilbertese dances have none of the sensual movements associated with the Tahitian tamure or the flowing grace of the Hawaiian hula. They are, instead, dances of slow and precise movements of the hands, head, and arms, accompanied by a rhythmic shuffle of the feet. The dances portray stories—historical sagas of the people—or they may depict the action of the frigate bird, the country's national emblem. Even the conservative Tabuaerans have some fire in their veins, and an occasional impromptu solo dancer will throw dignity to the winds and perform an enthusiastic dance that sets the crowd cheering and clapping.

Singing is also important in I-Kiribati social life, and other than solo dance songs, is usually performed a capella. Some songs are adapted from the Western world—mostly church hymns—and others are original pieces. The composer will fashion the song in his or her mind and then transfer it orally to the singing group. Memory and repetition make it popular.

— Guam & Micronesia Glimpses

Pastor Joe and his eel trap, Fanning Atoll

228

A VISIT TO TABUAERAN

Not unexpectedly, Tabuaeran's principal village, Paelau, is located at the one navigable pass into the lagoon, and we found its English Harbor to have both good and bad points. The anchorage, located just inside the pass, has flood currents to 4½ knots and ebb to 7 knots. On flood, the incoming flow bucks the tradewind and produces a dramatic race in the channel. Your anchored boat tends to forget all about weathervaning and swings with the tidal currents precluding the use of any landmarks to determine whether your anchor is holding or not.

You really needn't worry about the anchor holding in this coral sand bottom. Properly set, it will stay forever. We hung on our anchor for 17 days against strong tradewinds blowing across 5 miles of lagoon combined with the swinging of the boat following each change of tidal current. When we were ready to leave, our 60-pound CQR broke out cleanly on short stay and we were on our way.

Whaler Anchorage, in the lee of the atoll at the site of the Trans-Pacific cable station, was used in the heyday of the cable's operation. At that time it had a pier jutting out from the beach between the breakers, but it has since been battered into oblivion by waves. We observed that location on a calm day and thought it an impossible place to land, and certainly a rolly anchorage for any small boat that elected to anchor there.

Upon *Horizon's* arrival at English Harbor, the officials were Johnny-on-the-spot as soon as they saw the Q-flag. They came out to greet us in one of those marvelous Yamaha-built fiberglass fishing skiffs that are so common throughout Micronesia. They were wearing the official dress for men—lap laps or shorts and they courteously introduced themselves to us as they came aboard. Gilbertese have their own native tongue, but most of them also speak English, a heritage of their former British colonial days.

Following a brief look at the boat's papers and the grubby-looking crew who hadn't had a chance to spruce up before their arrival, the officials settled down to casual conversation spurred on by a cold beer and some of Betty's tailor-made cigarettes. The rest of the formalities were forgotten since they would be taken up on shore the following Monday. We were to see these people many times during our stay, since on shore there was no visible difference in behavior between government officials and copra cutters. They were one big happy family.

A note on smoking: The one vice that all Tabuaerans seem to have is smoking. Not chain-smoking, but social smoking by both men and women. A vice like that can be near tragedy when the supply ship fails to bring in tobacco for the store. Such was the situation when we arrived. The Tongan freighter, *Sammy*, had recently been there, but someone had forgotten to order tobacco. Tabuaeran was near the cold-turkey state.

Roll-your-own smokes using pandanus leaf papers was favored over tailor-mades by the adults of this isolated community. Long smokes are frowned upon, short-smokes shared with others is the norm. When every-

one has had a satisfying puff or two, the cigarette goes back to its owner who snuffs it out on the leathery sole of his foot and then stores it behind his ear.

In this well-disciplined colony there is a definite order of doing things and not until the officials had departed were we visited by another local person who became instrumental in setting the tenor of our entire visit, namely, socializing with the people. He arrived from shore in an outrigger canoe to invite, us on behalf of the Catholic Church, to come to a feast the next day at the church maneaba. This fellow's name was Ets and he is one of five schoolteachers on the atoll. His English was impeccable, and that is probably why he has become the greeter for the community.

We thought Ets to be an unusual man in more than one way. He could walk up a coconut palm with the best of the copra cutters; slice the top of a drinking nut with one swipe of his bush knife; and clean and skin a chicken on the aft deck of *Horizon* with all the ease of opening a can of Spam. Ets was raised on Nonuiti in the Southern Gilberts, educated on Abemama and then spent a year in Australia in further educational training. We could only guess how he came to be at Tabuaeran; but he did tell us that his former wives live on Nonuiti and Abemama atolls.

Our second visitor of the afternoon was on a "Welcome Wagon" mission. He was Jacob, another Yamaha skiff driver, and he brought us four loaves of delicious home-made bread as a gift. Shy and committed to getting his skiff back to official business, Jacob didn't come aboard, but he became our provider of fresh bread throughout our stay.

Between Ets and Jacob, we were invited to every social function that took place in Paepau and Jacob saw to it that we toured the lagoon and visited the village of Napari and the Cable Station. The days were busy but the nights quiet since their electric-generating system was turned on for only a few hours in the evening and then everyone went to bed.

Kiribati is one of the Third World countries striving to keep its society healthy and satisfied while it gets its economy in gear. It has been a free country for only a short time, and has few natural resources other than sun, rain, and the bountiful ocean. The cash economy is almost nil; but the people have learned how to live in harmony with nature and with a boundless enthusiasm for life.

Now life on Tabuaeran is taking on a different hue. In an effort to reduce the over-population of Tarawa, the capital island of Kiribati, additional settlers are being transplanted to both Kiritimati and Tabuaeran Islands. Numbers like 1,000 each are in the plans. While it should not affect a cruiser's visit to these islands, it may presage a long term tourist development as a means of supporting the increased population.

— Cruising World

TERAINA (Washington Island)

Between Tabuaeran and Palmyra atoll lies Teraina (Washington Island). It is a raised atoll about 2 miles long and 1 mile wide with a fresh water lake near its eastern end that has been stocked with the African tilapia fish. The island is covered with coconut palms and copra-making is the chief source of income. Like Tabuaeran, the lack of shipping keeps the copra economy from being a useful economic source.

"A little before noon, June 12th, the seaman at the masthead again called out, 'Land ho!' adding, that the same was half a point off the lee-bow. At meridian, this, newly discovered island bore west by north four leagues distance. This, was of a much greater elevation than Fanning's Island, and was, moreover, covered with plants or grass, presenting to our eyes a beautiful, green, and flourishng appearance.

With the unanimous approbation of every individual on board, both officers and seamen, and with feelings of pride for our country, we named this Washington Island, after President Washington, the father of his country."

— Edmund Fanning, "Voyages Round the World; Round the World; with selected Sketches of Voyages to the South Seas, North and South Pacific Oceans, China, etc., performed under the command and agency of the author," 1838

Teraina is rarely visited by cruising boats since it has a very difficult reef anchorage at West Point. Anchorage should only be taken there in fair weather and then a capable crew person should be left on board for safety. As the Sailing Directions say, "communications with the shore are always dangerous and should be left to the surf boats."

— Unpublished Note

CHAPTER 8

A LOOK BEYOND THE TRADEWINDS

"We are inclined to view nature as constant, the earth solid, the sea eternal, the climate dependable, on any timescale that matters to us, though sometimes perturbed by landslides, storms, or earthquakes. Geologists, too, have long regarded the earth as well-behaved, its evolution slow and driven by the same forces, with the same intensities and in the same combinations, that drive it still. Rather a dull history, were it not for the excitement provided by the evolution of life.

This view seems no longer valid today. More probably, the history of the earth was a history of many brief intervals of change between longer periods of quiescence. Mountains rose, then disappeared; ice ages came and went; even the positions of the continents changed continuously.

Tjeerd H. van Andel, "New Views of an Old Planet"

HOW PACIFIC IS THE WEATHER?

Most cruising in the Pacific takes place in the tropics where balmy tradewinds drive your boat between enticing ports of call. Although tradewinds receive most of the attention, they are not the only natural phenomenon of importance. The cruiser should be aware of others which can influence his cruise. They come in the form of both wind and wave, some are good and others well, let's talk about them.

High Pressure Cells

Weather of the Pacific Ocean east of 165° east longitude is governed by atmospheric high pressure cells in both northern and southern hemispheres. The northern cell, commonly called the "Pacific high," lies about 1300 miles west of Los Angeles during the boreal (northern hemisphere) summer. During the winter months, it lies considerably south and east of this position, but still dominates North Pacific weather patterns. The fact that it has moved south accounts for the winter weather "lows" being able to penetrate farther south during the winter bringing rain, wind and snow to the West Coast as far south as Los Angeles. The steady winds to the south of the Pacific high are the northeast tradewinds that extend far into the Western Pacific where they become modified by monsoonal winds from the Asian subcontinent.

In the South Pacific a comparable high pressure cell lies about 1800 miles off Valparaiso, Chile, and it generates the southeast trades on its

equatorial side and enhances the westerlies on its southern perimeter. The South Pacific westerlies below 45° south tend to be stronger and more consistent than their northern hemisphere counterparts because of an almost unimpeded flow around the world.

Currents

It is well known that open ocean currnts are generated by winds and the steady trades produce current circulations somewhat matching the wind patterns. Within the tropics in both hemispheres, the equatorial currents flow westward, while above the highs, the North Pacific current (Kuroshio) and its counterpart, the "west wind drift," or South Pacific current flow easterly. Like the southern hemisphere winds and for the same reason, the west wind drift is markedly stronger and better defined than North Pacific currents.

Between the equatorial currents lies a maverick, the equatorial countercurrent flowing eastward. It is only 50 or so miles in width and resides primarily in the northern hemisphere between 6° and 10° north latitude. It disappears entirely at its eastern and western ends.

Intertropical Convergence Zone (ITCZ)

Where the northeast and southeast tradewinds meet, generally north of the equator, atmospheric confusion reigns. The region is formally called the Intertropical Convergence Zone, but more popularly known as the doldrums. The ITCZ is a region where the northeast tradewinds converge with the southeast tradewinds. When they 'bump heads', something has to give. What happens is that the air rises leaving little wind for the poor sailor and generally causing cloudiness and rain. It is most pronounced where the angle at which the tradewinds meet is greatest. That occurs near Central America, narrowing in the central Pacific and almost disappearing in the Western Pacific.

In thinking of the doldrums most people have visions of the luckless sailing ship slatting away on oily seas for days on end with nary a breath of air stirring. The sun beats unmercifully down on the hapless sailors whose parched throats cry out for a drop of water. I have crossed the ITCZ many times and never suffered the infamous oily calm of sailors' tales. Some days, though, 60 miles was welcome progress.

To some extent, the ITCZ follows the sun, moving north and south, but with a lag of as much as three to four months. East of the dateline, it always stays north of the equator. West of the dateline, it will migrate south of the equator following the sun. When it does this, the western branch is sometimes called the South Pacific Convergence Zone (SPCZ).

During the austral (southern hemisphere) summer, the SPCZ extends east from Northern Australia across the Samoas and southeast to the Cooks. In the SPCZ the winds are often light and alternate between easterlies and westerlies. The SPCZ is very pronounced in western waters and that is why cruisers have to motor so much in the regions of the Solo-

mons, Vanuatu and Papua New Guinea. In the austral winter, the western portion of this doldrum belt again lies north of the equator and becomes the familiar ITCZ.

The SPCZ is also a belt of high rainfall with considerable seasonal variability. Cruisers who have passed through American Samoa know how much it can rain there any time of the year. That is because the SPCZ alternately moves north and south over the Samoas, never getting very far away.

Monsoons

In the western Pacific there is a unique wind pattern known as the "monsoon," a word derived from the Arabic "mausim" meaning season. These are, indeed, seasonal winds brought on by the alternate heating and cooling of the large Asian land mass. When it is summer in Asia (May-October), a large low pressure area builds up in central Asia. This produces a general flow of air from the southwest moving from the Bay of Bengal over southeast Asia, influencing the climate as far east as Japan and the western Caroline Islands.

The southwest monsoon usually brings with it the heavy rains that are the lifeblood of the Asian subcontinent. At the beginning of the southwest monsoon season, the winds are strong with squalls and thunderstorms. That is the season to do your sailing in the South Pacific. As the season wears on, the winds diminish, becoming variable in direction and the heat sets in.

The northeast monsoon takes over between October and April when the Asian land mass cools and a high pressure area builds up in central Asia. These are not tradewinds, but they do reinforce the northeast trades providing excellent sailing conditions in the western North Pacific.

During the October to April period of the northeast monsoon, the climate is much drier and the skies are clearer. In the latter half of the northeast monsoon season—February-April, the strong trades have moderated, typhoons are at a minimum and cyclones are absent from the Bay of Bengal making it the ideal time for sailing the waters of the mysterious Far East. January to March is the time of year for circumnavigators to make their passages from Singapore to the Red Sea. Just remember this monsoonal sailing ditty: "West on the east and east on the west."

Tropical Cyclones

A cyclone is a closed wind circulation around a low pressure cell. When that circulation builds up wind speeds greater than 63 knots, it is called a tropical cyclone in the South Pacific; a hurricane in the eastern North Pacific; and a typhoon in the western North Pacific. It is possible to have winds of over 63 knots in violent frontal activity in many places in the world; but they are not closed circulations, hence, they are not called cyclones. Tornados and waterspouts are both cyclones.

For a tropical cyclone to develop, you must have a destabilizing trough

of low pressure air referred to as a depression. You also need warm water—above 28° Celsius (keep this in mind when you read about El Niño later) and that is why they only occur in summer. Meteorologists also put other conditions on them, but if the water is too cool or there is no depression, then there is no cyclogenesis and tradewinds continue to blow.

One unique feature of cyclogenesis is that it rarely takes place closer than 6 to 10 degrees to the equator because you need a poleward component of force from the spin of the earth to cause the airflow to spiral into a closed circulation. In 1987, all 22 tropical cyclones recorded in the eastern North Pacific started above 10° N.

If you are looking for a place in the Pacific to cruise during cyclone season, try the waters near the equator. They are not only free of cyclogenesis, but they are also off the common cruising tracks and, therefore, less spoiled. Most cruisers carefully schedule their passages to avoid tropical cyclones, which pack more energy than nuclear bombs.

Both hemispheres are subject to cyclogenesis during their summer and fall seasons. In general, western Pacific typhoons are stronger and more prevalent than either eastern Pacific hurricanes or southwest Pacific tropical cyclones because of greater heating of the surface water that fuels the cyclonic activity. Cyclones are absent from the southeastern Pacific because of its colder water.

Weather and current patterns tend to move north and south with the sun although not in unison. This is most noticeable in the tropical cyclone seasons where the months of most intense activity follow two months behind the sun's movement.

El Niño

While most meteorological events of the world are cyclic, there is one that is not and that is the abnormal weather condition known as El Niño. It is a random occurrence manifested by a number of weather and ocean anomalies. The most noticeable is an increase in ocean surface temperatures in the eastern Pacific which can fuel cyclonic activity. A more subtle indicator and one of greater significance to the scientific community, is the increase in sea level height of the eastern Pacific and a corresponding decrease in the western Pacific, an anomaly called the Southern Oscillation.

The most recent manifestations of El Niño occurred in 1986-87; but they were barely felt compared to the 1982-83 event, which produced unusual cyclonic activity in French Polynesia and caused severe droughts in Australia and floods in South America. Prior to that, mild events had occurred in 1972 and 1976, but it took the dramatic 1982-83 event to set a worldwide scientific investigation into motion to seek a cause.

While science still does not have complete answers to what causes an El Niño, increased ocean surface temperatures and shifting sea level heights are now known to be precursors of one. They can be spotted in advance and the public forewarned. French Polynesia's current ban on

cruising boats in their waters from November to March no longer makes sense and should be eliminated. The scientific community is able to provide a one- to two-month advance warning of the possibility of an El Niño condition developing. With such warning, a boat could be long gone from French Polynesia. This archaic restriction on cruising boat visits to the Pacific's most popular cruising destination is no longer warranted.

— Cruising World

PACIFIC SAILING WINDOWS

The concept of "sailing windows" is a planning tool for taking advantage of the best weather for cruising and avoiding the worst. Commerical shipping has been routed for years by professional weather forecasters using this technique in order to avoid adverse weather which causes delays and increases fuel consumption. On a monthly basis significant weather events are plotted on a bar graph. This graph allows the route planner to make a quick assessment of whether a given ocean area may be subject to meteorological disturbances that would adversely impact the planned route.

Pacific Sailing Windows is an adaptation and expansion of that concept prepared exclusively for use by cruisers planning extensive Pacific passages.

Weather over the tropical Pacific is generally benign provided that the sailor selects his sailing windows properly. There is a tendency for today's cruiser equipped with a high tech boat and equipment fancy enough to go into space to think that he is impervious to adverse weather. Nothing could be further from the truth. While nautical technology may have changed significantly since Captain Cook's time, the weather has not and we have the same old tropical storms, tradewinds, moving lows, gales, etc. The only difference is that now we know more about their origin and seasonal patterns allowing us to avoid the worst and bask in the best.

— Cruising World

SAILING WINDOWS

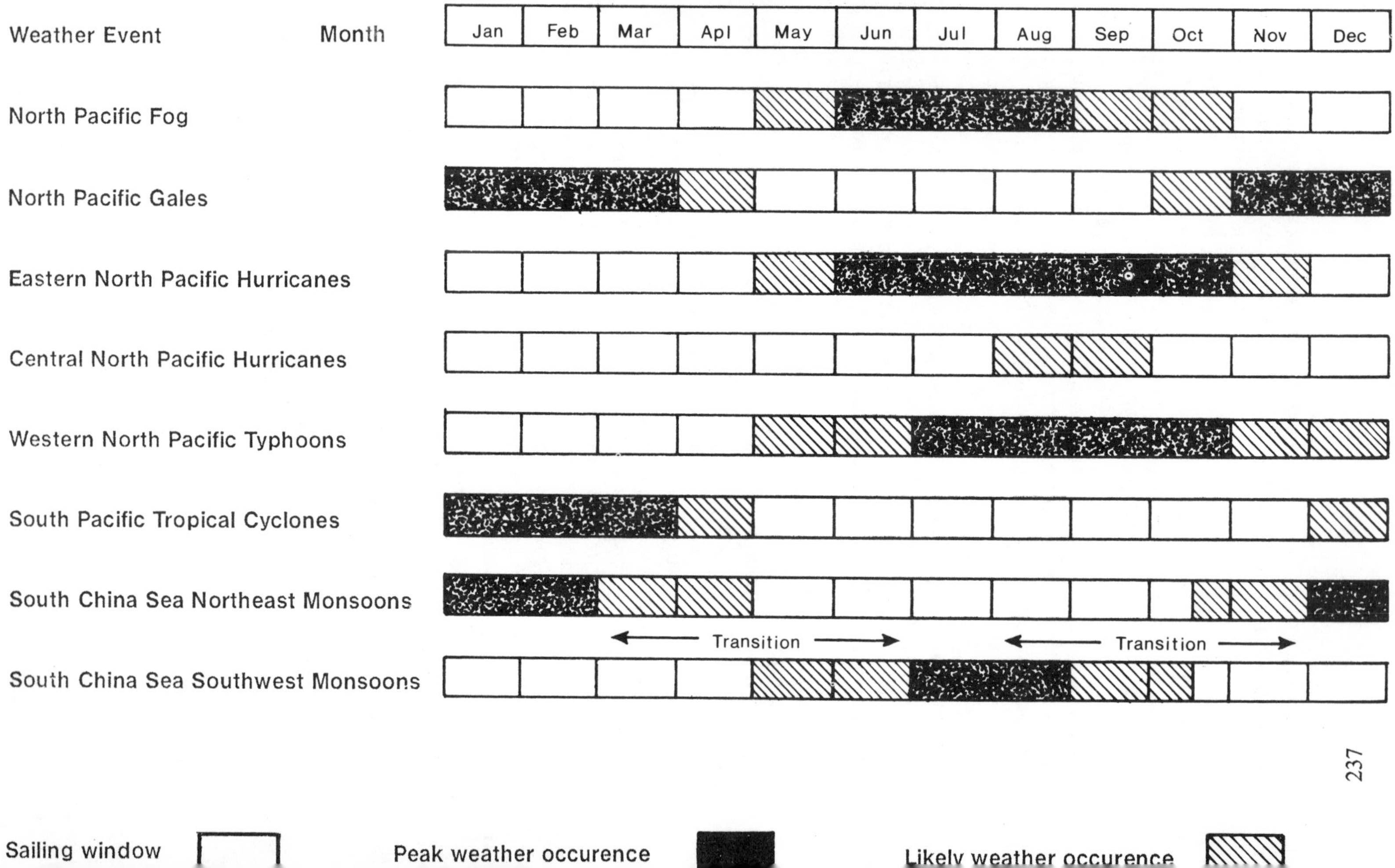

Weather Event	Jan	Feb	Mar	Apl	May	Jun	Jul	Aug	Sep	Oct	Nov	Dec
North Pacific Fog	□	□	□	□	▨	▓	▓	▓	▨	□	□	□
North Pacific Gales	▓	▓	▨	▨	□	□	□	□	□	□	▓	▓
Eastern North Pacific Hurricanes	□	□	□	□	▨	▓	▓	▓	▓	▓	▨	□
Central North Pacific Hurricanes	□	□	□	□	□	□	□	▨	▨	□	□	□
Western North Pacific Typhoons	□	□	□	□	▨	▓	▓	▓	▓	▓	▨	▨
Eastern North Pacific Hurricanes												
South Pacific Tropical Cyclones	▓	▓	▨	□	□	□	□	□	□	□	□	▨
South China Sea Northeast Monsoons	▓	▓	▨	□	□	□	□	□	□	▨	▓	▓
South China Sea Southwest Monsoons	□	□	□	□	▨	▨	▓	▨	▨	□	□	□

Transition ←→ (South China Sea Northeast Monsoons / South China Sea Southwest Monsoons)

Legend:
- □ Sailing window
- ▓ Peak weather occurrence
- ▨ Likely weather occurrence

237

THE DOWNBURST

This phenomenon exists the world over and is a strong vertical downdraft, one so subtle that it went unrecognized for years. Not until a number of landing and takeoff accidents by aircraft were investigated beyond "pilot error" did scientists come to realize that downdrafts near the ground existed and did play havoc with aircraft, trees, structures and boats. They were given the name "downbursts!"

The actual culprit was eventually identified as the horizontal rush of air radially outward from a descending column of air which slowed the aircraft down by as much as 30 to 70 knots. That was enough to put the airplane below stall speed in many cases and cause a crash. At a downburst's higher speed, swaths of trees, shrubs and buildings are blown down, not up-rooted as in a tornado.

Normally we think of winds as air in horizontal motion and that is what most winds are but there are also vertical disturbances to the atmosphere. The more common ones occur over land and are called cyclones and tornados. They are made up of rapidly rising air currents whose low pressure centers and violent peripheral winds cause extreme damage.

The maritime version of a tornado is a waterspout. It is eery to behold and can be quite dangerous if it is a tornadic type that generates along the leading edge of an advancing cold front, squall line or thunderstorm. A second type of waterspout is associated with fair weather and has little of the danger of the tornadic variety but all of its snake-like motion. In general, mariners should limit their waterspout investigations to taking pictures from a distance; the more distant, the safer. Tornados and waterspouts are visible during the day and also show up on radar so they can be avoided.

The downburst that can cause an airplane to lose its airspeed and capsize a boat at sea is larger than a tornado or waterspout. The original and still principal investigator of such weather phenomena is Dr. T. Fujita of the University of Chicago who has published the definitive text on them: "The Downburst," Univ./Chicago, 1985. In his book, Fujita describes downbursts as follows:

"A downburst is a strong downdraft which induces an outburst of damaging winds on or near the ground. Damaging winds, either straight or curved, are highly divergent. Sizes of the downbursts may vary from less than one kilometer to tens of kilometers."

Downbursts are further subdivided into macrobursts or microbursts. Macroburst winds extend in excess of 2½ miles in horizontal distance. They last from 5 to 30 minutes and have winds as high as 134 mph. Microbursts extend less than 2½ miles from the center and may have winds as high as 168 mph.

Downbursts are products of virga in an otherwise clear sky or from anvil or cumulus clouds associated with cold front activity. A roll cloud preced-

ing a cold front can be the precursor of downbursts. The roll cloud under a severe thunderstorm is called "arcus" by the meterologists and at sea it is known as a line squall. Unlike tornados and waterspouts, neither virga nor cloud-induced downbursts are clearly visible to the naked eye, but they can be seen on doppler radar. Generally the virga-induced downburst is without rain while the cloud downburst is immersed in considerable rainfall.

Airplane accidents became the frontline of the downburst investigation because more lives were at stake and the fact that overland there is much more comprehensive reporting of small-scale weather phenomena than over the water. But the maritime problem was not overlooked by the National Weather Service as noted in the "Mariners Weather Log" for Winter, 1987. In that issue, Jerry Nickerson, a marine weather consultant and former National Weather Service employee, described the downburst's role in the sinking of the *Pride of Baltimore* in May 1986 as well as several other sinkings formerly attributed to unknown causes.

Of the *Pride's* sinking he wrote: "Winds jumped (instantaneously) from about 30 knots to as high as 90 knots. Within an estimated 20 seconds the port gunwale and the lower part of the mainsail were in the water. Moments later, the *Pride* was in a full knockdown with the ship on its side. In only 60 to 90 seconds, the hull was flooded and the *Pride* was on its way to the bottom, 3 miles deep."

Such things don't happen only to large training sailing vessels, they can also happen to contemporary recreational sailboats. Robert O'Brien, also writing in the "Mariners Weather Log" (Summer, 1985), recalls his experience in sailing the Santa Cruz 50, *Scotch Mist*, on a Victoria to Maui race. He wrote: "About 2300 a whopper of a squall hits us and the wind goes up to 40 knots apparent. The boat responds by taking off on a screaming plane that seems to last half an hour—probable duration 5 min. We sustained speeds over 18 knots with bursts over 20 and finally a whopping 23 knots. Dave Knottage, who is steering, says in a voice about an octave higher than normal: 'We have too much sail up.' So we shortened down."

Then followed a second squall with a downburst in it: "It lasted for over two hours and with just a mainsail up our speed never dropped below 10 knots and we at times hit 18 knots. Wind speed was in the 40 kn range with gusts to 65 kn true. It was not a pleasant experience .... Although we did not encounter any extreme wave per se, the sea generally became substantially steeper during the whole occurence."

O'Brien goes on to say, "A heavy displacement vessel is more susceptible to this situation than lighter displacement vessels currently being raced. Lighter displacement allows sudden (wind) force to be translated rapidly into acceleration rather than heeling moment. You can still get into trouble, though, and the same recovery techniques (bearing off downwind and freeing the sheets) are applicable."

Downbursts don't last forever and they do not capsize the vessel beyond 90 degrees. A well-found hull closed against the intrusion of

seawater will eventually right itself. The training ships *Pride* (United States), *Marques* (British) and *Active* (Danish) were probably all lost because of open hatches and, possibly, holing of the hulls by loose internal ballast.

Downbursts have been with us since weather was invented, but we didn't recognize them as anything different than a squall. Nor did the boats probably suffer as much from them for in the days of manila lines and cotton sails, sails most likely tore relieving the loads and preventing a complete knockdown. Today's ultra-strong synthetic lines and sails can withstand such downbursts and now the whole boat is put in jeopardy.

— Cruising World

TSUNAMI!

Geologists tell us that the earth is armored with enormous stone slabs called "plates" floating on a denser liquid material of the mantle called "magma." The edges of the plates are constantly being ground away and renewed in a process called "plate tectonics." As the plates drift, they push and pull on the continents, displacing them from previous locations over long stretches of geologic time. This causes humongous accumulations of energy and sudden releases of it; earthquakes are the result.

Nowhere in the world is this more evident than around the rim of the Pacific Ocean—an area alive with volcanoes and seismic activity. There is nothing that shapes the earth's surface more dramatically than earthquakes and nothing creates larger ocean waves than earthquakes and submarine avalanches. This great ocean wave is referred to as a seismic wave; popularly called "tsunami"—a Japanese word meaning "great wave in the harbor" and erroneously called "tidal wave."

The tsunami presents no danger to boats at sea, in fact, it will probably go unnoticed. At sea the 600 mph tsunami wave is but a long period swell, hardly discernible. As the tsunami approaches shallow water, however, it slows and converts speed energy to enormous wave heights.

A U.S. Government publication notes: "Every island and coastal settlement in the Pacific Ocean area is vulnerable to the onslaught of the great waves. Those of 1868 and 1877 devastated towns in northern Chile, and caused death and damage across the Pacific. A series of waves generated

by the eruption and collapse of Krakatoa in 1883 killed more than 36,000 persons in the East Indies. Japan lost 27,000 lives to the wave of 1896 and 1,000 more to that of 1933. There have been hundreds more whose effects were less spectacular but which took many lives and did much damage. As late as 1983, a big earthquake and tsunami hit the west coast of Honshu, the main island of Japan."

The 1946 waves which struck Hawaii are a case in point as are the waves sent out by the 1960 Chilean earthquake. The great Alaskan earthquake's sea waves in 1964 caused damage as far away as California, Chile and Japan.

Warnings of tsunamis now come through a sophisticated warning network that covers the entire Pacific Basin. The Tsunami Warning Center at Ewa Beach, Oahu, Hawaii, maintains a 24 hours-a-day watch on seismological and tidal instruments strategically located throughout the Pacific Basin. When an earthquake of sufficient magnitude occurs to generate a tsunami in the Pacific Ocean, a watch is established in all areas to determine if a tsunami actually has been generated. If it has, a warning is issued to all areas of the potential arrival of a destructive sea wave including the estimated time of arrival.

Twice I have been on the receiving ends of tsunami warnings. In New Zealand, I naively thought I could ride out the wave in the Bay of Islands.

Fishing fleet damage from Tsunami at Seward, Alaska

Luckily, it never developed. Later, in Hawaii, I exercised better judgement and took *Horizon* to sea until the waves passed. They were only 1½ feet. high in the harbor; but they could have been 10 to 20 times that. There is only one safe place for a boat to be when a tsunami strikes and that is in at least 100 fathoms of water. No harbor or breakwater is safe when a tsunami strikes. Warnings will be given from one to four hours ahead of the tsunami's arrival depending on the distance from its origin.

— Sea

TONGA'S CYCLONE SEASON

Tonga lies in the southwest Pacific hurricane region whose normal season is December through April; but it also has been known to have occurrences in May, June and November. The southwest Pacific region is large, however, stretching from French Polynesia to Australia and from the Solomon Islands to New Zealand. Tonga is just a small part of it and, fortunately, not subject to the consistent annual cyclones that seem to hit Fiji and Vanuatu. Nevertheless, there is sufficient activity to make it of concern to cruising sailboats.

In September 1982, the Center for Disaster Studies, James Cook University of North Queensland, Australia, published a comprehensive review of the impact of Cyclone Isaac on the society and economy of the Kingdom of Tonga. It contained the most succinct analysis of historical cyclonic events in Tonga that is available. It drew on Tongan, Australian, New Zealand, Fijian and American sources. There were some enlightening facts presented regarding cyclonic storms in Tonga over the period March 1830 through March 1982. Let me summarize some of the more pertinent points.

First, note that a tropical cyclone (a revolving wind system) comes in different strength levels. It can have steady state winds of gale strength (34 to 47 knots), tropical storm strength (48 to 63 knots) or hurricane strength (64 knots and over). So when we talk about cyclones, we are talking about a wide range of wind speeds. Also note that gusts can increase wind speed sporadically by 25 to 50 percent.

In the 153 years of record keeping, Tonga has been affected by 108 tropical cyclones, or approximately one every 1.4 years. Unfortunately, they come randomly with none some years and as many as three in other years. There is no pattern. This number is slightly more optimistic than that given in the "Mariners Worldwide Climatic Guide to Tropical Storms at Sea" published by the U.S. Navy. It says that the frequency of tropical storms plus hurricanes in the 5° geographic square area that includes Tonga, is one occurrence every 1.1 years. This compares with an overall frequency for the entire southwest Pacific region of one occurrence every 0.8 years. So Tonga is definitely better off than the southwest Pacific in general.

One source of historical data used by the James Cook University suggested that there has been an increase in the numbers of tropical

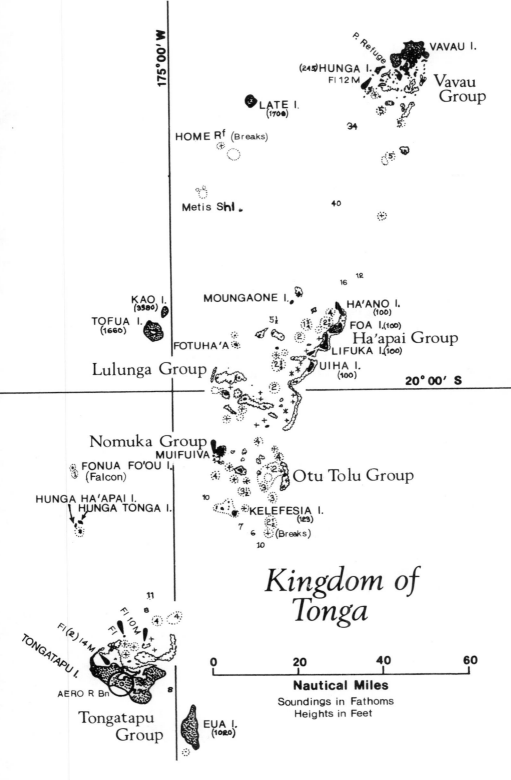

175°00′ W

P. Refuge

VAVAU I.

(245) HUNGA I.
Fl 12 M

Vavau
Group

2 LATE I.
(1700)

34

HOME Rf (Breaks)

5

Metis Shl

40

16 12

KAO I.
(3580)

MOUNGAONE I.

HA'ANO I.
(100)

5½

TOFUA I.
(1660)

FOA I. (100)

2

FOTUHA'A

LIFUKA I. (100)

Lulunga Group

2½

UIHA I.
(100)

20°00′ S

2

Nomuka Group

MUIFUIVA

4

4

FONUA FO'OU I.
(Falcon)

4

2

Otu Tolu Group

HUNGA HA'APAI I.

10

3½

HUNGA TONGA I.

3

KELEFESIA I.
(123)

7 6 (Breaks)

10

*Kingdom of
Tonga*

11

8

Fl 10 M

4 4

Fl (2) 14 M

Fl

TONGATAPU I.

0   20   40   60

Nautical Miles

AERO R Bn

250

8

Soundings in Fathoms
Heights in Feet

Tongatapu
Group

EUA I.
(1020)

cyclones in the overall southwest Pacific in recent decades. The New Zealand Meteorological Service provided the following tropical cyclone data by decade:

1939-1949	58 cyclones
1949-1959	64 cyclones
1959-1969	72 cyclones

I wasn't able to find later years and I hope that the trend has reversed itself. Whether this trend also applies to Tongan waters is not clear since that is too fine-grained an element to uncover at this time.

The same New Zealand source also indicated the following return periods for different intensity tropical cyclones, viz, those with gale force winds (over 34 knots)—3 years; storm force (over 48 knots)—7 years; and hurricane force (over 64 knots)—14 years. (These were described as sustained wind speeds for a ten-minute period over the open sea. Gusts were liable to be 25 to 50 percent higher.)

Prior to Isaac (March 1982), the records show that the last severe cyclone to impact Vava'u was in March 1961, a 21-year interval. The last severe cyclone to hit any of Tonga was Annie, which hit Ha'apai in December 1977, a five year interval.

Although the hurricane season is defined as December through April, there is actually a distribution over many months. The 49 storm force or greater cyclones that affected Tonga from 1923 to 1982 occurred as follows:

Oct.	Nov.	Dec.	Jan.	Feb.	Mar.	Apr.	May	No Record
1	2	8	10	13	7	6	1	1

The Tongan archipelago is a long north-south string of islands and every tropical cyclone does not affect every island equally, if at all. In fact, just the opposite is true. The "preferred path" for tropical cyclones that reach Tonga is from the northwest to the southeast passing generally through the Ha'apai group in central Tonga. Isaac had to be different and pass almost straight down the entire Tonga group of islands, wreaking havoc among all of them. It was, however, the exception.

James Cook University listed the following distribution of geographical areas in Tonga affected by tropical cyclones over 153 years. These will add up to more than the recorded events since some of the cyclones affected more than one geographic area:

Islands to the north	Vava'u	Ha'apai	Tongatapu	E,S, or W of Tonga	All of Tonga	Without specific record
21	20	24	30	18	3	9

This says, historically, that Vava'u has been in the path of only 16 percent of all tropical cyclones that have affected Tonga in 153 years.

Although Vava'u is affected less by cyclones than, say, the Ha'apai or Tongatapu groups, cruising boats tend to wander throughout the islands of Tonga and they have to consider an overall weather picture.

As for Vava'u being a good hurricane haven, it does have high hills surrounding it and a lagoon with good holding ground almost totally enclosed from the sea; the anchorage did not come through the storm force winds of Isaac as well as expected. The one vulnerable area of this harbor is probably Ahanga passage to the east and, since Isaac passed to the east, I suspect this may have been its Achilles heel. Any break in the protective shoreline can be breached by storm surge and waves that accompany a major cyclone. It is not the wind but the waves that ultimately do the damage.

You can see by the rather comprehensive records that tropical cyclones in Tonga (as elsewhere) are erratic in strength, time and path. At best, we can use averages over long periods of time. If you think Tonga is erratic, look at what happened to Tahiti during the infamous 1982/83 El Niño period. Tahiti had not been affected by a hurricane for 22 years and then it was hit by five in a four-month period. The unique situation with Tahiti, though, is that cyclonic occurrences seem to be tied to a bigger problem—the El Niño/Southern Oscillation phenomenon.

I don't think that statistics even as well founded as these, or opinions of experts, are worth a damn to the guy whose boat and dreams lie shattered on a reef due to an unexpected cyclone. He is the one that must make the decision to cruise an area of known cyclonic activity.

Don Coleman's boatyard at Neiafu, Vava'u, Tonga

Each skipper must make his own evaluation of the weather risk no matter where he is sailing, especially when he is sailing in an area of known cyclonic activity during its cyclone season. Nobody else can prescribe his course or assure his weather. In the final analysis, the safety of a cruising boat and crew is in the hands of the skipper.

— Personal letter to a resident of Vava'u

VULCANISM

Is there a connection between vulcanism and cruising? In 1985, the answer was yes and cruising folk should note two events for future reference. The first was the underwater eruption of a volcano at Home Reef in Tongan waters (19° S, 174° 47' W). Even before the eruption, Home Reef was known to break in big seas even though the surrounding waters are 600 fathoms deep. Then, on March 2, 1984, it did more than break—it blew! The eruption plume reached a height of 7 miles and by March 5th a new island had formed. The dimensions of the new cinder island are estimated at 0.8 miles long by 0.3 miles wide and between 100 and 165 feet high. There is a boiling lagoon in the center which is expected to disappear with time.

Volcanoes in Tongan waters are not new. In May 1979, a volcano erupted at Metis Shoal (about 13 miles southeast of Home Reef), producing a cinder island about one-third the size of the new Home Reef island. The Metis Shoal island was named Lateiki by the King of Tonga. Metis Shoal has produced three islands in the past 100 years; but the two previous ones have eroded away.

The chances of your boat being attacked by an erupting volcano are slim indeed; but you might have a problem with the after effects. The Home Reef event spread pumice over a large area. On May 1, almost two months after the eruption, one yacht reported on the Maritime Mobile Net that it was sailing through a patch of pumice about 1 mile in diameter and 2 inches thick. Many boats and ships operating in the Tonga-Fiji-Samoa triangle complained that the floating pumice was so thick that it

clogged their engine water intakes. Think of what that would do to water pumps! Fortunately, no tsunami was generated by the Home Reef eruption.

The second major volcanic event, which appears to be neverending, but occasionally in remission, is at Rabaul, New Britain Island, Papua New Guinea. Volcanologists who have been watching Rabaul believe that should it erupt, it could be a greater cataclysm than that of Mount St. Helens of a few years ago.

Rabaul's Simpson and Matupi Harbors lie in the caldera created by an old eruption that took place about 1,500 years ago in a Krakatoa-like explosion. As late as 1937, a major eruption took place on the western flank of the harbor creating what is now 2,600-foot-high Vulcan Mountain. Center of the current seismic activity is Matupi Island, over which a plume of sulphurous smoke is rising and thickening. Something will give someday. In the meantime, the Volcanological Observatory in the hills above Rabaul keeps a 24 hours-a-day watch on its seis- mological instruments.

Rabaul Harbor and town have been longtime favorites of cruising yachts. Rabaul is a port of entry to Papua New Guinea, and a fairly good provisioning stop. It is one of the best harbors in the world for ships and small craft alike; but it lives under a volcanic threat. Cruising yachts should not tarry long in Rabaul. An eruption would trap and destroy them in Simpson Harbor. Yachts throughout the Pacific should stay alert to the possibility of a tsunami developing as a result of a major earthquake in Rabaul. The whole ocean region south of New Britain into the Solomon Sea is seismically active and a Rabaul event could trigger another earthquake or eruption in the area.

We can only hope that the vulcanologists are wrong on this one.

— Cruising World

Mount Vulcan, Rabaul, Papua New Guinea

247

WHEN CROSSING THE LINE

Ever since cartographers drew a line around the earth creating northern and southern hemispheres, sailors have had to "cross the line" in traveling north and south. The line is invisible, except where drawn on world globes and nautical charts, but pollywogs still search for it in their quest to join the hallowed ranks of shellbacks. On the serious side, though, is the navigator's search for an accurate position. In this region of the world, he must ponder such uncertainties as counter currents, an overhead sun, weather anomalies and, as he penetrates farther into the new hemisphere, a compass reaction called magnetic dip.

The Overhead Sun

When equatorial bound, the time will come that you find the sun overhead and the usual noon sun sight just doesn't work out. At that time the complete navigator resorts to the simple, but not often used, high altitude sight technique.

A high altitude sight taken on a small boat can be the ultimate challenge to the navigator's sextant skill and it can be done. Taking two high altitude sights when the sun is within, say, 3 degrees of its zenith, can give you all the ingredients you need for a mid-day fix—something you cannot get out of an ordinary meridian sun sight. The big difference in sight reduction is the use of a circle of position rather than a Sumner line. (See Bowditch for an example.) Although the sights require more sextant skill than conventional noon sights, the subsequent sight reduction is no more difficult and a lot more satisfying.

My first chance to make a high altitude sun fix was in the 1970 Los Angeles-Tahiti TransPac race. The sun was moving north as we sailed south towards the equator. While the rest of the crew gathered for lunch one day, I took up the challenge of the noon sun fix. Fortunately, the sky was clear and the 48-foot cutter provided a steady sighting platform. The results were just as advertised and well worth the late lunch. All navigators should try this one for satisfaction.

Equatorial Weather

Weather near the equator is not always conducive to taking sights and you may run for days through overcast, squalls and shifting winds. These are the doldrums, where the tradewinds meet. Its significance to the navigator is a probable loss of visibility of the sky for a few days and the need to resort to dead reckoning techniques. The latter requires some knowledge of equatorial surface currents and how to handle them.

Another interesting feature of equatorial weather to keep in mind is that tropical cyclones do not exist near the equator. A beneficial rule of thumb for the navigator to remember when sailing in tropical cyclone regions is to stay near the equator or at least head there when you hear of cyclonic trouble brewing.

Equatorial Currents

Open ocean currents are primarily wind-driven, following the wind patterns of each hemisphere. Water, however, is not as free as the wind to circulate in a three-dimensional manner. Hence, when west-flowing equatorial currents approach leeward land masses, they are redirected north and south and, surprisingly, also back along the equator. This very narrow band of east-flowing water is called the equatorial countercurrent. It is only 50 or so miles in width and resides primarily in the northern hemisphere between 6° and 10° north latitude. Sometimes it is not there at all, as if it submerged and was passing beneath the equatorial currents themselves. Other times it can be very noticeable. It disappears entirely at its eastern and western ends.

If you are crossing the countercurrent, it will warp your track the same as when you cross the Gulf Stream, although in a lesser manner. The navigator of a boat sailing under overcast skies in the ITCZ must make allowances in his dead reckoning for these currents or incur a significant (and embarrassing) error in position.

I recall in the early 1970s, the Seven Seas Cruising Association Commodore's Bulletins carried numerous letters regarding the mysteries of the equatorial countercurrent. Why, boats were even going backwards in light winds! I thought it would be fun to investigate this current as we crossed its estimated latitude from the Pilot Chart. So, on a 1975 passage from Mexico to the Marquesas, I concentrated on getting good celestial fixes as we passed through the region of the countercurrent. With careful celestial sightings and good dead reckoning, I was actually able to track its direction and strength day by day. (The results are illustrated in my book "Sail Before Sunset.")

From that experience, the countercurrent became indelibly etched in my mind years later, when we were returning to Hawaii from Abemama, we deliberately rode the countercurrent for nearly 900 miles staying just north of the equator. It accounted for almost 30 miles per day of our progress which was slow in beating against the light easterlies of the Intertropical Convergence Zone. Without knowledge of the equatorial countercurrent, I would not have chosen this route to Hawaii.

Magnetic Dip

A hemisphere-unique phenomenon is compass card tilt which you will notice as you take your northern hemisphere compass across the line. It is a result of the earth's magnetic lines of force having an inclination that varies from zero at the magnetic equator (horizontal) to near 90° at the magnetic poles (vertical). Since the magnet in a compass tends to align itself with these lines, they significantly influence compass operation.

First, as these lines deviate from the horizontal, they diminish the north-seeking ability of the compass. Second, the compass card tends to tilt in aligning itself with the curving lines of force—in the extreme causing the pivot to bind. The former we can do nothing about except resort to a

gyro compass when at high latitudes. The tilting of the compass card, however, can be corrected during construction.

Manufacturers of quality compasses produce two models—one adjusted for the northern hemisphere and one for the southern hemisphere. Each is magnetically balanced to minimize card tilt for that hemisphere. This is not evident simply by looking at a compass, you have to ask. If you do most of your sailing in one hemisphere, get a compass corrected for that hemisphere's magnetic dip.

How big a problem is magnetic dip? That depends on the freedom of the compass card to tilt. My Ritchie Globemaster, made for the northern hemisphere, sits level in Hawaii, but in New Zealand it had a noticeable southern tilt. There was no evidence, however, that it was ever binding. If I were to do all of my sailing in the southern hemisphere, I would surely prefer looking at a card that was level.

Other Equatorial Concerns

There are still other problems for the navigator to consider when crossing the line. One is the obvious, but often forgotten, change of north-south designations of latitude. Another is the change in procedure for determining zenith distance in the noon sun sight. Failure to incorporate these changes can negate otherwise good sight reductions. For the northern hemisphere navigator, there is also the loss of Polaris as a latitude determinant when sailing out of the northern hemisphere. Nothing like it exists in the Southern Hemisphere.

— Ocean Navigator

CHAPTER 9

NOTES ON PACIFIC CRUISING

"When sharing an anchorage with a handsome yacht which we know has found her way across the oceans to faraway places, Susan (my wife) and I usually row over to have a closer look, and if there happens to be someone on deck we probably make a complimentary remark. How pleased we then are if he proves to be the owner and says 'Come Aboard', for such an invitation will give us the opportunity not only to examine the details on deck and aloft and the general arrangement below, but perhaps a chance to hear the ideal impressions, practices and experiences of another voyager; the methods of navigation he uses; his procedure in heavy weather; how he makes a living as he goes; what his thoughts are on compasses, flags, other people's children, writing letters, port officials, yacht clubs, self-steering systems, the environment, the Panama Canal . . . There is a lot that we would like to know, and his answers may give us much to think and talk about, and perhaps even incorporate, when we return to our own vessel."

— Eric Hiscock, "Come Aboard"

HITCHHIKING THROUGH PARADISE

Two of my "Pacific Tidings" readers had asked me how to get on a cruising boat crew for which I gave them these suggestions: First you check your local marinas for leads on boats headed out to the Pacific. Read bulletin boards and classified ads in boating publications. Talk to everyone you can. Seek out the mainland ports from which boats depart and let it be known that you are available. Perseverance will win.

If you want to gamble a little, fly out to cruising nodal points such as Honolulu, Papeete, Pago Pago, Suva, Noumea, Honiara, Whangarei, Guam and the like. That's where crew changes take place and you can simply walk the docks asking who is going where. The secret of the whole thing is to be in the right place at the right time since cruising tends to be somewhat seasonal as to where boats are at any given time.

Here are some typical examples of migration patterns:

San Diego, California	October to December to the south
La Paz, Mexico	December to April to the south and west
Honolulu, Hawaii	March to May to the south and west
Honolulu, Hawaii	June to August to the mainland
Papeete, Tahiti	June to August to the west
Papeete, Tahiti	May to June to the north
Pago Pago, American Samoa	August and September to the west
Suva, Fiji, and Noumea, New Caledonia	October and November to the west and south
Suva, Fiji, and Noumea, New Caledonia	May to the east
Whangarei, New Zealand	April and May going any direction
Guam, Mariana Is.	January to March to the east, west and south. May and June to the north.

— Cruising World

Vegetables at market, Papeete, Tahiti

252

GETTING ALONG IN OCEANIC CULTURES

Differences in cultures can be pretty subtle and it is a wise cruiser who tries to blend in with the local people during his stay on an island. Let me give you some representative examples from around Oceania.

Tahiti

French Polynesia is the most visited of South Seas islands and it has its own cultural personality. Some differences exist in cultures between the four island groups that make up French Polynesia, but the following guidelines on getting along in Tahiti can help you through all of the islands:

- There is no tipping in Tahiti and it can be insulting to a Tahitian to offer him a tip.
- Tahitians should not be encouraged to drink liquor, wine or beer which are expensive in relation to their income.
- Tahitian natural medicine practices should not be ridiculed. Their herbal cures kept them healthy long before the Europeans showed up. However, most Western diseases should be treated by modern medicines.
- Tahitians are generally reserved and wait for the visitor to set the mood of the meeting. If you show friendliness, they will respond with warmth. If you are demanding and arrogant, you will miss the spirit of Tahiti.
- If you are fortunate enough to be invited to dine with Tahitians, remember that their menus will be different from yours. Breakfast is usually fresh French bread and coffee. Lunch is the main meal built around hot meat and fish dishes prepared in a number of ways greatly different from what you are used to. Supper is usually leftovers from the noon meal.
- The Tahitian work ethic differs from the European in that Tahitians are not driven by financial greed or the amassing of material wealth for show. They work when they need to and not just to accumulate wealth. (It is said that the Chinese do all the work and the Tahitians have all the fun.)

— Sea

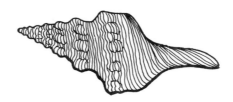

253

SAMOA

Although the Samoas are politically divided, the people are of one stock and continue a common heritage. They are among the last remaining true Polynesians and they steadfastly cling to their Samoan culture and traditions. This is called "Fa'a Samoa." it means "the Samoan Way." Fa'a Samoa has kept Samoans strongly nationalistic and cautious about changes that might threaten the traditional structure of their lives. Visitors should consider the following:

- Samoans revel in speech-making. When entering a home, expect a formal speech of welcome and be prepared to respond with a speech of equal formality.
- Oral communications are important in the Samoan culture and respect for the visitor often causes Samoans to give answers which they think the visitor wants to hear.
- When speaking, do not gesture with the hands. If standing, stand still and do not sway back and forth, for to do so indicates contempt or anger.
- Visitors to Samoan homes should not enter until mats have been put in place. Leave shoes outside and sit cross-legged on the mats. It is impolite to stretch the legs or point the feet at any other person. If a sitting posture other than cross-legged is needed, then the legs and feet should be covered with a mat.
- Personal belongings are felt to be for sharing and should freely be offered to others if admired. Gift-giving is important and appreciation of one received should be vocally expressed and followed up with a reciprocal gift.
- If offered food, the guest should partake of a little even though not hungry .
- Meals are usually eaten without utensils. To lick fingers is impolite and bowls of water are provided for washing the hands. Compliments on the meal are greatly appreciated.
- Samoan dress is conversative. Men wear lava lavas or trousers with a shirt. Women wear long dresses, arms covered and never pants or slacks except as athletic dress.
- The Samoan hierarchal order dominates and permission from a "matai" (chief) will smooth the way of the visitor in enjoying Samoa. It is "Fa'a Samoa" to be respectful to your Samoan hosts.

— Unpublished Note

Serving lunch, Western Samoa

TONGA

Tonga is the biggest paradox in the Pacific. While it conducts its business, communications and foreign policy in a modern manner, it sticks to some pretty traditional customs as far as its social, religious and homelife practices are concerned. These are people to be admired and the best way for a visitor to get along with them is to respect their customs and join in their way of life. Let me offer a few pointers on getting along in Tonga:

- Conservative dress is the most obvious requirement for the visitor.
- Women should not wear short skirts, low-necked dresses or bathing suits in any public area, street or gathering place. Pants are not considered proper women's dress. Men may wear walking shorts and must always wear a shirt; in fact it is against the law for a man not to wear a shirt in a public place. At formal gatherings, it is tie, coat, long pants (or lava lava), shoes and socks. Long hair on men is not acceptable.
- Tongans are warm, friendly and jovial people but they do not display affection in public. Shaking hands and a verbal greeting is the usual way of meeting people and it is not improper to call a person by his or her first name.
- Speechmaking is not a Tongan trait. Tongans like to receive compliments but they hesitate in giving compliments. It is sometimes difficult to establish conversational rapport with them in a group meeting as they tend to be passive.

• Eating has its own social restrictions. Do not eat out on the street—that goes for ice cream cones and candy bars. Also do not eat or drink while standing.

• Sunday is a day of rest in Tonga. It is improper, if not illegal, even to play or go swimming on Sunday.

• Tonga is a constitutional monarchy with a king and nobles. There are no political parties and the people have great respect for their nobility. Do not criticize their government, traditions or society. They like it the way it is and I think you will too.

• Tipping is not encouraged in Tonga. As in most of Polynesia, the Tongans consider it a privilege to give service to a visitor.

— Sea

Street scene, Neiafu, Vava'u, Tonga. Note conservative dress

POHNPEI

Cruising yachts should attempt to avoid the "ugly American" image when visiting the low-keyed islands of the Pacific in order to preserve the warm welcome given to yachts by the islanders. Although common sense can guide you much of the time, each island group has some unique cultural aspects of its life which should be observed. Following are suggestions on getting along in Pohnpei:

• Don't appear unexpectedly in a Pohnpean village or gathering. Have a local person introduce you to the ranking chief and the other prominent villagers.

• Pohnpean women often go topless in rural areas. Don't make anything of it and do not take pictures of them.

• Short shorts or bikinis are improper female attire in town because they expose the thighs. A wraparound skirt is a handy item of dress for a woman when going ashore.

• Almost all land is privately owned. Walking across the land is permissible, but a picnic requires permission of the owner. Do not pick fruit because all trees are private property.

- Be generous with time allowances as Pohnpei's pace is leisurely.
- Keep your cool when dealing with Micronesians in general. A flare of temper only increases resistance. Try another tack when communications do not seem to be making headway.
- Pohnpeans will not show open disapproval if you violate their social codes, but it will hinder your stay.
- The Pohnpean word for greeting and salutation is "kaselehlia". It is used much as the word "aloha" in the Hawaiian language.
- Nan Madol is still sacred ground to the Pohnpeans, so tread respectfully in the ruins.
- The chief (Nahnmwarki) of the district of Madolenihmw, where Nan Madol is located, is the senior chief of the island and lives on Temwen Island. When passing in sight of his residence, stay seated in the boat to show respect.

— Cruising World

Picking pepper, Pohnpei

PAPUA NEW GUINEA

Papua New Guinea spans the ages. In some places it is not far removed from the Stone Age, while in others it is as modern as jet aircraft and high-tech electronics can make it. The cultural diversity of such a country carries with it social customs and protocol that are every bit as interesting as the people themselves. Let me give you a number of Emily Post guidelines to getting along in Papua New Guinea:

- Social tradition in some villages call for the women to walk different footpaths; they may not be permitted to witness certain initiation ceremonies or to enter spirit houses. Visitors should try to understand these local customs.
- In some areas, taking pictures of a person is taboo, in others it may be done for a charge. Ask before photographing individuals.
- Niuguineans will show a deference to Caucasians, but do not take advantage of it since you are a guest in their country.
- White women should not travel alone at night. Every society has its rascals.
- If you want to walk off the beaten path, ask permission and advice from the local provincial government office; they may know something that you don't.
- If offered a ride when hitchhiking along a road, consider giving the driver a pack of cigarettes as a goodwill gesture.
- Don't pick fruit indiscriminately; it belongs to someone else.
- Don't be afraid to bargain when buying artifacts in the villages. Always ask for the "number two" price.
- Never step over a baby. Superstition says that it will not grow anymore.
- Proper men's dress at a club is shorts, knee socks and a light shirt.
- Bikinis and super-tight shorts are frowned on away from swimming pools.
- Signs of affection, including hand-holding, are frowned on in public.
- Don't tip in Papua New Guinea. To give service to a stranger is an honor in Melanesian culture.
- If you show exceptional interest in a privately owned object, the Niuguinean may feel obligated to give it to you at some loss to himself.
- Be patient with the local people, the pace of life is more leisurely than in European communities, which is one of the reasons you are going there.

— Cruising World

BLACK PEARLS

History often repeats itself and the South Seas pearling industry is going through another development cycle. In the late 1800s and early 1900s, pearl diving in the lagoons of the Pacific was a big business. Native divers would free dive to 80 or 90 feet, descending with a big rock for ballast and ascending with natural pearl oysters for the trader. It was always the trader who got the pearls because he had the sale outlet for them.

Pearling activities diminished as the beds were stripped and native divers became wary of the physical dangers of such deep free diving. Then came World War II and the natives forsook pearling completely in favor of eight-to-five jobs. Forgotten were the pearl beds of the atolls and Nature, in her own way, began to replenish the crop. Recently, a 17-carat natural black pearl (diameter ½ inch) was found in 3 feet of water at Penrhyn Atoll in the Cook Islands. The finder is holding out for A$30,000. (Ordinary black pearls sell for A$50 to A$5,000.) Island entrepreneurs have found, that cultured pearls also have a good market even if the quality is not as high. Japanese pearl specialists, working for the famous cultured pearl company of Mikimoto, implant black oysters in the atolls and in return receive 20 percent of the cutlured pearl market price.

Many Pacific cruisers' favorite atolls, such as Ahe, Manihi and Penrhyn are active pearling sites. The black pearl has become an economic resource for the islanders. Black pearl oysters are fragile creatures and they don't like to be disturbed by anchors. Just sailing over a shallow bed of the giant black-lipped oyster will disturb its natural functions. To say the least, islanders are very suspicious of boats with scuba gear on board. Interestingly, the islanders have come to suspect that interisland trading vessels may be among the worst poachers of their livelihood.

A cruising boat with scuba gear can create a lot of goodwill when properly used. Elmer Adams of the Cal-46 *Summer Breeze* helped the people of Raraka Atoll in the Tuamotus set pearl culture frames in 60 feet of water. Adams noted that the pearl beds are usually left unmarked to protect them from poachers. He advises that when you arrive in an atoll lagoon, get anchoring directions from the local people so you don't damage a hidden oyster crop.

We cruisers have had an easy time of moving around the Pacific, but there are signs that things are tightening up. Some atoll governments are restricting boats to specific anchorages and not allowing them to wander freely in the lagoon. Don't feel harassed if you cannot move freely about in someone else's backyard. After all, there is a need for a local economy and black pearls are becoming an increasingly important part of it.

— Cruising World

OF POLLYWOGS AND SHELLBACKS

While we pity the poor navigator who has to guide our vessel across this region of eccentric hospitality, the captain has the task of preparing the crew for presentation to King Neptune, Ruler of the Deep.

This "cleansing" ceremony was originally a superstitious rite having its beginning in French ships in the 16th century. At first the rites were performed when a ship rounded a major cape for the first time. By the 17th century, the French had extended the rite to sailors crossing the equator for the first time. The English picked up the practice in the 1700s and even the exalted Captain James Cook deferred to maritime superstition on equatorial crossing.

Although by Cook's time paganism had given way to Christianity, sailing unknown seas still evoked trepidation in sailors. They were eager to take all possible precautions to appease the ancient god of the sea, Neptune. Humiliation and physical discomfort afforded by the rite of passage across the line were a small price to pay for gaining Neptune's blessing.

In Cook's day, the ship was hove-to, weather permitting, and the candidates hoisted outboard on the main yard and allowed to drop 35 feet into the ocean — a real trial for most sailors couldn't swim. Those whose rank, dignity or personality got in the way of the fun, such as the captain and distinguished supercargo, had to pay a forfeit, usually in the way of bottles of spirits to fuel the post-dunking party. Today ships no longer heave-to in order to splash the candidate; instead they use a tub or bucketsful of salt water for the cleansing.

The original crossing-the-line ceremony was a serious affair, but today it is an event to break the boredom of long passages. Since it takes place at the equator, the vessel is sometimes becalmed and a bit of horseplay is welcome to relieve the monotony of drifting on an oily sea under a baking sun. Sailors consider it a test of the man to endure the hazing and the candidates have to be good sports or suffer the consequences for the rest of the passage.

The cleansing ceremony cannot take place without a King Neptune attired in seaweed and piped on board with a conch shell. The lowly pollywogs grovel on the deck at his feet as they are presented by Davy Jones, the senior shellback present. In the old days, Mercury was the aide to Neptune and insured that proper protocol was followed, but with so many boats crossing the equator these days, Davy Jones, Neptune's scribe, handles most of the protocol. Other shellbacks present act as sideboys (bears and nymphs).

Lacking any shellbacks aboard, it is up to the captain to perform the ceremony and then receive his just deserts for daring to bring his vessel into King Neptune's dommain with such an ill-chosen crew. The captain throws a good party to atone for his sins.

The cleansing of pollywogs often includes searching for the "line" and,

On board outhor's *Horizon*, looking for the line when crossing the equator

when found, lifting it over the vessel; the eating of "fish," usually a devilish concoction of the cook; a liberal dousing of sea water; making a tithe to Neptune with a coin from the last port of call; and posting a letter at King Neptune's mailbox which, in essence, is putting a note in a bottle recording the event and setting it adrift at the equator.

There can be any number of variations in the ceremony tailored to the personality of the vessel. For instance, on Irving Johnson's *Yankee*, pollywogs were "tattooed" by the shellbacks with iodine swabs. On John Guzzwell's *Treasure*, the event was planned before leaving port and a supply of outrageous second hand clothing was procured to adorn Neptune and his followers. *Treasure's* ceremony included sea water drenchings and shaving cream attacks. As Dorothy Guzzwell wrote: "For one brief flash in time, a speck on the planet was utterly happy."

Once a sailor has paid his debt to Neptune, he receives an elaborate certificate to attest to that fact and to save him from undergoing a repeat cleansing in the future.

The 180th Meridian

Cartographers have drawn and quartered the earth by creating the equator and the prime meridian including its antipodal counterpart, the 180th meridian. The 180th meridian is considerably younger than the equator. It didn't officially exist until after Harrison had invented the chronometer (about 1735) and Greenwich had been selected as the prime meridian (1884).

The 180th meridian is the most unique of all meridians for it establishes the dates of the two hemispheres. Crossing it to the west, you move into tomorrow and crossing it to the east, you move into yesterday.

It is up to the navigator to keep this straight or he will get the wrong data from his Nautical Alamanac. The International Date Line, however, does not rigorously follow the 180th meridian and some countries near it arbitrarily select their own date. Tonga, for instance, uses a time difference of -13 hours and its slogan is "Where time begins." Who can argue?

Once the 180th meridian was identified, it rapidly became a status symbol for sailors who crossed it. They were awarded the Order of the Golden Dragon.

The most prized of all line crossing awards, however, is the Order of the Royal Dragon or Golden Shellback. A sailor qualifies for this when he crosses the equator right at the 180th meridian. Since few boats sail in those waters, you won't see many Golden Shellback certificates on display.

Although crossing the line can be a serious problem for the navigator, a little horseplay accompanying it can break the tedium of a long passage. After you have returned home, breaking out King Neptune's certificate (or an equivalent in authenticity, a wallet-size card) at gatherings will make you the life of the party, for how many of your friends have crossed the line and can prove it?

— Ocean Navigator

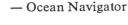

SEARCH AND RESCUE

A person has a right to be adventurous as long as it does not impact on others. Clearly, a mysterious disappearance does affect others—family, friends and taxpayer-supported organizations whose duty it is to protect life and property. There is both a humanitarian and a monetary side to a mysterious disappearance whether on land or sea.

Ocean cruising is the last refuge for persons who want to make their mark in life free of the restraints of civilization that are hemming in the masses. A person sets forth on a cruise with little bother to others and few favors asked—just the freedom to do it on his own. He realizes the dreams of many, which are consummated by so few.

Thousands of people every year seek out cruising as a way to free themselves of the fetters of civilization for a short time. Most return to society with a greater appreciation of life. Many are so taken by the casual cruising life that they never return to society, but seem to just keep on cruising. A few never return.

The year 1985 was a particularly bad year for cruising boats in the Pacific, five were posted missing. The boat *Mainstay*, completing a circumnavigation, departed the Galapagos Islands for Nuku Hiva in the

Marquesas in April 1985 and never arrived. The American yacht *Hummingbird* departed Pago Pago for Honolulu in May 1985 and never arrived. In June 1985, Bill Dunlop on *Wind's Will* started a singlehanded passage from Aitutaki, Cook Islands, to Australia and never arrived. A singlehander on *Antares* was due in Huahine, French Polynesia, in July 1985 from Honolulu, but was posted missing when weeks overdue. (He showed up after 58 days having broken a headstay along the way.) The Cal Cruising 46 yacht *Azilia* went missing on a passage from Rarotonga, Cook Islands, to New Zealand in October 1985.

There are lessons to be learned which may prevent you from being posted missing. The first thing to recognize is that the Pacific Ocean is vast in all directions. It measures 11,000 miles east to west and 9,000 miles north to south. There are 64 million square miles of it, with another six million square miles of adjoining seas. Approximately 30 million square miles of it lie within the tropics, where we do most of our cruising. A boat is but an infinitesimal speck in that vastness.

If you don't believe that the Pacific is large, consider this: *Marara* went missing for seven months and was seen by no one in all that time. Initially she must have drifted west with the south equatorial current, then found its way into the equatorial countercurrent and was drifting east at a speed of 35 miles per day when found. Had it drifted through the Tokelau and Phoenix Islands? And maybe others? Why had nobody seen it in seven months of drifting?

Just what are your chances of being found if you do need assistance? Good, if searchers have some idea of where to start looking, otherwise, from poor to impossible. But aren't there other cruising boats out there? Why can't they spot you? On the majority of my Pacific passages, I did not see another boat, ship or airplane until I closed on land. You must remember that the curvature of the earth, high waves and swells, 12 hours of daily darkness and rain all diminish your chances of being seen by another vessel.

Your chances of being found are better if you are a ham radio operator and have checked in with one of the maritime nets on a regular basis. That provides a positive starting point in time and place for a search in case your boat is posted missing. Further, the net will have some idea of your sailing intentions, a description of the boat and crew and an indication of their ability to hang on in an emergency. Not every skipper, though, has made the effort to get his license as part of his boat's insurance policy. What then?

Well, your EPIRB will work, won't it? Yes—if you have one and if the battery is fresh. My information indicates that less than half of the cruising boats in the Pacific carry an EPIRB and practically none carry one in the life raft.

One set of EPIRB listening posts is the airplane flying overhead. At 37,000-foot altitude it can provide a listening coverage of 166,000 square

miles—assuming perfect propagation and good receiving equipment, but is there an airplane in the vicinity to receive your EPIRB's chirping? That is another problem.

The Los Angeles-to-Honolulu air route probably has the greatest concentration of air traffic (military and civilian) over the Pacific. There are an estimated 75 commercial flights daily between Los Angeles and Honolulu, but how close is your position to their flight paths? Other flight paths like the Papeete-to-Honolulu route are flown less frequently, only 6 to 10 flights per week, so your chances of being within range of an active flight path are greatly diminished.

There is a 24-hour listening post in the sky, however, thanks to the space programs. It is called SARSAT/COSPAS. (SARSAT is an acronym for the United States Search and Rescue Satellite-Aided Tracking Project and COSPAS is the English phonetic spelling of the Russian acronym for its Space Project for Searching for Vessels and Aircraft in Distress.) SARSAT/COSPAS satellites operate in polar orbit at about 600 miles altitude. Three of the satellites are Russian and two are American.

The SARSAT/COSPAS sentinels can reach out for EPIRB signals as far as 1,800 miles on each side of their ground tracks with reasonable accuracy. With diminished accuracy, they occasionally can receive signals from even greater distances. As with all navigation fixes on earth, it takes two pieces of information to pinpoint the EPIRB's chirp. That is accomplished with two passes of a satellite occurring anywhere from 45 seconds to 2½ hours apart.

The value of an EPIRB and the SARSAT/COSPAS system was amply demonstrated when the 38-foot sailboat *Cherokee* ran into rudder trouble on a passage from Honolulu to Bellingham, Washington. Five satellite passes picked up the EPIRB's persistent chirping and pinpointed its location within five miles. Soon a Coast Guard C-130 airplane was on its way and two ships were diverted to the scene via the AMVER (Voluntary Automated Mutual Assistance Vessel Rescue) program. While the boat could not be saved, the crew was rescued and returned to Portland, Oregon.

Although SARSAT/COSPAS gives worldwide coverage, it depends on a real time down link to relay the distress data to earth stations and therein lies our Pacific problem. Worldwide, there are 10 "local user terminals" (LUT), but only three of them service any part of the Pacific. (A fourth operated by Russia covers the far northwest corner of the Pacific where few cruising boats operate.)

The present LUTs are at Kodiak, Alaska; Point Reyes, California; and Scott Air Force Base, Illinois. If you draw effective listening circles of about 2,200 miles radius from these bases, you get segments of the three circles overlapping in the northeast quadrant of the Pacific with Hawaii on the edge. That leaves three-fourths of the Pacific without active SARSAT/COSPAS coverage. Since the most popular cruising grounds are west and south of Hawaii, the Pacific cruiser can expect to be out of

bounds of SARSAT/COSPAS coverage most of the time. His EPIRB coverage will only be that provided by airplanes.

Future SARSAT/COSPAS developments will include LUTs in New Zealand and Australia plus the addition of new technology in the form of a 406 mHz frequency EPIRB which will allow the satellites to store EPIRB distress signal data and then read it out when interrogated by a ground station, effectively making worldwide coverage with only short delays. Of course, to take advantage of this new rescue monitor, boats will have to carry an EPIRB having the new frequency, but that will be a small price to pay for having a new watchdog in the sky. Since it will only react when you activate your EPIRB, it will not be an intrusion on your sailing freedom—only a helping hand when asked.

Lt. Cdr. Phil Dyer, Public Affairs Officer, 14th Coast Guard District, Honolulu, says: "Having overdue boats is a common occurrence. Information is almost always sketchy in the early going of the search and often gets worse when we talk to different groups of family and friends left on the beach. Usually the information conflicts on the facts we need to know to initiate a search. In many cases, basic information on the description of the boat, its equipment and knowledge of the skipper and crew varies tremendously. The next step is trying to determine where and when the boat left, its intended course, speed and next port of call. A lack of or conflicting information makes search pattern planning impossible when you have such a huge area as the Pacific Ocean."

Let's be optimistic and assume that your EPIRB's chirping has been heard by either an airplane or satellite and your position is relatively well determined. What then? It depends on where you are. If you are near shipping lanes, it is entirely possible that a ship can be diverted to your aid. If not, then the Coast Guard may dispatch an airplane to seek you out, but once again, the vastness of the Pacific Ocean enters the picture. With a firm known position for the vessel in distress, a C-130 aircraft could fly directly to it with emergency equipment—pumps, food, medical supplies, life rafts, etc., and airdrop them to the vessel in distress. However, it can't lend a helping hand on the surface or even slow down to pick up survivors by any technique. That is a job for ships. If the Coast Guard has found you and the weather doesn't deteriorate, chances are good to excellent that you can be rescued by a ship. It may take days, so plan on hanging in there.

At a search altitude of 1,500 feet and flying at 210 knots, the C-130 crew can visually examine a 14,000-square-mile area in one sortie. That may seem like a lot, but it is a mere drop in the bucket compared with the Pacific's 64 million square miles. Worse still is the case where the distressed vessel is not found in the initial search pattern. Subsequent patterns will then be at greater distances requiring more fuel for transit and less fuel for the low altitude search. The situation never gets better, only worse.

In addition to the impracticality of mounting searches based on dubious position data, is the exorbitant cost of searching. It is estimated that the taxpayers' cost for the *Marara* search and recovery was over $580,000 for the C-130 aircraft and the Cutter *Sassafras*. That makes the posted reward money of $40,000 look like petty cash.

The 14th Coast Guard District, which handles the Central and Western Pacific areas plus Samoa, responds to 900 SAR incidents a year saving as many as 150 lives and over $45 million worth of property. While many of these are near-shore incidents, a large number involve vessels in distress on the high seas. On average, there is one overdue vessel a month reported year after year. *Marara* was one, others are sailing and fishing vessels, mostly small. Vessels become overdue with distressing regularity in this large ocean.

The bottom line is that if a missing vessel is to be given aid, it first has to be located and that starts with the missing vessel itself. The skipper must have provided some hint as to its whereabouts by a float plan, radio communication or an EPIRB.

But wouldn't it be wiser to ensure against the need for rescue in the first place by preparing yourself and your boat in advance for all eventualities? Learn your seamanship, study the weather patterns and take appropriate action when it turns bad. Avoid hurricanes. Buy yourself good insurance in the form of quality gear for the boat, emergency equipment like pumps and rerigging tools, long-term provisions, emergency medical gear, a good life raft with an EPIRB and get yourself a general ham radio operator's license. If you are smart enough to get the money and free time to go cruising, then you are also smart enough to pass the simple amateur radio tests.

Lt. Terry Walsh, Search and Rescue Coordinator for the Joint Rescue Center, 14th Coast Guard District, Honolulu, says: "The most important survival equipment doesn't come with your life raft, it comes in your head. Being a survivor is a 'mind set' you establish ahead of time. It's 99 percent being prepared. You can only do so much with the remaining one percent of time and effort, which usually is done in moments of terror."
—Cruising World

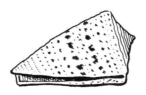

POSTED MISSING

The time to think about the unthinkable is before you start on your cruise. It is when you are outfitting your boat and getting ready for that adventure of a lifetime that you need to inventory your preparedness for the unthinkable possibility of being "Posted Missing." Along with your other considerations of medical problems, fire, grounding and hurricanes, give some thought to a mysterious disappearance. Why? Because it can and does happen and the people you leave behind are faced with a traumatic predicament.

Take the case of Manning Eldridge, 42, a singlehander from California who, after two years of sailing in the Pacific, went missing on a passage from Papeete to Honolulu. He cleared his boat, *Marara*, with the Papeete Port Captain on January 8, 1987, but never arrived in Honolulu. Relatives reported him overdue on February 15th. It was believed that he was heading for Kiritimati (Christmas Island) with a stop at Caroline Island along the way, but someone else thought he was sailing via Rangiroa Atoll to get his easting.

The French searched their corner of the Pacific to no avail. The U.S. Coast Guard made a comprehensive communications check using telephone, marine radio, ham nets, HydroPacs and other two-way radio systems to scour all possible landing places north of the equator. An initial air search was made from Kiritimati to Honolulu, but to no avail. In the meantime, worried relatives and friends were trying other means to locate him, including posting a $40,000 reward for information. No takers. And then the story turns bizarre.

It started out as just another day for the Korean fishing vessel *Neptune 101* searching for increasingly scarce fish for the canneries at Pago Pago. She had reached a position 810 miles north northeast of Pago Pago on July 25, 1987, when the crew saw a floating apparition on the horizon. These waters near the equator are rarely visited by other boats for it is hot, humid and without much wind.

The crew gathered at the rail and chattered in their native tongue trying to make sense out of the apparition. It appeared to be a sailboat wallowing in the waves, with sails shredded and loose rigging slapping the mast as the boat rolled rythmically in the troughs of the waves. No sign of life could be seen through binoculars. It appeared to be a floating derelict. *Neptune 101* warily circled the apparition, looking for signs of life, calling out to anyone on board. No response only the gentle lapping of water.

Paint was seen to be peeling from the hull and rust was streaking the once proud topsides of this derelict sloop. The portlights in the cabin trunk were closed as were the hatches. Lifelines drooped over bent stanchions. The stern pulpit was wrenched loose, but still hung tenaciously to the deck as if to avoid that final 2000 fathom plunge to the bottom. The mainsail boom had been wrenched free of the mast by some giant hand and lay tangled with sail and lines on the portside deck. Only the vacant

Abandoned S/V *Marara* at 1° 07' S, 165° 38' W on 7-26-87

cockpit looked unmarred. On the foredeck a dinghy was lashed down in an inverted position. Everything said that this derelict was once a proud sailing vessel, but now . . . . . . ?

Neptune 101 closed in on the sloop for a close look. Peering under the main hatch, whose vertical bin boards were the only cabin closure not in place, a scene of horror greeted Korean eyes. Bones, once the skeletal frame of a human being, were sloshing loosely about the interior while a multitude of cockroaches and surface dwelling sea crabs scurried about in search of food. This boat was a 20th century Flying Dutchman destined to sail eternally on Pacific waters had it not been for the chance sighting by a sharp lookout on *Neptune 101*.

Superstition and fear seized the crew. They shied away from boarding the boat or taking it in tow. A primitive reaction that may have cost them a $40,000 reward. Instead, *Neptune 101* contacted the U.S. Coast Guard Liaison Office at Pago Pago describing their find. As best they could decipher the name on the transom, it said *Marara*. That struck a bell with the Coast Guard Liaison Officer. He remembered a missing vessel report on a California sailboat which had departed Papeete, January 8th, bound for Honolulu but never arrived. Could this be it?

Early the next day, a long range Coast Guard search and rescue C-130 airplane from Honolulu flew over the drifting sailboat and verified that it was the *Marara*. Photographs taken from a mast-high flyby later showed it to have all the characteristics of the missing 41-foot sloop even though the name was a blur in the picture.

Normally, a derelict would be sunk on the spot as a hazard to navigation, but the *Marara* contained human remains. For humanitarian reasons,

the Coast Guard dispatched the Cutter *Sassafras* from Honolulu to tow the *Marara* back for positive identification of the skeletal remains aboard. It was a long tow at a maximum towing speed of 5 knots. On August 14th, the sloop *Marara* finally reached her original destination of Honolulu, but in the tow of a big Coast Guard buoy tender.

It took the Honolulu Medical Examiner only a short time to verify that the remains were those of the intrepid single-handed sailor, Manning Eldridge, who had departed Papeete in *Marara* bound for Honolulu over seven months earlier, but had never arrived—until now.

What could have gone wrong? We may never know since dead men tell no tales, but the wrenched-off boom attachment to the mast and the almost totally closed cabin suggests that the skipper may have suffered a serious physical injury and was only able to crawl down into the cabin and close the hatch behind him before becoming unconscious. Possibly he bled to death or starved in reach of food, but unable to prepare it and he had no means to call for help on this boat.

A close examination of the boat interior is being made by the U.S. Coast Guard in hopes of uncovering some clue to the last days of the unlucky skipper. Chances are, however, that his demise may yet become another mystery of the sea.

Postscript to the *Marara* mystery: The State of Hawaii Medical Examiner's report stated the cause of death was undetermined because of the advanced state of decomposition and skeletonization. The cause of incapacitation of the individual was never established. Another mystery of the sea.

— Pacific Magazine

The *Marara* after being towed to Honolulu

VAGABONDS OF THE PACIFIC

Orphaned by storms and failed nets, glass fishing floats dot the waters of the North Pacific, like a sparkling string of pearls. Once set free of their moorings in the Western Pacific, they start an eternal drift around this vast ocean. Some come to rest along the beaches of North America, while others pick a Pacific Island on which to finally rest. Still others simply ride the ocean currents to oblivion.

The pearls of the Orient have been traversing Pacific sea lanes since the early 1900s. They are runaways from life, for their real purpose is to support fishing nets and lines and not to cruise aimlessly in this largest of all oceans.

While today's glass fishing floats are of Japanese origin, the Japanese did not invent them. They came from the Scandinavian countries in the mid 1800s, spread to other European countries around 1900 and were taken up by American fisherman during World War II, but it is to the credit of the Japanese to have perfected their use. Today's Oriental fishing fleets still use them in abundance.

Improvements have been tried such as a hollow orange plastic sphere with an attaching eye molded onto it. The weight and cost of these impersonators seem to be hampering their popularity, which is just as well, for they are ugly compared to glass.

The Japanese glass fishing floats come in a variety of sizes and colors but always in a spherical shape. Small floats (tennis ball size) are used for gillnet salmon fishing and are the most commonly found size (approximately one-half of all finds). Medium floats (grapefruit size) are next most common and are used for supporting bottom nets. Large floats (basketball size or larger) are used for longline tuna fishing.

Like all glass, the color of a float is dependent on the trace chemical elements found in manufacture. The most common color is blue-green, similar to a Coca Cola bottle, which is the result of traces of iron salts in the glass. Floats are also found in other shades of green as well as pale pink and light gold, but they are less common.

Glass floats formerly made in the United States were machine blown, but those from Japan are hand blown and that is what gives them their character. Each tends to be a bit different with varying patterns of entrapped bubbles in the glass, possibly a patch on the surface somewhere, maybe a glass thread across the interior and, of course, a variety of trademarks or other imprints which identify the manufacturer or the glass blower.

The currents that bring the glass floats to the eastern Pacific are part of a gigantic water circulation system in the North Pacific. Far to the west is the north-flowing Kuroshio current (Kuroshio in Japanese means "black stream" because of the dark color of the water). This current has been likened to the Gulf Stream because it carries warm tropical water to the

higher latitudes. It is this current mingling with the Alaska current that moderates the air temperatures along the southern Alaska coastline.

As the North Pacific current approaches the American continent, it is deflected to the south along the coastline, eventually broadening out to a large fan whose easternmost boundary is the California current. The current then turns west and the drift becomes the North Equatorial current running westerly above the equator until it is deflected north near the Philippine islands and, once again, becomes the Kuroshio current.

For the Hawaii-Mainland voyager, it is the immense current gyre located approximately underneath the Pacific "high" that is both adversary and benefactor to the navigator. At its worst, the gyre retards sailing progress if you cut the corner too closely in rounding the Pacific "high." At its best, it gives you a little boost along the homeward route when winds are characteristically light. It is in this gyre that the homeward bound voyager can do his "beachcombing" and find these treasured Japanese fishing floats.

In this area the waters are all too often an oily calm and the iron genny must furnish the motive power. Squinting eyes will suddenly glimpse a concentrated light reflection. Keep an eye on that reflection for it is, most likely, a glass fishing float. The helmsman steers the boat alongside the float so it can be recovered by a boat hook or gaff (if the net is still on the float) or by using a fish net or long arm over the gunn'l if it is bare. You will now have in your possession the prize for patiently sailing the Pacific "high." There are thousands of floats out there, so keep right on looking until every crew member has this unusual souvenir of a homeward bound passage.

Hundreds of thousands of glass floats are lost each year by the fishermen. These vagabonds of the currents keep circulating around the Pacific until picked up by some lucky cruiser or they are cast ashore on the North American coast or one of the thousands of islands of the Pacific.

Some floats may still have a sound net surrounding the glass ball. If you are more patient than squeamish, you can pick off the hitchhiking barnacles and mussels one by one. Eventually, the fishy odor, too, will disappear so that they can be displayed indoors. More often than not, the float will be sans its net or the net will be torn because the fishing gear was a victim of a violent storm. That does not reduce the value of the find because bare floats can be equally well displayed in a macrame sling made for the job.

To the shoreline beachcomber as well as the mariner on the Hawaii-North America passage, glass fishing floats are treasured finds— something to take home that will spark sea stories and conversations for years to come.

— Western Boatman

Glass fishing float decorating a tree

HANDICRAFTS AS CRUISING MEMORIES

All the fun of cruising is not in the action itself, but in the memories which the cruiser brings home from faraway places. Everybody uses photography and some video to supplement what the mind remembers. For those whose travels take them to the islands of the Pacific, there is yet another choice and that is handicrafts. These are the wood carvings, woven baskets, painted wood cloth and knitted bags that are handcrafted by the island people.

Handicrafts have become a major source of income to island people enabling every person to share in the generation of income from visitors, not just hotel, restaurant and tour operators. Other than for a few scattered islands like New Caledonia and Nauru which have mineral resources, there are few ways for native people to supplement their copra income other than to produce handicrafts for the tourist trade. If there are trees and shrubs and shoreline, then there are raw materials for handicrafts and the ingenuity of the local people takes it from there.

The problem in collecting artifacts is determining those that are truly handcrafted and have traditional values. As islanders host increasing number of visitors, they tend towards mass production for the creation of handicrafts. That is popularly called airport art being sold at airport stores that cater to the traveler who is in a hurry to buy something—anything for a memento.

It is wise to recognize some of the other differences in native art. In the field of handicrafts, there is traditional art that was created before the ar-

272

rival of the western influence. This period essentially pre-dates World War II in the Pacific. Prior to that, most native endeavors at handicrafts were devoted to making items useful to their own existence or as religious articles. Many of these found their way into the museums of the world by way of explorers, whalers and adventurers and are now priceless historical artifacts.

Some of the more isolated places of the Pacific such as the Highlands of New Guinea, the atolls of Ontong Java and the island of Rapa are still producing handicrafts in the traditional mode for they are not overly tainted by western contact. Few of them, however, could be called museum pieces for they do not have pedigree of story, maker or materials. Most countries are jealously protecting anything that smacks of art with a pedigree. If, while traveling, you should come into possession of a piece of art that appears to have a pedigree, judiciously inquire about exporting it. Many countries have laws against that and you may be faced with a smuggling charge trying to take it out of the country. By government edict in Papua New Guinea, for instance, any piece of native art that predates 1962 is an artifact and cannot be removed from the country.

Excluding traditional art with a pedigree and avoiding airport art like a plague, we are left with an art form that is called classic art—a blend of traditional design and materials with contemporary handcrafting. In this category are replicas of traditional art, many on a smaller scale than the original for lack of enough material resources to make an original size replica. Oftentimes substitute materials are used, for many ancient craft materials have already disappeared from the face of the earth. (Sandlewood was rapaciously gathered on all islands of the Pacific to satisfy a Chinese demand for this fragrant wood. Now it is all but extinct on most islands.)

The wise cruiser will visit a local museum to get some idea of what is traditional art before he makes his purchase from a street vendor or in a remote village. Some museums now publish books displaying authentic artifacts and their stories. These can be very helpful. With local guidance the buyer will have some chance of separating airport from traditional art. While it is almost impossible to get traditional art anymore, there are some very good replicas available which fall in the category of classic art.

The popular forms of contemporary classic handicrafts in the Pacific are wood carvings, weavings and textiles. Not all are available throughout the Pacific because of varying materials, skills and people to produce the products. Not surprisingly, the skills of the older generation of island peoples are disappearing the same as craftspeople are disappearing in the industrialized world. The best places to find capable workers are in outer islands of a group where a subsistence economy still prevails.

It should not be unexpected that wood carvings are available only on the high islands of the Pacific where substantial numbers of trees grow. In most cases the woods used will be unfamiliar to cruisers since they are probably indigenous to the local islands, but that adds to the allure of a carving. Wood carvers on Nuku Hiva use toewood, which is similar to black

Fan made for Betty Hinz by woman at Abemama, Gilbert Islands

walnut, and rosewood which is common in many parts of the Pacific. The toewood is harvested once a year by the carvers in Baie Marquisienne and is relatively scarce, therefore they have a self-rationing program to preserve this resource. Toewood is used for smaller carvings like replicas of spears, swords and tikis and for bowls. Larger items like chess boards and tables are made out of the more plentiful rosewood.

Pitcairn produces some excellent carvings of miro wood. While it is not exactly uncommon in the Pacific, there is none on Pitcairn so once or twice a year the Pitcairners make an expedition to Henderson Island about 100 miles away to collect wood for carving. That also adds to the value of the carving.

I have a large collection of carvings to remember my Pacific travels for years to come. Unfortunately, they remain in storage since a boat has very limited display space. My favorite is a shark carved out of red mangrove wood by a wood carver in the little Polynesian enclave residing on Pohnpei. This is classic art created as a source of income by the people from Kapingamarangi atoll who are now living on Pohnpei.

My second favorite is a replica of a canoe prow ornament from the Solomon Islands. It is the classic "noosa noosa" carved out of king ebony with nautilus shell inlays. Although I bought it in Gizo, it was carved on near-by Kohigo Island. The carver had come to Gizo, to take a member of his family to the district hospital and he brought along a few carvings to help pay the bill. The Solomon Islands as a group, probably have the finest collection of wood carvers in the Pacific. Their high, well-wooded islands provide excellent materials.

When you get to an island like New Caledonia where a rich monetary economy exists, do not expect to get good handicrafts of any kind. The best I could do in New Caledonia was get a poor quality wood mask carving in a Noumea store where handicrafts were lined up on shelves like ducks in a shooting gallery. I wouldn't have bought it except it was a good example of airport art.

Another example of airport art which I will defend. It is the "stick chart" of the Marshall Islands. Made of epoxy-glued sticks with typewritten atoll names next to small shells representing atolls, it is a poor quality replica that sells well at Majuro's airport. It is certainly not quality indigenous art, but it is symbolic of a unique talent that still exists only in Micronesia—non-instrument navigation between islands. The Marshall Islands are the only ones, however, that developed the stick chart and as a conversation piece after your cruise, it can't be beat—even if it is airport art.

Weaving is a handicraft that is common on all atolls and islands of the Pacific where grow the pandanus trees. The leaves of this tree are the raw materials of baskets, fans and mats. I have seen so many good woven products that it is difficult to choose a favorite one. The peoples of Micronesia as a group probably produce the best baskets. They are colorful, made with precision, and they are functional. The pure white, finely woven "Kili bag" made by the displaced Bikini islanders now living on Kili Atoll is a favorite handicraft at the Marshalls Handicraft Co-op. (While I recommend buying handicrafts in the place where they are made, that is not always possible and co-op stores are the next best places to look.)

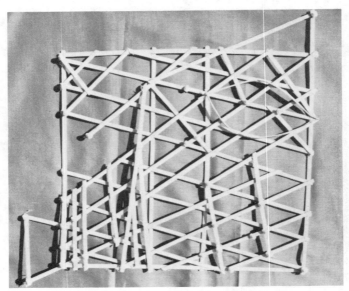

Stick chart from Arno Atoll, Marshall Islands

The woven product most treasured by my wife is a fan made for her by a woman on Abemama Atoll. We had anchored in the lagoon off her property and became good friends with her and her family to the extent of exchanging visits. She brought the fan out to Betty the night before we were to depart for Howland Island. The spontaneity of the gift added to its crafted value.

Another favorite handicraft collected by cruisers is *tapa* cloth (a Marquesan name, it is called *kapa* in Hawaii, *masi* in Fiji and *seapo* in Samoan). Tapa is made from the inner bark of the paper mulberry tree. This is a very labor-intensive product and, hence, has almost disappeared from the island scene, as has the paper mulberry tree. Many hours of beating are required to make a thin strip of bark into a large piece of cloth which is then layered to form the right size and desired thickness. In Fiji, the largest known masi was 30 feet wide and one-half mile long. The best tapa cloth (and the only tapa available in any quantity) comes from Fiji and Tonga. As you would expect, tapa cloth is only made on the outer islands of these groups.

There is an ersatz tapa cloth made on Fatu Hiva in the Marquesas Islands out of the inner bark of the breadfruit tree. I do not believe that any tapa cloth of whatever origin is found on the other islands of the Marquesas even though the name originated there. It has none of the softness, color or usefulness of true tapa cloth. Its only use is as a wall

Tapa cloth, fly whisk and bailer from Fiji

decoration because it is stiff and porous, a victim of the demise of the paper mulberry tree in the Marquesas.

Of all the handicrafts, tapa cloth is the most difficult to preserve after you arrive home. Following are some suggestions on maintaining your tapa cloth:

Store flat or rolled. Iron on wrong side to remove creases.

Do not wash or wipe with a damp cloth. Avoid direct sunlight.

Protect from insects but do not use chemical sprays on it.

Do not varnish or coat with plastics.

Avoid sticky tapes, glues, cements and tacks.

Buying handicraft products at your different ports of call not only adds to your cruise memory bank, but it greatly helps the local economy. Copra income is pretty meager even in the best of times and the purchase of a handicraft item from a local person can make them feel wealthy, if but for a moment. For you, it may be the beginning of an island freindship that can lead to more enjoyment at a port of call.

— Cruising World

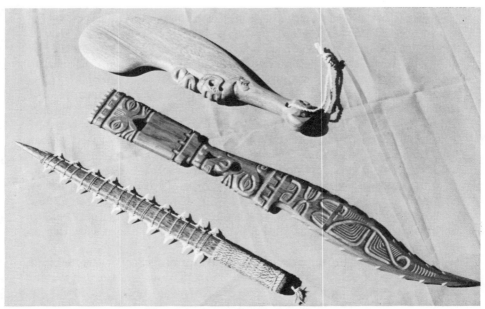

Weapons of early Pacific Islanders
"Mere" from New Zealand at top
Ceremonial sword from the Marquesas
Shark tooth sword from the Gilberts at bottom

CHAPTER 10

PATHS OF THE PACIFIC

"The routine of long passages makes one delightful day
at sea like the next, but always leading to that smudge on
the horizon that says you have navigated to a new land.
Anticipation of new scenery, interesting people, and days
swinging lazily at anchor in sparkling waters makes you
quickly forget the 24-hour schedule that you lived with
enroute. You are pleased with yourself, your crew, and
your boat, and your confidence is subtly bolstered by yet
another passage to still another island paradise. It can
become an endless way of life and the Pacific Ocean
could occupy your days to eternity."

— Earl Hinz, "Sail Before Sunset"

DESTINATION HAWAII

Sailing to Hawaii can be the highlight of cruising boat ownership. You
do not need to be a racing buff taking part in one of the many races to
Polynesia, USA, nor must you be a dedicated cruiser with years to spend
sailing the world's oceans. The requirements are a well-found boat, sailing knowledge and a few months of time during the summer.

For the casual cruiser, this is definitely a seasonal event because of a
peculiarity in the Pacific weather pattern known as the Pacific "high."
This is a major atmospheric high pressure cell that lies off the coast of
Mainland USA creating the fabulous northeast tradewinds of the tropical
North Pacific. The "high" spends the summer season at its most
northwesterly position making it practical to sail from the Mainland to
Hawaii and return in relative comfort. In the winter, it is at a lower
latitude and closer to the Mainland allowing frigid low pressure weather
to come down from Arctic waters. Although it is reasonable for a boat to
sail to Hawaii in the winter, it usually is a masochistic event to attempt
the return sail at that time.

There is another intruder on the normally tranquil Pacific weather and
that is the occasional tropical cyclone that generates in Mexican waters
and wanders west. Sometimes it drifts as far west as Hawaii, although the
numbers that do are relatively small. It is the occasional one that changes
course to the northwest before reaching the longitude of Hawaii, thereby
crossing the usual cruising path to the islands, that must be avoided.

The main season for eastern North Pacific tropical cyclones is June
through October and the earlier storms are usually not numerous or of

great intensity. One should not worry about tropical cyclones but objectively plan the route and schedule keeping in touch with the weather situation.

Whether coming from the Pacific Northwest or Southern California, the initial days and nights of the passage will be the same—cold, wet and, possibly, foggy with winds from the northwest. This is the prevailing weather along the coast and a potential Hawaii cruiser will be familiar with it. Be prepared with warm clothing, plenty of hot drinks and a stable stomach. If you have any tendency to *mal de mer*, take precautions well before you start the passage. The roughest going will be getting offshore into the tradewinds. Once you have entered the tradewinds, you will be in a world of pleasant sailing and balmy breezes and that is what cruising is all about.

Navigation to Pineappleland is no different than other bluewater cruising except it goes on for a longer period of time. In a sense, the Mainland-Hawaii passage is the longest passage in the world with no practical way of shortening—about 2200 NM, so you must be prepared to find your way over a lot of ocean. Avoid the derring-do attitude of "I can find it by watching the jet contrails." Some boats have completely missed the archipelago and others have run out of supplies trying to get there. Do your homework well. Celestial has to be your navigation backbone. You can back it up with Loran C for the first 1000 miles or so and with SatNav all the way.

Equip yourself with the latest editions of charts, sailing directions and other government publications for weather and radio. Ignore the cost, for these are the best insurance you can buy. If you are willing to put thousands of dollars into black box navigation, you should also be willing to invest hundreds of dollars in the charts that can make or break your bluewater cruise. You are on the verge of making personal history, don't blow it by penny-pinching on the one hand, or excessive high tech reliance on the other hand.

Getting There

The route you take and the time of departure depends on where your home port is and what else you want to do. A recommended departure time directly to Hawaii from the West Coast is not earlier than May for weather reasons and no later than June, if you want ample time in Hawaii.

Cruisers from the Pacific Northwest have the longest outbound passage, but only by a few days. Their course should swing south of the rhumbline crossing longitude 140° W at about 30° N. The first one-third of the passage will be made under the influence of the Westerlies. It is also possible to sail farther down the coast before turning west, but ship traffic and often heavy coastal weather makes that a less attractive alternative. An average cruising boat should make the passage in 18 to 30 days, and coming from far north there will be only a brief period of good downwind sailing. The rest will be reaching, which isn't all that bad.

From California the preferred route swings a bit south of the rhumbline from Los Angeles to Hawaii. There are always great debates before the several Mainland-Hawaii yacht races about which route to take. Generally, it is agreed that a great circle is too far north, but there is little agreement on where to go from there. It becomes dependent on where the "high" is sitting and how closely its isobars are stacked together. While we all like to make sharp passages, a day or two longer in the Tropics isn't all that bad, so just work hard to get out of the coastal Northwesterlies. From San Francisco the passage will take 15 to 25 days and from Los Angeles/San Diego it may take a day longer.

For those who can get away, say in November, there awaits much fun and good cruising down Mexico way during the winter. That means, of course, that you will sail down the coast all the way to Cabo San Lucas, but be of good cheer, the last part of the trip will be in the tropics and that is when the cruising life begins. Your timing for the Mexican detour should consider the annual cruisers bash at Pacific Marine Supply store in San Diego held in late October. At any rate, you should be in the La Paz area of the Sea of Cortez by March for the annual Sea of Cortez Race Week—not a very serious affair, which is why it is so popular.

Your departure for Hawaii from the Sea of Cortez should take place no later than May, for the eastern North Pacific hurricane season starts by June and it is best to be out of Mexican waters by then. The route from Cabo San Lucas to Hawaii is almost a perfect great circle and will take 19 to 28 days, all in the tropics!

Cruising boats from the East Coast who come through the Panama Canal have an opportunity to stop at a couple of rarely visited islands along the way—Cocos and Clipperton. The departure from Panama should be made early enough to allow for these stops and also to beat the eastern Pacific hurricanes which may cross the cruising track later. If you arrive in Hawaii before the rest of the cruising fleet does, make the most of less crowded facilities. Your passage time will be 35 to 49 days, so you can see that the Cocos-Clipperton stops may be very welcome. These are not reprovisioning stops, though, so prepare yourself in Panama for the long haul.

Your Arrival In Hawaii

No matter where you depart from for Hawaii from the mainland, there is really only one place to make landfall and that is Hilo on the Big Island (Hawaii). Doing this, you have nothing but downwind sailing as you later work your way through the Hawaiian Archipelago. The Big Island is the most windward of the group as well as the largest and youngest island.

Clearing into Hawaii is not difficult but does depend on whether you made a stop at a foreign port or not on your way from Mainland USA. If you did, then you must enter at one of the five official Ports of Entry, but again pick Hilo for more pleasant sailing later. After you are moored in

Diamond Head Lighthouse, Oahu, welcomes boats to Hawaii

Hilo's Radio Bay, the skipper checks in with the harbormaster who calls U.S. Customs, Immigration, Health and Agriculture (oftentimes Customs will handle it all).

If you come directly from another United States port, you can enter Hawaii at any port, but the skipper must then call Hawaii State Agriculture for inspection. They will confiscate any remaining fruits or veggies that you have on board. A word of good advice to dog and cat lovers—don't bring the animals along. Hawaii Agricultural Regulations state that cats and dogs arriving from anywhere must be put into a 120-day quarantine in Honolulu and the cost of doing that is about $500 per animal. After your vessel and crew are cleared by the inspectors, you are free to roam the islands. Foreign vessels, however, must have a cruising permit which is obtained from Customs.

The Return Home

Certainly the time will fly while you are cruising the Islands and you will need to make some early plans for you homeward passage. Most boats depart the Hawaiian Islands for the Mainland in August to avoid the buildup in North Pacific winter weather and possible gales that come down the West Coast from Alaska. September is still all right, but by October the weather starts to get nasty and some insurers will not allow such a late passage.

Departure is best taken from either Honolulu or Hanalei Bay. The latter is an ideal last port of call and will leave you with a more satisfied feeling of having cruised tropical waters. Honolulu is where you should do your return-leg provisioning. Hopefully you stocked your boat well with non-perishables before leaving the Mainland and only have to replenish per-

ishable goods. Foodstuff prices in Hawaii are 20 to 30 percent higher than Mainland prices and that can dent the cruising budget already strained by all the nice places you found to spend money in the Islands.

The usual cruising boat route from Hawaii to the Mainland passes north of the Pacific "high." The location of the corner to turn east is a matter of guessing and luck. If you turn east too soon, you will find yourself in the plateau of high pressure in which there is little wind. When that happens you turn on your "iron genny" and motor on while searching for glass fishing floats. Boats with extremely good windward performance can beat their way under the Pacific "high" and shorten the overall distance home; but they run the risk of an excessive motoring time if they get trapped. Typical passage times are 21 to 29 days to Seattle/Vancouver or San Francisco and 20 to 34 days to Los Angeles.

Once you have squeezed all you can out of your Hawaii cruise, then the trip home will be one of good memories, but don't relax on your navigation for you are approaching a dangerous coast often wreathed in fog. Your navigation will again be tested to the limit and your lookout system must be alert for you are also sailing into busy shippng lanes and fishing grounds and this would be no time to let your guard down.

Once back at your homeport, you will be the envy of all who could not get away that year. You are the old sea dog who has experienced blue water cruising at its best. Be kind to the others, they will need your help next year to make the same cruise.

— Cruising World

Snug anchorage off Molokai, good only in prevailing winds

TO THE SOUTH SEAS

The Pacific Ocean offers the cruising yachtsman unparalleled advantages in space, exotic ports of call, fine sailing weather and hospitable people. It is the largest ocean of the world covering 64 million square miles and that does not include another 6 million square miles of adjoining seas. At the equator the Pacific Ocean measures 11,000 miles east to west and it is over 9,000 miles north to south. Approximately 30 million square miles of Pacific Ocean lie between the Tropics of Cancer and Capricorn, making it the world's largest cruising ground.

This is where the people of Melanesia, Micronesia and Polynesia live. The notable exception is New Zealand which is ethnically part of Polynesia; but outside of the tropics. The early Polynesians sailed to and populated the islands of the Polynesian Triangle in their marvelous sailing canoes using primitive navigation techniques. They were great seamen propelling themselves over vast distances, often to windward, using only wind power.

In the Age of Discovery, these were the waters of Tasman, Mendana, Cook, Bouganville, and Bligh. This is also today's Coconut Milk Run made famous by such early cruisers as Slocum, Voss, Gerbault, Pidgeon, Robinson, Hiscock, Roth and a host of latter day sailors. In story, it has been made famous by Stevenson, London, Nordhoff and Hall, Heyerdahl and Michener.

The joys of cruising the tropical waters of the Pacific are found not only in the atolls, islands and peopls of Oceania, but in its seasons of normally fine weather. Northern and Southern Hemispheres have opposite seasons, ie., when it is summer in Hawaii, it is winter in Tahiti. This gives a remarkable flexibility to cruise scheduling provided that the cruiser understands the governing weather patterns and how they shift throughout the year.

The Outbound Voyage

It is within the tropics that blue water sailors have enjoyed accumulated centuries of cruising, following weather patterns that take them safely from the North Pacific to the South Pacific and return. It is entirely feasible, using sailing windows, to depart the West Coast of North America early in the year, spend several months in French Polynesia and then return to the West Coast before winter sets in, all the time avoiding tropical cyclones and gales. Such a six-month cruise, however, is only a teaser. For all the investment in time and money you will have made, it comes up far short of full cruising satisfaction.

One should bite the bullet and add a year to it in order to see a more varied geography as far away as New Zealand with dozens of exotic ports of call along the way. Once you have entered the tropics, you will become so enamored with tradewind sailing and the people of Oceania that you

will not want to go home too soon. Full appreciation of the pleasures along the Coconut Milk Run to New Zealand takes at least 18 months and out of it comes a lifetime of happy memories.

Departure time from the West Coast is set by the ending of the South Pacific hurricane (tropical cyclone) season. Even though French Polynesia, your first landfall, has relatively few cyclonic occurences, it is best to be cautious the first time around and not arrive before the weather is quiescent. May is the best month for arriving in French Polynesia. Any earlier will put you at the tail end of the hurricane season, while arriving later compromises the amount of time for your leisurely cruise to Kiwiland.

Regardless of your departure port along the West Coast—California, Mexico or the Panama Canal—you should be provisioned for a minimum of three months, more if you have room to stow everything. You will not find many provisions in your first port of call except local fruits and vegetables. Once you reach Papeete, the supply is better but prices will be higher than back home.

From Los Angeles, typical passage times to the Marquesas are 21 to 29 days, initially sailing in familiar northwesterly coastal winds. About one-third of the way to the Marquesas Islands you will enter the tropics and simultaneously pick up the northeast trades. That is when the cruising life begins!

Departure from Mexico to join the Coconut Milk Run should be taken by early May to avoid the Eastern Pacific hurricane season. It can be taken from a variety of ports along Mexico's west coast as far south as Acapulco. Cabo San Lucas, however, seems to be the most popular. From there typical cruising times to the Marquesas are 21 to 28 days, all in the tropics. This passage can be broken up with a stop at Soccorro Island in the Revilla-gigido group 600 miles along the way.

The Atlantic connection to the Coconut Milk Run is made from the Panama Canal and offers a wonderful opportunity to visit the "Enchanted Islands"—the Galapagos. They are just south of the rhumbline to the Marquesas and will take 9 to 16 days to reach them. Although only 845 miles from the Canal, this slow passage is the result of light and variable winds in the eastern ITCZ, to say nothing of some erratic currents. You cannot avoid these sailing conditions even if you bypass nature's wonderland, so you might as well take it in.

At present, only a limited number of long term cruising permits for the Galapagos Islands are being offered by the Ecuadorian government, but you can still stay for three-day periods at Wreck Bay and Academy Bay, long enough to see some of the flora and fauna and rest up for the longer passage to the Marquesas Islands. The Galapagos are sparsely settled islands, so do not expect to get services, provisions or even water in any significant amount.

Sailing improves after leaving the Galapagos Islands for you soon enter the southeast tradewinds to sail on a broad reach the rest of the way to the

Marquesas. Transit times vary between 22 and 32 days for this 3055-mile leg in what is normally a pictureperfect passage.

Although distances from the Americas to the Marquesas Islands are great, the three- to four-week passage is treasured by most cruisers. Weather enroute is normally good and it is a time to unwind from the trauma of months or years of preparing for the blue water cruise of a lifetime. You are now on your way to the South Seas and becoming a blue water cruiser to be envied.

Cruising The Golden Triangle

Over the years, a golden triangle of atolls and islands has attracted thousands of cruisers and earned a reputation as the finest cruising grounds in the South Seas. It starts in the east with the tropical islands and atolls of French Polynesia and stretches southwest all the way to New Zealand. All of it lies within Polynesia except for Fiji whose people have a Melanesian heritage. Although it is only a small part of the Pacific, this region has over the years been able to satiate the cruiser's demand for adventure, challenge of blue water sailing and an ample sampling of native cultures.

The golden triangle begins in the Marquesas Islands, which are generally the first ports of call made by cruisers on their outbound leg from North or Central American ports. These are the islands of Melville, Gauguin and Heyerdahl—high islands with lush growth and just a touch of 20th century civilization. After a long downwind passage, the Marquesas offer good navigation targets with no tricky currents or passes and they are just sophisticated enough so that the cruiser doesn't suffer cultural shock at his first landfall. Yet these islands remain mysterious and relatively unspoiled by local ambition or tourism.

The cruiser is cautioned to make formal entry at designated Ports of Entry here and in all subsequent island groups. Here is where you learn the procedures of inbound clearance under the Q-flag. Most island countries follow the same inbound clearance procedures involving health (the reason for the Q-flag) as well as immigration, customs, agriculture, and port control. Depending on the sophistication of the island country, these may be handled by separate persons or by one person acting for all the others. At this time you should inquire about the need for obtaining a cruising license or special permission to visit other islands of the group. An inbound clearance by itself does not always imply freedom to visit other islands in the group.

The Marquesas are the cruiser's first major contact with other cruising boats and the start of many gams. He will learn to swap yarns, trade advice and spare parts and make cruising friends for life.

Whatever your longer range plans, the Tuamotus come next in the itinerary and this is where the cruiser cuts his teeth on atoll navigation. Atolls present three navigational challenges—currents outside the atoll, currents in the passes and coral growth inside the lagoon. Approaching a group of atolls, like the Tuamotus, requires care lest the currents sweep the boat into or past the atoll. Local currents are variable in both direction and

strength and very unpredictable. The neophyte should approach his first atoll with great care and attempt the passage into the lagoon only in daylight with the sun astern to enhance both land and water visibility. Atolls are not easily seen from great distances and should not be approached at night. Although atolls can be picked up on radar, implicit faith in the radar return without eyeball contact is asking for trouble.

Slack water is the best time to enter the lagoons, if at all possible. Sometimes there is no slack water because waves breaking over the windward barrier reef keep the lagoon filled to overflowing and the leeward passes are continually emptying the lagoon. In this event good visibility and ample speed are mandatory to a safe entry.

In all probability the cruiser will make the Marquesas–Tahiti leg by passing through the westernmost atolls of the Tuamotus. This has led to a growing popularity of Ahe, Manihi and Rangiroa atolls as ports of call, but there are another two dozen inhabited atolls that could be considered and which will be found less "crowded." Do not, however, expect to be hospitably received at Mururoa, Fangataupa or Hao atolls, France's nuclear test bases. This is the only place in the Pacific where such strict nuclear restrictions are in effect.

All of the wonders of French Polynesia are not contained in the Marquesas or Tuamotu Archipelagos. Continue sailing on a broad reach to the southwest and you come to the Society Islands and Papeete, the capital of all French Polynesia. The Society Islands turn out to be the most cruised of all French Polynesia. Not only do they have the South Seas' metropolis of Papeete, but they include the popular tourist island of Moorea; legendary Raiatea; glamorous Bora Bora; and the garden island of Huahine.

Dance troupe, Papeete, Tahiti

286

Papeete is a necessary stop for administrative reasons as well as provisioning, boat services and sightseeing. These taken care of, most boats then head for the outer islands, away from the hustle and bustle of a capital city. If you do not plan on later returning home via Tahiti, then you may want to take a two-week diversionary cruise south to the Austral Islands. It is a sailing reach both ways and these rarely-visited islands will set you apart from other Coconut Milk Run cruisers. If you intend to come back to Tahiti from New Zealand, then you can see these islands on the return passage. Before you leave the Society Islands, however, be certain to retrieve your posted bond. If you have deposited it in a bank with a Bora Bora branch, you can pick it up when you take leave from French Polynesia.

Now it is decision time again. The cruiser heading west will most certainly want to make a landfall at Pago Pago to take advantage of all its services; but first he will pass through the Cook Islands. These islands and atolls are equally as beautiful as French Polynesia and they are populated by English-speaking Polynesians. There are two basic choices on visiting the Cooks—reach southwest to Rarotonga and Aitutaki or run west northwest to visit Suvarov Atoll. In the first instance, you will be visiting the southern group where most of the people live; in the second instance you will be visiting an atoll inhabited by only a few persons who act as administrators of the National Park. Suvarov was the home of Tom Neale, widely known as a hermit, but he was a pleasant host to all cruising boats. Although Suvarov is not a Port of Entry, the administrators there can give permission to land and spend a few pleasant days.

Cruising the islands of Polynesia during the austral winter months of May to November gives you the best possible climate for cruising. It is comfortably cool; rainfall is at a minimum (except for Pago Pago where it really never quits raining); irritating insects are absent except for the no-no flies of the Marquesas and parts of the Societies; and good, even stiff tradewinds blow. This is not the season for cyclones anywhere in the southern hemisphere so you can sail with impunity. Gales?—only at the beginning and end of the season and then not severe.

American Samoa is a highly recommended stop on the Coconut Milk Run because of the logistics, communications and maintenance services available. Pago Pago is a beautiful, if dirty, harbor. It is on the "American Plan" and that makes life much simpler for the cruiser, who by this time has been away from the States for possibly as long as three months. Mail, telephone and airlines are U.S. domestic services and food products are mostly familiar names at case lot prices.

Eighty miles to the west of Americanized Samoa are the islands of Western Samoa. While larger in area and population, they are more traditional in their culture and provide a chance to get back to the Polynesian way of life. They have even managed to keep a treasure in the form of Aggie Grey's Hotel on the waterfront—a famous hotel and eatery from World War II days. There is also the former home and the grave of Robert Louis

Stevenson. Sailing visits to other parts of Upolu and Savai'i require written permission and do not expect to find good harbors, only small anchorages, but rental cars and buses can take you around Upolu.

Leaving the Samoas, there are three choices to continue the outbound cruise—via Niue Island, Fiji or Tonga. These are not mutually exclusive, but if you want to visit Niue, as well as either of the other two, you had better go there first or you will face an unnecessary sail to windward. To see all three, route yourself to Niue first, followed by Vava'u, Tonga, and then Fiji. If you choose to omit Niue, then shape your itinerary to enter Fijian waters through Nanuku Passage and later head for Vava'u, Tonga.

Suva will be your last good logistics, communications and maintenance port until you reach New Zealand. There are over 300 islands and atolls in Fiji but the most liked seem to be the Yasawa and Lau groups, however, don't be restrained by what others have done. The recent political machinatons in Fiji did not affect cruising boats which are not only welcome in Fiji, but as safe as any place in the world—safer than some.

Your last stop in the golden triangle will be Tonga; it shouldn't be missed. These are probably the least spoiled (by Westernization standards) of the major island groups. Vava'u is a must and if you still have time a beautiful overnight reach down to Nuku'alofa brings rewards in seeing the last true kingdom of the Pacific.

Now it is time to talk weather again for it is, probably, late October, and near the beginning of the austral summer. In the austral summer cyclones (hurricanes) generate in this part of the South Pacific and some head west to the vicinity of Fiji and Tonga. Unless you deliberately intend to stay in these island groups through the hurricane season, you should think about getting to New Zealand by the end of November. Passage times vary between 10 to 16 days, with sometimes confusing winds due to the fact you are departing the tradewind zone and passing into a region of variable winds. Make westing at least to the longitude of New Zealand's North Cape before turning due south. That way you will be able to ride potential southwesterlies more comfortably.

Most boats spend the austral summer in New Zealand. A better place to refurbish boat and selves does not exist. The Bay of Islands, Whangarei, and Auckland are home to hundreds of transient cruising boats every year. Sailing the length and breadth of New Zealand's North and South Islands is recommended only for the hardy, but touring them by land could be the highpoint of your Pacific cruise. The weather up until April or May is generally good, being interrupted only occasionally by fringes of tropical cyclone winds or gale winds from low pressure cells which come across the Tasman Sea from Australia. With all of the natural harbors along New Zealand's shorelines, your boat is never far from a safe haven.

Escaping The South Seas

Breaking away from Kiwiland will not be easy, for all who have visited

this land of peaches and cream have gained a fond attachment to both country and people; but by March or April you and your boat should be refurbished enough to get on with the cruise. It is decision time again. Do you go west, north or east for your next leg? One thing is for certain, you do not go south.

If you are planning to circumnavigate, this is where you leave the Coconut Milk Run and strike out to the west for the Indian Ocean. Those intending to sail via the southern Indian Ocean usually exit through Torres Strait in July or August and head for Africa via Cocos-Keeling and Mauritius Islands. Those who choose to sail the North Indian Ocean have until January before entering the Bay of Bengal and heading for the Red Sea via Sri Lanka and the Maldive Islands. In both instances there is ample time for the circumnavigators to see more of the islands of Melanesia and Indonesia before poking their bows into the Indian Ocean.

But if you can spend another year away from home (making a 2½ year cruise) and have no desire to circumnavigate, you can take advantage of a more complete South Seas itinerary. Your second cruising season can take you from New Zealand to New Caledonia, Vanuatu, Solomon Islands, Papua New Guinea and thence to Australia with its Great Barrier Reef, hospitable people and many wonderful harbors along the Tasman Sea. Plan on spending the second cyclone season (December through April) in Australia. When it is time, the way back to Mainland USA will be similar to that from New Zealand, but starting 1000 miles (about 10 days) farther west.

So what is the best way home from Down Under? There are choices and they all involve windward work. That is where your sailing abilities bring out the performance claims of your boat's manufacturer. You have enjoyed langorous days of sailing downwind through the golden triangle of the Pacific, now you must pay the piper. Do not fall into the trap of thinking that the fun is over and what is left is merely a delivery trip home. The return voyage can be pleasant, if properly planned, and to make it more interesting add some new island stops along the way.

All practical routes home lead through Honolulu, but you should plan on stopping at one of the logistic nodes of Suva, Pago Pago or Papeete along the way. One route option is to head for Papeete staying well south on the edge of the westerlies, (about 40° south) until you can lay the Austral Islands. You will find both Raivavae and Tubuai are well worth a visit. For this passage you can leave from New Zealand as early as April getting back into the tropics before the austral winter sets in.

From Papeete, make your easting to about 145° W at the equator visiting more of the Tuamotus along the way. Done properly, you will have a pleasant close reach from the equator north to Hilo, Hawaii. Typical passage times from New Zealand to Papeete are 18 to 27 days and from Papeete to Hilo, 16 to 26 days. An R and R stop in Papeete is well worthwhile.

Another route of interest to those who bypassed Suva on the outbound leg is to first take a leg from New Zealand to Suva (9 to 12 days) and then one from Suva to Honolulu (20 to 33 days). Do not, however, plan on leaving New Zealand before May since the cyclone season to the north is still active. On the Suva to Honolulu leg, you can add the Wallis and Tuvalu islands to your logbook. They see very little cruising traffic.

The idea behind this "looping" route from Suva to Honolulu is to avoid sailing hard on the wind by making use of the variables and westerlies north of 40° north to gain easting. It is an old sailing ship route and square riggers could not point close to the wind. You will have a more comfortable passage, albeit longer, by not trying to "Sunday race" your way home. Crack those sheets and foot along in comfort being kind to boat and crew alike.

The route from Pago Pago to Honolulu takes its easting across the southeast trades with the possibility of visiting the Line Islands along the way. This route typically takes between 22 and 31 days. It is designed for those who prefer to island-hop to weather, breaking up the long passages into tolerable, convenient legs.

When you reach Honolulu, you are almost home—at least you are back in the USA. Although you are still in the tropics and Polynesia, Americanization of these islands is so great that you may think you are really home—some of us are. Here you will find all the comforts of life as well as the necessities to make ready for the final leg around the Pacific high.

This leg should be undertaken no later than September, for after that the North Pacific gales start building up. The leg consists of sailing north from Honolulu as close to the wind as is comfortable and rounding the Pacific high at 35° to 40° north. From there it is pretty much a straight shot sailing the westerlies to any of the coastal ports of Canada and the United States as presented in "Destination Hawaii."

Now you have done it. You have sailed to the legendary South Seas and back in your boat. You have joined the fraternity of blue water sailors and seen the best of the tropics. You have sailed before sunset.

— Cruising World

DESTINATION MICRONESIA

Mention the North Pacific to most sailors and they go into a paroxysm of shivering. Their minds ignore the fact that the North Pacific Ocean extends all the way to the equator and within the tropical North Pacific lies a vast array of islands and atolls waiting visits by adventurous cruising folk. One region alone, a part of Oceania, lays claim to over 2,000 of these islands. It is the area called Micronesia, a Greek term for "small islands." Indeed, these are small islands for their total land area measures only 1200 square miles and they are sprinkled over 4 million square miles of ocean. The inhabitants of these islands are Micronesians, a race of people related to, but distinctive from, both the Polynesians and the Melanesians of the southern hemisphere.

In recorded history the islands of Micronesia have been the pawns of Spain, Germany, Japan, Australia, Great Britain and the United States. Except for the phosphate rich islands of Nauru and Angaur (Palau group), they have no natural resources except sun and sand. Their value to World Powers was more of political dominance than social development. Spain wanted them for its religious empire; Germany for their copra; Japan to relieve its over-populated home islands; Australia for phosphate; Great Britain as colonies; and the United States to prevent any repetition of World War II.

Now most of the island groups of Micronesia are independent to a degree. Nauru with its vast but waning phosphate deposits, is an independent island-country. The Gilbert Islands are a part of the Republic of Kiribati which sprawls along the equator for 2400 miles penetrating deeply into the Polynesian "triangle." Guam and the Northern Mariana Islands are U.S. Territories. Other former islands of the "United States Trust Territory of the Pacific Islands" are now the countries of the Republic of the Marshall Islands; Federated States of Micronesia and Republic of Palau; all still having some political connections to the United States. It is important to understand the political status of these different island countries, for you will have to clear in with them when you cruise the waters of Micronesia.

The Micronesians evolved from the peoples of the Asian corridor area of Malaysia and they are ethnically more akin to the Polynesians than they are to the Melanesians. Occupying such a vast area of ocean, the Micronesians became great navigators and today are the last practicing non-instrument navigators of the Pacific.

Unlike the Coconut Milk Run through the South Pacific, relatively few cruisers have enjoyed the distinctive character of the islands of Micronesia. There are many reasons for this. Cruisers transitting the Panama Canal are practically in the South Pacific when they leave the Canal and they just continue on into Polynésia. Cruisers from the West Coast of North America head south down through Mexico and just continue south like

everybody else not realizing there are other options. It has only been the cruisers with Hawaii on their minds that have been exposed to the potential for cruising Micronesian waters.

One of the interesting things about heading off into Micronesia from Hawaii is the possibility of seeing most of Oceania without backtracking by following a counterclockwise route through Oceania. Another is the opportunity to minimize the tortures of returning to Mainland USA without resorting to circumnavigating either the Pacific or the world. It has often been said that the return passage from the South Pacific to the United States is dull and hard sailing to weather. It needn't be if you plan your total cruise with the return passage in mind and that's where Microniesia enters your cruising itinerary.

Micronesia is rarely a destination in itself, it is part of a longer cruising itinerary. As you progress through it east to west, bear in mind that there are many ways to leave these "micro islands" depending on your overall cruising goals. You can literally go north, south, east, or west without backtracking on your passages. Let's take a look at some of these strategies.

Return To Hawaii

Should you want to go back to Hawaii, there are two possible routes, one north taking advantage of the westerlies, and the other south riding the countercurrent home. If you have gone as far west as, say, Guam, then getting your easting back by sailing above 30° north is probably the best choice. It will get you out of the Western Pacific typhoon region quickly and in the summer has a minimum of North Pacific gales to contend with. The northern route carries you well to the north of Hawaii while getting your easting, and you turn south to Honolulu when you are able to comfortably sail on a reach on the northeast trades. Typical passage times are 28 to 32 days along this route.

The second route back to Hawaii takes you south into the equatorial countercurrent which will give you an easterly boost to supplement the light southeast trades blowing along this route. If you choose to cut your Micronesia cruise short of Guam, this is the best route back to Hawaii and it is free of tropical cyclones at all seasons of the year. It will give you an opportunity to stop at such little visited atolls as Tarawa, Abemama, Kanton, and the Line islands south of Hawaii. The countercurrent should not be ignored as a useful means of easterly passage-making when near the equator.

To Polynesia Or Melanesia

If you are not returning to Hawaii, then other options exist for exiting from Micronesia. One of them is to drop south into either Polynesia or Melanesia depending on whether your next major country of call is New Zealand or Australia. If it is New Zealand, then you have the option of sailing south through the islands of Tuvalu, Samoa, Tonga and Fiji, bringing you right onto the Coconut Milk Run itself. This should not be

attempted until after April in order to avoid the South Pacific cyclone season.

If you are very far west into Micronesia, say, Palau, then head south into the waters of Papua New Guinea, Solomons, Vanuatu and New Caledonia for an eventual landfall on Australia. Again, don't do it before the South Pacific cyclone season is over and do not go into Indonesian waters unless you have procured a cruising permit from the Indonesian government.

On To The Orient

At the western end of Micronesia, you are also within easy sailing distance of the Philippines and the mysterious Orient. To proceed to those destinations, however, your timing must be right. It is properly done before or after the typhoon season for these waters of the Philippine Sea and the South and East China Seas are home to typhoons. Judiciously avoiding the typhoon season also means you will be sailing the northeast monsoons which are not as wet as the southwest monsoons.

A visit to Japan from Micronesia is best done between April and June after the cold winter is over and before the typhoon season starts. Circumnavigators could consider staying in Japan for the entire summer and then, following the typhoon season and with the return of the northeast monsoons, sail south to Hong Kong and on to Singapore to be ready to cross the Bay of Bengal in January.

Boats planning on returning directly to the United States will want to depart Japan by July for the long sail back, either to Hawaii or the Mainland. They will certainly want to clear the waters of the North Pacific before October when gales start to form in earnest. Typical passage times from Japan to Hawaii are 34 to 51 days and from Japan to North America, 39 to 55 days. Record cruising passages are 30 and 34 days, respectively.

Cruising Eastbound Through Micronesia

Until now we have assumed that your cruise is westbound through Micronesia, but what if you are entering Micronesia from the west having come from Papua New Guinea or, possibly, from a cruise of Indonesia? The islands of Micronesia are so numerous and so close together that it is entirely feasible to tack your way east through them all the way to Majuro. In doing so, you will be seeing many atolls off the beaten path for your tacks will take you away from the capital islands. Remember, regardless of which direction you are traveling, you will need those all-important visas and vessel entry permits in many countries of Micronesia. When you get to Majuro, take a big breath and be ready for a long haul to windward to reach Hawaii. Again, it can either be done by a long tack north into the westerlies, or a shorter tack south into the equatorial countercurrent. Forget motorsailing from Majuro to Honolulu, it is not a viable option as proven by several boats in the past.

A Two-Year Cruise Scenario

Consider the following plan for a nominal two-year Pacific cruise: depart the Panama Canal or Mexico in May just before the Eastern North Pacific hurricane season begins. Spend the summer cruising Hawaii and then take off for Micronesia in October or November. (West Coast cruisers could also depart from home as late as October, heading directly for Hawaii and be in a position after reprovisioning to continue right on into Micronesia.)

Depart Hawaii in November for at least five months of good cruising in Micronesia before turning south into Melanesia. The timing of your turn south is controlled by the beginning of the summer typhoon season north of the equator (May). If you want to leave Micronesia earlier than May, then plan on cruising the equatorial islands until the South Pacific cyclone season is over in April. (The equatorial islands between ± six degrees of the equator are free of cyclonic activity the year around.) Then, from May to November, you cruise the islands of Melanesia ending up in New Zealand for the South Pacific hurricane season.

The following May, head east through the islands of Polynesia and this is where you benefit from a reverse flow concept. Boats which follow the usual westward Coconut Milk Run strive to see all the islands of Polynesia on the downhill passage. As a result, when they get ready to return home, they unmercifully beat themselves and their boats on the upwind passage skipping islands and forgetting about the delights of lazy passages through the South Seas. The incentive to stop along the way and visit is gone.

Instead of such a sadistic return, the cruiser approaching Polynesia for the first time from the west will want to stop at as many of the islands of Polynesia as possible and intersperse sailing with sightseeing, thereby relieving the trauma of the upwind passage. He can do this by a tacking route eastward from, say, New Zealand to Tahiti, enjoying short passages, some only a day or two long. Many will be on a reach as he first goes to a northern island followed next by a southern island, all the time making his easting until he reaches Tahiti for the turn north through the Tuamotus and a stop at the Marquesas Islands on his way to Hawaii and the Mainland. This is exactly the itinerary used by Kiwis and Aussies when they head for North America and it is a proven one.

In Conclusion . . . . .

For those cruisers who want to get off the beaten path and see a part of the Pacific that is different from the common Coconut Milk Run of the southern hemisphere, Micronesia is an exciting alternative. It is a part of the great South Seas where you can challenge your skills as a navigator, adventurer and romantic. Few places in the Pacific remain untouched by adventurous cruisers and Micronesia is one of the last. It is isolated only by ignorance of geography, but readily accessible to the sailing adventurer. Certainly it is less well publicized than Polynesia or even Melanesia.

While off the beaten path, it is still readily accessible to the cruising boat and it holds strong ties with mainstream America by means of all the communications invented by man.

—Cruising World

"Yacht Clearance" dock at Malaloa Marina, well inside
Pago Pago Harbor, American Samoa

THE TAIWAN CONNECTION

Practically all boats built in Taiwan that are not shipped to North America sail to Hong Kong first as a sort of shakedown cruise, but more importantly, to get to a port where essential boat finishing services are available and proper provisioning can be done. From Keelung, the major exit port from Taiwan, the distance to Hong Kong sailing down the west coast of Taiwan is about 500 miles and nominal sailing time is 4 days.

The best time to depart Keelung for Hong Kong is winter, say between December and March. That's when the northeast trades are blowing and the current in the Formosa Strait is running to the southwest. In that time period, a beeline can be made for Hong Kong with favorable wind and current. This timing, incidently, also allows some time for outfitting and provisioning before having to get underway for the North Pacific crossing. You should depart Hong Kong near the turn of monsoons and before the western Pacific typhoon season starts in earnest.

Should departure be made from Taiwan for Hong Kong after April, southwest monsoons will be starting and a reversed current may be found in the Formosa Strait. Fighting both of them, your passage will certainly

295

be more difficult. The current can be ameliorated to some extent by staying within 15 miles of the coast until south of the Pescadores Islands and then heading straight for the mainland. It all depends on local wind direction for this routing. Bear in mind that the Territorial Sea limit of Taiwan is 12 NM and sailing inside the Pescadores may make your vessel very suspect in the eyes of a very suspicious people. Wind permitting, it may be better to head out earlier into the Formosa Strait.

Whatever your choice, when you leave Keelung Harbor, plan on going all the way. The Taiwan Defense Force does not take kindly to yachts sailing in and out of their harbors. It's an old phobia of theirs.

Weather

Any passage from the Far East to North America is a seasonal affair for three very good weather reasons: monsoons, typhoons and winter. The southwest monsoon blows from May to October and that is the best time to make a passage from Hong Kong to Japan. The southwest monsoon is strongest in the early part of the season but, unfortunately, it is also accompanied by more rain. As the season progresses, the winds lighten and the rainfall diminishes. The northeast monsoon blows from about October to April and, as it ends, there is a period between monsoons when the winds are variable.

Taiohae Bay, Nuku Hiva

Starting from Hong Kong much before April will certainly involve more windward work, but do not depart from Hong Kong later than May because it is important to get out of Far East waters before the typhoon season begins in earnest. The typhoon season may start as early as April, but in an average season the month of April has less than one typhoon in all the western Pacific, so it should not be a big worry. In May, there is the possibility of over one typhoon and June is closer to two for the month. It's certainly time to leave by then.

Winter weather becomes an important consideration at the eastern end of the passage. From October on, there is a noticeable buildup in gales over the North Pacific and those gales tend to move at more southern latitudes. That is the time to be off the open ocean.

Northern Sailing Routes To North America

The Hong Kong to North America passage should be made in two or three segments. The first, Hong Kong to Japan. The second, Japan to North America direct, or a Hawaii stopover. The third, if a Hawaii stopover is chosen, Honolulu to the Mainland. Comparative great circle distances and historically recorded passage times are:

Leg	Distance NM	Sailing time – days*		
		shortest	average	longest
Hong Kong-Vancouver	5530	(not available)		
Hong Kong-Tokyo	1560	(not available)		
Tokyo-Vancouver	4070	34	39-55	58
Tokyo-Honolulu	3350	30	34-51	65
Honolulu-Vancouver	2355	18	20-30	41

*From my records. Average sailing time represents middle two-thirds of all passage times.

A non-stop passage, Hong Kong to North America, would be the shortest total sailing distance, but also the most grueling and least interesting. A call at a Japanese port is surely in order since the great circle route closely approaches the east coast of Japan. A little rest and resupply plus a look at Cherry Blossom Land would boost your morale for the subsequent long passage whether to North America direct or via Honolulu.

There are many places to stop in Japan and, although yachting is not yet big there, cruisers report the people to be very friendly and interested in their welfare. Although the foregoing distance table identifies Yokohama as the Japanese stopover port, that is only because it is the major port of Japan and not the best port for cruisers unless you really want to see crowded Tokyo (Pop. 12 million).

As for the Honolulu option, it is a matter of how important you feel about the need for more R and R before arriving home. The total passage time will be two to three weeks longer by stopping at Honolulu than sailing direct, but you have a nice break in which to refurbish crew and boat

in Polynesia, USA. Even though you plan a nonstop passage, it is possible to make a change in routing after crossing the Date Line and drop down to Hawaii. Certainly, Honolulu must be considered for any emergency that may develop in the early part of the passage.

Yet another route is possible although not strongly recommended. Instead of dropping south to Honolulu, your route can swing farther north and sail just south of the Aleutian Chain stopping at Dutch Harbor or Kodiak Island for a break. In doing that, I highly recommend that your boat be equipped with radar. Unless you really want to see Alaska, that route is longer, may have more vigorous winds or oft-times more variable winds, and it is fraught with cold and fog.

From Japan, most boats follow a modified great circle to Vancouver, staying south of the Aleutian Islands. Plan on passing through two waypoints along the route. Cross latitude 40° north at 156° east on your way to 45° north, there most of your easting will be done, hopefully with west winds. Then when you reach 150° west, head directly for Juan de Fuca Strait and home! (Note: A true great circle route from Tokyo to Vancouver reaches to 55° north and that would meld with some dog sled trails in the Aleutians!) You should not have to go above 45° north to get good westerlies, if they exist at all. From Japan to Vancouver you will also be boosted along by the Kuroshio current which will help shorten the passage time. Along this leg however, considerable fog can be expected from the warm Kuroshio current reacting with cold Arctic air, a hazard familiar to North Pacific sailors.

Whether a stop is planned at Honolulu or not, your passage should be scheduled to arrive in Vancouver by the end of September at the latest. In October there is a noticeable buildup of gales in the North Pacific. They come all the way from Japan, which you left behind. So, the problem of starting time from Hong Kong has to be worked within the timing windows of monsoons, typhoons and winter gales. There is also an increment of time that must be allowed in Hong Kong to do whatever boat work is necessary and that sets the latest time at which departure can be taken from your starting point of Taiwan.

Pirates

I think the subject of pirates can be ignored for this route. I have only heard of one instance of piracy as far north as Hong Kong and that was near the entrance to Hong Kong Harbor, itself. It seems that some local fishermen didn't have anything else to do so they stopped a boat but got nothing and did nothing. Taiwan, China, Hong Kong and Japan are all so suspicious of each other that they have numerous naval patrols in local waters that suppress any piratical ideas just by their presence. Piracy, in the Far East, what there is, is concentrated in the waters south of Hong Kong, but that's a whole different story.

— Personal Letter to a "Cruising World" reader

POSTSCRIPT

"On an ancient wall in China
where a brooding Buddha blinks,
Deeply graven is this message —
it is later than you think.
The clock of life is wound but once
and no man has the power
To tell just when the hands will stop,
at late or early hour.
Now is all the time you own,
the past a golden link.
Go cruising now my brother —
It is later than you think."

Anon., courtesy ELYSIUM III

Point Cruz Yacht Club, Honiara

INDEX

Street scene, Port-Vila, Vanuatu, Chapter 5

Opening drinking coconuts, Fanning Atoll, (Tabuareran),
Kiribati's Line Islands, Chapter 7

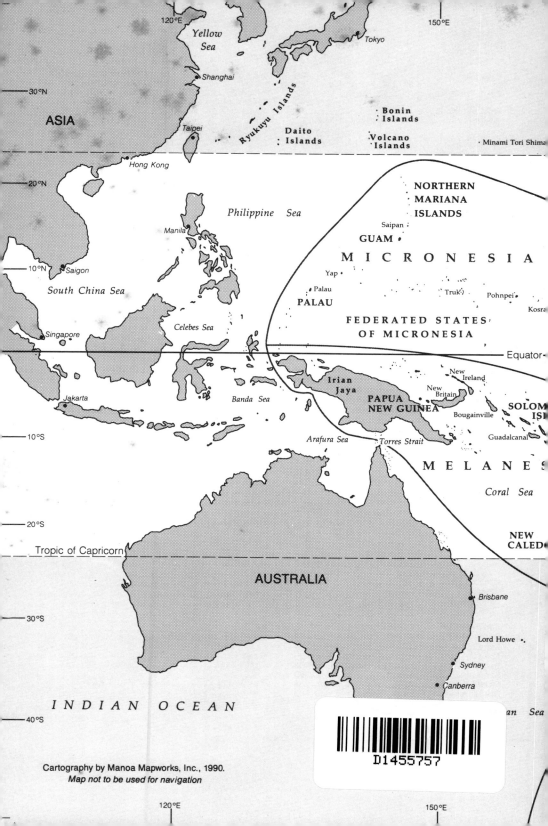

D1455757